OFF NORTHAMPTON SHED

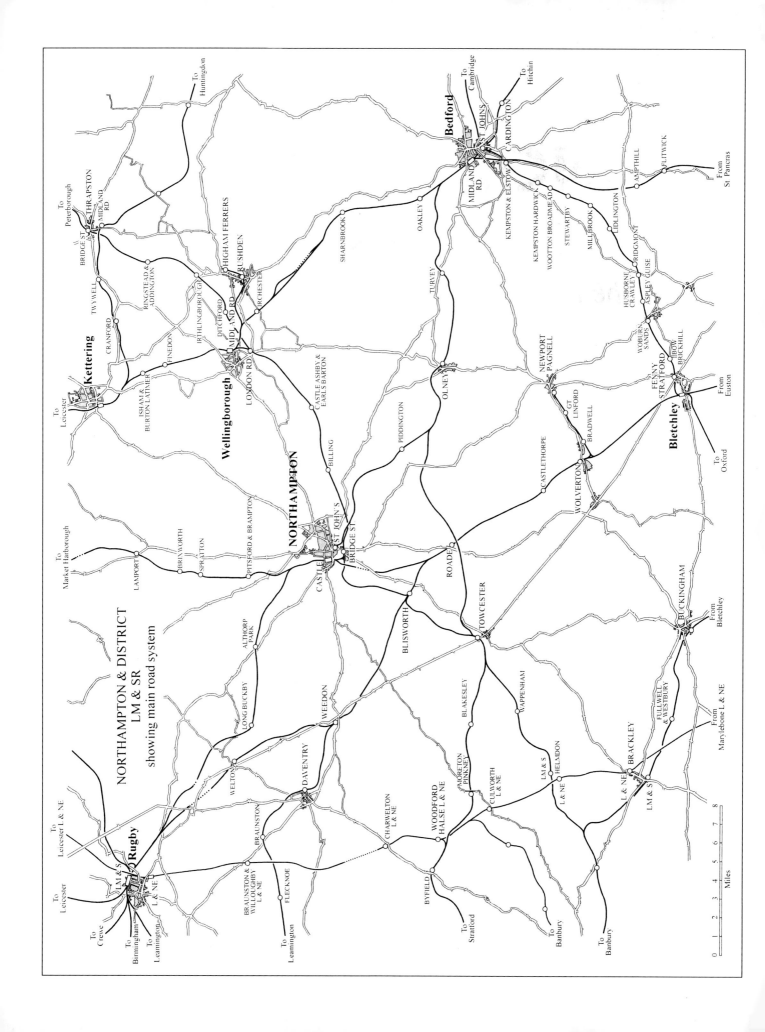

NORTHAMPTON & DISTRICT
LM & SR
showing main road system

OFF NORTHAMPTON SHED

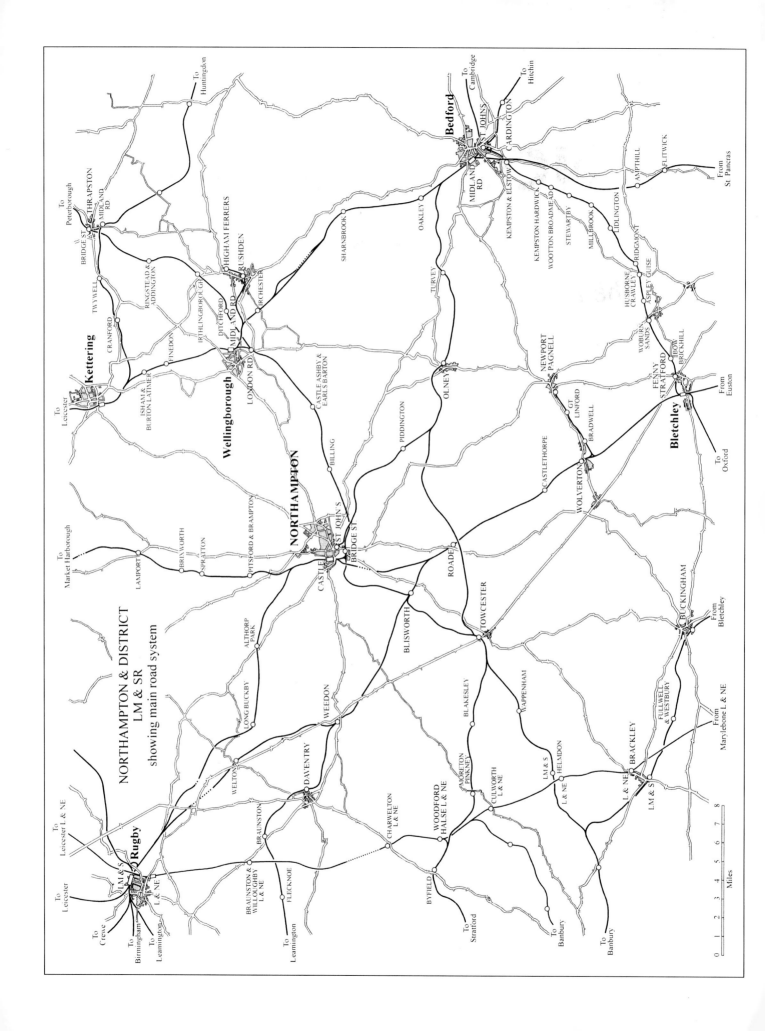

NORTHAMPTON & DISTRICT
LM & SR
showing main road system

OFF NORTHAMPTON SHED

The Reminiscences of an LMS Fireman

BY

DEREK MUTTON

WILD SWAN PUBLICATIONS

In Memory of
NORMAN QUENNELL
and
BILL ALLEN

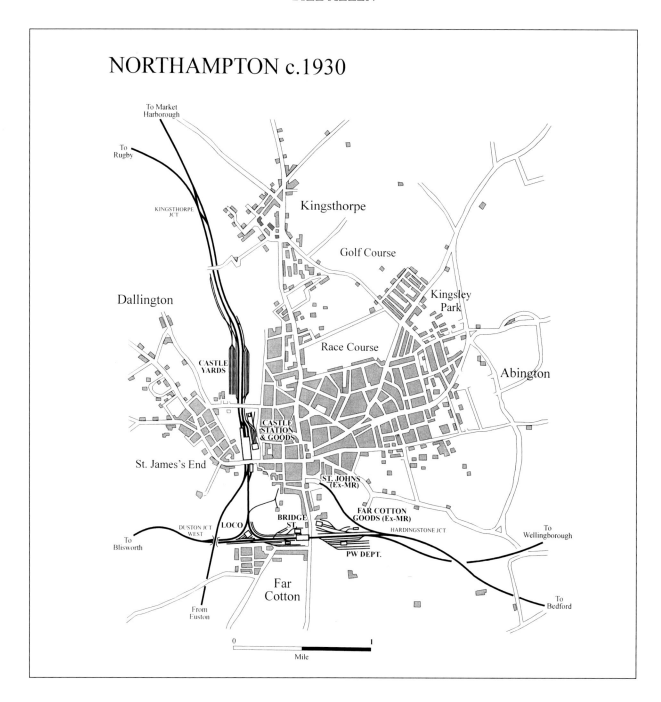

NORTHAMPTON c.1930

To Market
Harborough

To
Rugby

KINGSTHORPE
JCT

Kingsthorpe

Golf Course

Dallington

Kingsley
Park

Race Course

Abington

CASTLE
YARDS

CASTLE
STATION
& GOODS

St. James's End

ST. JOHNS
(Ex-MR)

FAR COTTON
GOODS (Ex-MR)

BRIDGE
ST.

HARDINGSTONE JCT

To
Wellingborough

DUSTON JCT
WEST

LOCO

PW DEPT.

To
Blisworth

Far
Cotton

From
Euston

To
Bedford

0   1

Mile

Designed by Paul Karau
Printed by Amadeus Press, Cleckheaton

Published by
WILD SWAN PUBLICATIONS LTD.
1-3 Hagbourne Road, Didcot, Oxon, OX11 8DP

CONTENTS

Some youngsters at Gayton loop just northwest of Blisworth watching a 'Jube' thundering northwards. I, too, had perched on the fence here when 'requested' to leave the station at Blisworth whilst 'number snatching', but I can see no notebooks or pencils, so think these must have been local children 'playing the wag' from school.

W. MALLARD

One can see what a naive gormless lump I was at fourteen — and so easily diverted to be 'fitters apprentice' by Gaffer Breasley.

CHAPTER ONE
THE BEGINNING

Main Road looking towards Duston West with Crown Foundry on the right and the broken wall of the old chapel in the foreground. The photographer was standing near the entrance to the loco walkway on the right out of the picture. The Working Men's Club features on the left and in the middle distance "Dick Ford's" pub, the Rose & Crown.
G. ONLEY

DURING the early part of the war, Northampton was inundated with evacuees, and schooling was affected. When I went to senior school (Campbell Square Intermediate) we had lessons for only half of each day – mornings one week and afternoons the next, alternating with the evacuee children. Our 'school time' when not at school was spent under supervision of a teacher or, more usually, a Land Army lady, in 'digging for victory' at allotments in the Billing Road area, or harvesting, either there or at local farms.

After Dunkerque life became quite exciting for us children around where I then lived – my family had by this time moved to a part of town not far from Weston Favell. Not only did we have many of the evacuees with us still, there arrived also several groups of soldiers who camped in the fields and woods not far from the end of the street in which I lived. I remember the 'Free Czechs' were a very boisterous group. There was also a large detachment of Canadians, from whom we children sometimes managed to cadge chewing gum, and occasionally chocolate – luxury indeed!

By 1942, many of the evacuee children had either returned to their homes or had been 'adopted' by relatives in equally peaceful areas of the country as Northampton. But the war continued, and as my 14th birthday drew near, I and three school chums decided that we would leave school and join the Merchant Navy. I was slightly older than the others and was able to leave prior to Christmas, whilst they had to wait until Easter 1943. It was then that I had what I thought was a brilliant idea – if I went to work on the railway until Easter I could learn about boilers, etc., and thus perhaps more easily gain employment as a stoker when I joined ship.

With this in view, I attended Northampton Loco Department where I was interviewed by the Manager (The Gaffer), a Mr. Breasley. He convinced me that I should become a Fitters' Apprentice, in which position I would be able to learn everything I wished about boilers, steam raising, and the mechanics of steam engines. I was so naïve that I swallowed all he said hook line and sinker.

Thus in December 1942, wearing a too small second-hand brown boiler suit (brown being the cheapest mother could buy) and a pair of second-hand boots, I presented myself at the loco-shed, where I was placed in the care of a charge-hand fitter, a man named Archie Harris.

In fact there appeared to be three charge-hands, Mr. Harris, Billy Egan, a diminutive Irishman with a great sense of humour, and Glynn Hughes, a quiet serious Welshman. They occupied what was known as the 'glass house', a small

1

box') Smith, the senior fitter; Percy ('gas man') Freeman; Horace ('bookie') Williams, the lubrication expert; and some of the fitter's mates, such as Charlie ('moon man') Watts; Tommy ('full moon') Jay; Billy ('jolly') Evans; plus boiler men 'Fanny' Sutton; Colin Blick, who was also the shed First Aid man; and Bert Reed, with whom later I was to learn how to build brick arches in fire-boxes. Most of the nicknames given meant little to me at that time, except for Charlie Watts, whose protuberant chin and thin features

The entrance to the shed from Main Road with the wall of the derelict 'chapel' on the left. The post in the centre of the walkway was not there when I started. The path turned left to the footbridge.   G. ONLEY

From the bridge, looking back towards the entrance path, showing the right-angled turn to the right. Bridge Street (old CMD) sidings are also shown.   G. ONLEY

office, which was a half-glazed lean-to against the wall adjacent to the 'fitters shop' doors. I learned later that Mr. Egan was the foreman, Archie and Glynn being his deputies.

The fitters shop had in former times obviously been the domain of the blacksmith – when more making and heavy repairing had been done at the shed. The room was dominated by the forge, with its cowl and chimney, with the giant bellows behind, all of which were to the right as one entered the double doors which were at the end of one of the longer walls of the rectangular-shaped room, and opposite the two windows. In the centre of the uneven brick floor stood a large anvil, with a rack of tools and a water bin nearby. Along the shorter wall to the left as one entered, and opposite to the forge end of the room, were several small wooden lockers stacked one on the other like so many rabbit hutches. These were where the fitters kept their own tools and personal items.

Along the two longer walls, and facing each side of the forge, were wooden benches for seating. Above these on the wall opposite the windows were hooks for hanging clothes upon. The two windows were in the wall opposite the doors. These were tall, narrow, with small panes and rounded tops – reminiscent of chapel windows. However, these were so blackened with years of grime that even those panes which had non-frosted glass were so opaque that the gas lighting in the room had to be on permanently.

I was allotted a hook for my clothes, and then introduced by Archie to those present: such characters as Albert ('snuff

The view on the bridge, with the steps down to the shed, and Bridge Street junction box visible.   G. ONLEY

A view from inside the shed yard of the footbridge and Bridge Street Junction signal box. The 'dolly' signal for leaving the shed and going onto the running line can be seen in the centre of the picture. Someone had been a little rough with the capstan in the foreground — not there in my day. The wagons on the two sidings roads would have been for coal to the shed, and then utilized for ashes disposal, etc. when empty.
*   G. ONLEY*

The shed appears a lot lighter in this picture of the mid-thirties, than it did as I remember it ten years later. The gas lamps remained, but the only daylight that came through the roof was where the glass was broken or missing.

W. J. S. MEREDITH

were self evident of his likeness to a new moon when observed side faced.

After introductions, during which I was questioned about my sanity in wanting to work on the railway, it was indicated by Archie that I would be under his supervision for an initial period, for which I was very thankful, as he appeared to be a kindly man. He took me on a tour of the shed, introducing me to the stores personnel – the lovely Ivy Weatherell, and old Fred (whose last name I think was Willets) who, Archie said, had retired as an engine driver before the war but who had come back to 'do his bit'. I was to have many a chastising word from him in the days ahead ! I was also taken to the shed offices where I was presented with a metal disc, about the size of a half-crown, on which was stamped the number 354 and with a hole near the edge. The disc was my identity and was normally kept hanging on a board of hooks in the glass-house, blank side showing when one was off duty, and reversed when one 'booked on'. It was also to be presented to the clerk on payday in exchange for a small metal tubular tin (marked 354) containing my wages.

That first day went by in a blur of faces and locations, but it was very clear that although attached to Archie, I was to be a 'go-for', and during the first weeks I was kept very much occupied with fetching and carrying tools, mostly for Archie, but also for anyone else who happened to see me apparently 'doing nothing'!

Although in these early days I was not crawling about in the motions of engines, my brown overalls soon began to look distinctly grimy. Just sitting in the fitters shop on the greasy benches and leaning against absent men's overalls hanging on the pegs was enough to put grease and oil stains on my new clothing.

The inside of the shed itself was very dark, the only daylight penetrating the gloom being where parts of the roofing glass were missing or broken, and from the open end of the shed, although there were nearly always engines stabled outside which reduced the amount of daylight available from

This 1960s picture of the re-roofed shed shows the end wall (left) much as it was in my day, although none of the paraphernalia seen here was there, except the first-aid box seen attached to the wall. The stores 'counter' door is visible in the left foreground (just off the picture on the left was the booking-on lobby). The archway entrance to the shed for pedestrians is apparent just beyond the ladder leaning against the wall, and below the fourth smoke flute. The wagon furthest from the camera was on the road which went through the arch to a small area where the heavy metal (brake blocks, baffle plates, superheater tubes, etc.) were stored, and scrap metal retained to await collection, and where a wagon could be positioned to facilitate unloading/loading. The double doors to the fitters shop were just beyond the archway, with the 'glasshouse' (foreman's office) just beyond them. On the other side of that was a recessed area where sand bags, and other 'dry' commodities were stored. In front of the glasshouse was the large tool rack to which I trudged back and forth at the orders of one or other of the fitters. The wagon nearest the camera appears to be one that was part of the breakdown train, which was normally housed on No. 10 road, furthest from the camera.
G. ONLEY

there. There was also an archway next to the fitters' shop, which gave access to the heavy metal (brake blocks, baffle plates, super-heater tubes, etc.) storage area, and to the very primitive toilets – no doors or seats, and a wall to urinate against – also the offices, plus the footpath to/from the shed. Some daylight filtered in via this archway, but the general gloom within the shed necessitated the lighting being on at all times. The lighting was mainly by gas, although there were one or two electric points around the shed, but these were often found to be defective. Thus the only light one usually had to work with was from either a paraffin torch - with its yellow smoky flame – or a carbide lamp.

Archie Harris was the footplate fitter, and any reported defects, such as badly-leaking steam glands, loose valve handles (regulator etc.) or extra stiff operation of any of those components, was Archie's to cure. I guess it was classed as a cushy job because his clothing seemed hardly to get soiled.

After being the 'go-for' for a couple of weeks or so, I had learned which spanners were which, so that when sent by one of the fitters, or their mate, for a particular item from the rack near the glasshouse, I usually returned with the correct one. Some of these spanners were quite large (the gudgeon-pin-nut spanner for instance), and as much as a skinny fourteen year old could comfortably carry for any distance. I was therefore quite pleased when Archie rescued me from being a general dogsbody and showed me how to do footplate work, which mainly involved the removal of the old asbestos packing from the various steam glands, and repacking with new lengths of asbestos rope or string. These came in various thicknesses – from three-quarter inch for the regulator gland, down to three-eighths inch string for such glands as the blower or ejector.

It was while engaged on this work, and attending the stores for more packing, that I fell foul of old Fred. He was obviously of the impression that I was wasting the asbestos, and refused to let me have more. After negotiations by Archie, further lengths were obtained, but I was told not to dispose of all the old packing within the glands (probably five or six rounds), only discarding two or three rounds which were to be replaced by the new pieces. The rest of the old rounds – suitably soaked in thick oil and grease – should be replaced in the gland and the nuts given an extra tightening, just allowing movement of the valve. Very good for waste-conscious wartime, but, as I learned when I later became a fireman, very seldom did the footplate glands not leak prior to an engine being due for its next 'X scheme' service. Another renewing that was done at X scheme time was that of the boiler water gauge glasses. These glass tubes often became quite thin during the time between renewals, and could burst, with at least 'uncomfortable' consequences, as I found on one or two occasions during my later firing days.

For about two months I continued to do this reasonably clean work and was left on my own while Archie was else-

where, but I was conscious that I was not really learning a great deal about boilers and steam generation – for which I had originally chosen railway employment – even though I questioned Archie about all aspects I could think of, and to which I'm sure he became somewhat fed up. However, Easter was approaching and I thought it would be a suitable time to tender my resignation to Gaffer Breasley, so to be ready, together with my chums, to seek employment in the Merchant Navy. It was then that I received a rude awakening. Because of the war, the railway had been declared a reserved occupation, and I was unable to leave until the end of hostilities. Although very disheartened at the time, I later gave thanks for having to continue my current employment – the ship of one of the lads with whom I had planned to join the navy was torpedoed, and before he was sixteen he was lost at sea.

So, resigned to working on the railway – at least until the end of the war – I went home that evening to tell my mother. I think she had somewhat mixed feelings when she heard the news. She had already made it known that my take home pay of 14 shillings and ten pence per week 'hardly pays for the soap to clean your clothes', as she put it. However, I think she was secretly glad I wasn't going off to war at such a tender age – especially as Father had been called up for military service and was 'somewhere in Britain' as a despatch rider with the Royal Military Police (because of his hammer toes he had not been suitable for the infantry !).

It was shortly after this setback that I joined a scheme supported by most of the fitting staff whereby overalls were provided, and laundered, by a professional firm. Although this cost me half-a-crown every two weeks, mother was certainly more than a little pleased with this development, as it saved her from the drudgery of boiling and then scrubbing the overalls as they were laid flat on the concrete outside the back door of our house.

However, I was having second thoughts about becoming a railway fitter, and had been talking with some of the cleaners – youngsters not much older than myself – with whom I had come in contact around the shed, often while they were cleaning an engine on which I was working. I learned that their pay was almost double mine, and they certainly appeared to be less supervised than we apprentices were. Often when I was sent to the cabin (the locomen's mess room) to make tea for one or other of the fitters, I would see some of the cleaners playing shove ha'penny on one of the two long zinc-topped tables, which had been specially marked out with a sharp tool for the purpose.

I resolved to attempt a transfer as soon as possible, perhaps after my fifteenth birthday, although at my initial enquiry of Gaffer Breasley I was informed that as an apprentice such a transfer was more or less out of the question.

So again somewhat naively I knuckled down to my fitting role, but with the resolve that I would keep trying. Being a railway fireman, and perhaps one day a driver, held far more attraction for me than becoming a fully-fledged fitter.

CHAPTER TWO

FITTER'S APPRENTICE – STILL

I continued the work of packing the footplate steam glands under Archie's supervision, interspersed with other jobs such as fetching and carrying for other fitters, and other activities which a supple youth was more able to perform than the somewhat rotund fitters who had been allocated the work. One particularly unpleasant ancillary job given to the apprentices was that of cleaning the water feed valves in the tender tanks of engines which were on shed for their X scheme service.

This, of course, entailed the tank being emptied, and then the person detailed to do the job – as mentioned above, usually one of the young apprentices – lowering himself through the open tank lid, and with, if he was lucky, a boilersmith's carbide lamp, making his way to the front of the tank where the feed valves were positioned. If there was no carbide lamp available, he had to make do with a smoky oil torch, which in the very confined space of the tank quickly fouled the air. Everything inside the tank was invariably covered with a thick pinkish deposit of slime created by the water-softening agent added to the water used in the engines. Invariably, too, there was water covering the bottom of the tank, so by the time he had negotiated the support plates of the coal bunker part of the tender and crawled in the ever-decreasing headroom to the feed valves, he was quite wet, and covered in slime.

When the offending valve was reached, it was usual to find it clogged with particles of coal, which had fallen in to the tank and been drawn to the valve by the movement of the water. These were scooped out by hand, and transferred to a bucket, which you took in to the tank as you entered. In my mind's eye I always likened the experience of cleaning tanks to that of sub-mariners trapped in a sinking submarine. This became especially realistic when, as sometimes happened, some wag would put a hose pipe through the tank lid and water began cascading through the only escape route!

By this time there were two other apprentices at the shed, one from Carlisle, and the other from Chester, and they were known by those names (I never could remember their real names). I was always known as Mutt, a name I had from school days. We apprentices were of a similar age and, as one can imagine, we used to get up to juvenile pranks when we were not under one of the fitters' direct control – such as the water treatment mentioned above, or perhaps putting a fog detonator on the line close to one of the wheels as one of the fitters' mates was using a pinch bar to reposition an engine to get at a particular part of the motion or brake gear.

Using a pinch bar was very heavy work, and it usually took two of us youngsters to drag one around the shed and position it under an engine wheel. Another somewhat heavy task we apprentices were usually 'requested' to do was to operate the bellows behind the forge when one of the fitters was heating a piece of metal – a leaf of a spring being

repaired, or perhaps a distorted cotter pin for a spring or brake block. The bellows, the concertina body of which was nearly three feet in diameter, and more than that in depth, housed in a metal frame, was operated by means of a long wooden handle about five feet from the floor. To operate this contraption by hand for more than a few minutes was more than I and the other apprentices could manage, so we used to climb on the framework around the bellows and pump air by stepping on and off the handle, using our weight and leg muscles to press the handle down, then stepping off to allow it to return to its original position before repeating the operation. We would support ourselves by bracing our arms against the adjacent wall and the chimney-breast, and continue thus until the fitter working the piece of metal was satisfied with the heating of it.

One 'perk' of being Archie's protégé was that I was able to accompany him, and other fitters, when the breakdown train was required – usually because of a derailment of an engine, or perhaps a wagon – in one of the shunting yards, or even in the shed yard. The breakdown train of Northampton loco department was a very simple affair, merely two old carriage brake vans loaded with jacks, special metal ramps, pinch bars, crow bars, heavy chains, and plenty of old broken sleepers. We had no crane, but it was surprising what could be achieved with the equipment to hand, and during the times that I attended with Archie the men were never thwarted for very long in 'persuading' an engine back on track – aided of course, if necessary, by the engine of the breakdown train.

My job on these excursions was mostly confined to humping packing wood to where it was required, and after the job was complete to return any reusable pieces back to the van. Sometimes, if the operation was taking longer than had been anticipated, I was called upon to mash tea – the 'makings' always being stored in one of the vans – water being taken with us each time. A large iron kettle was also part of the furniture of the van, and heat was obtained via 'adapted' welding equipment. I was never sure how safe this strategy was, but at least the kettle boiled reasonably quickly!

After being seconded to Archie for some ten weeks or so, my pleasant footplate job came to a rather dramatic end. I had been engaged on one of our old 0–6–0 engines (I believe it was number 22916) during the course of which I had inserted a shim, cut from an old piece of tin, into the square hole of the regulator handle which was loose on its seating on the valve spindle. Unfortunately, I had inadvertently rammed in the shim in such a way that when the regulator handle was closed against its stop, the valve was still slightly open. Next day the engine was re-lit ready for use, and was moved outside the shed into the daylight by the preparation crew when it had about 40 lbs of steam. As the steam pressure increased under the efforts of the fireman, the

The streets of Far Cotton with St. Mary's Church, the school and Delapre Street at the centre. The small terraced houses are typical of the area, and most were in situ in 1886. The foundry roof is seen in the foreground and Main Road is seen where the cars are.
G. ONLEY

This engine, No. 22916, is typical of the type of engine used for shunting in the Castle Yard. The injector clack was housed on the boiler just in front of the central driving wheel. When the clack stuck (which it did frequently) we had to give the clack housing an almighty clout with the coal pick. The clack would then invariably drop and close off the rush of steam and noise — much to the shunter's relief.
COLLECTION R. J. ESSERY

engine slowly trundled back into the shed while both crew members were absent, and hit one of our many 'D's on which Albert Smith was working in the motion. This engine was moved slightly by the impact, causing one of the big ends to rise and thrust Albert towards the underside of the boiler. Fortunately, he was not seriously hurt, and the incident had an amusing twist to it. Albert alleged that his glass eye popped out as his body was squeezed, and it took him half an hour sorting amongst the general mess in the bottom of the pit under the engine to find it! I guess it was very lucky that the driver of 22916 was not oiling in the motions of that engine when it began to move. No damage was done to either engine – only to my pride.

However, an enquiry was held, and Archie was chastised for not supervising me properly. I was removed from my packing job and given into Bert Reed and Fanny Sutton's care to learn about the inside of firebox work and boiler washouts respectively.

Fanny Sutton was a tubby little man, who, with his wife, also ran a small grocery shop at the house where they lived in one of the streets of Far Cotton, not far from the loco shed. I later learned (somewhat to my discomfort) that he also pulled teeth should anyone have a molar that was paining them – his wife apparently ready to hold the patient's head firmly against the back of the chair should such action be necessary. His mate was a man named George, who always seemed to be looking for Horace Williams, who 'ran a book' when there was any racing. My job with Fanny and George mainly consisted of pulling a long, heavy, wire-reinforced hose pipe to wherever they wanted it, coupling it to a hydrant, and turning on the water when they shouted to me to do so. I also learned how to remove and replace boiler plugs without damaging the fine copper thread, and how to manoeuvre the long hooked copper rods they used to dislodge the scale within the boiler so that it could be washed out via the plug holes. The time with them was what one might describe as rather damp. In

fact, my lower half was usually soaked each day. They wore special clogs and waterproof leggings, but there was no spare equipment for young apprentices, so while holding the nozzle of the hose (if it was a non-threaded nozzle) into one plug hole, the water would be gushing from an adjacent hole – usually over my legs and feet, whilst scale from within the boiler was raked out together with the water by use of one of the hooked rods.

However, my two weeks stint with them was soon over, and I then passed on to Bert. He was a jovial man, also quite rotund, which meant that even when the baffle plate and rim plate were removed from the fire-hole, he had quite a struggle to squeeze himself into the firebox. Here was his domain, and I quickly became almost as enthusiastic as he in sealing leaking stays and tube ends. Bert's colleague was Colin Blick, the shed First-Aid man, who always wore brown overalls – so that he could readily be seen, he told me. He was a very conscientious man, and took great pride in his building of brick arches in the fireboxes. From these two worthies I learned how to install the wooden formers in the firebox, and mix the fire clay to the right consistency. However, as you might guess, my main task was to collect both the wooden formers and the fire bricks from where they were kept, barrow them to whichever engine we were working on, and to pass them on to the footplate and thence into the firebox to Bert or Colin. The bricks were of different shapes and sizes, depending on the type of engine, and were numbered for identification. Most were tongued and grooved to create rigidity in the arch, so I would be told to collect so many 31s and so many 40s, etc. As the bricks weighed about 20 lbs each, it was no light task not only to collect them, but also heave them on to the footplate and thence into the firebox. No wonder I found that I was building muscle, and from a very skinny child I was developing into quite a strong youth, although I was nowhere near as strong as Bert's other mate, Tommy Jay. He was a very large man, who walked a little like an ape with his arms

View of Main Road with "Dick Ford's" pub, the Rose & Crown, visible on the corner of Henley Street. Rickard Street was the first turning beyond. The houses to the left, on the hill, are in Rothersthorpe Road. Harry Stevens used to live in one. This 1960s view was taken from the top of the Ash plant.
G. ONLEY

hanging in front of him. At a certain time of the moon's cycle he would sometimes take it into his head to demonstrate his strength by ambling around the shed carrying six or seven baffle plates, or two or three brake blocks, which would be hurled at anyone who was foolish enough to make a remark to which Tom took exception. We all tried to keep out of his way at those times!

Understandably, the heavy work I was doing also made me hungry and I never seemed to have enough to eat. I think mother despaired of ever satisfying me, and, being wartime, it was not always easy to obtain extras, especially if such items were rationed. Two of the usual stand-by's were baked beans and powdered egg flapjacks, which I had in sandwiches. These I would toast at the forge using a long-handled homemade two-pronged fork. Of course one had to be careful when toasting the baked bean sandwiches, balancing them carefully on the fork so as not to allow the beans to dribble out and into the fire.

Following my time with Bert and Colin, I was given in to the charge of Horace Williams, who, when not running his 'book', was the lubrication man. I learned how to clean out oil pipes and runs, and how to thread the needles with the wicks, via which oil was transferred from its small reservoir down the tubes to the lubrication points. We also serviced the mechanical lubricators on the more modern engines (black fives and eights), and the steam pressure cylinder lubricators on the footplates of the older engines that appeared on shed. It also became my job while with Horace to refurbish the pads in tender axle boxes of some of the engines in for their big service. I found the time with Horace very interesting (and relatively clean), plus I learned something which has stood me in good stead all my life, namely, never skimp on oil in machinery and if possible change it regularly.

After Horace I had a week or two with Albert Smith, who luckily seemed to have forgotten the runaway engine incident. He was affectionately known as 'Snuffbox' by the less reverend of his colleagues – because of his addiction to the brown powder. The nostril area of his face seemed always to be black with grease from his fingers and, with the snuff adhering to the grease as he tried to sniff it up his nose, he presented quite an amusing picture! He once or twice enticed me to take a pinch, but it invariably made me sneeze, to put it mildly. In fact, it nearly blew my head off!

My time with Albert was spent mainly in the motions of engines, positioning eccentrics, or carrying and using quite large and heavy spanners (the gudgeon-pin-nut spanner previously mentioned), that had to be collected from the rack by the shop, or holding cotter pins while Albert hammered them into position, hopefully seeing them clearly with his one good eye in the gloom of an inside motion lit only by a paraffin torch.

Following my relatively short time with Albert, I was seconded to work with little Percy Freeman. Whenever I had seen Percy, whether it was around the shed, or sitting in the fitters shop eating his sandwiches, I had invariably wondered how he managed to get so filthy. His short tubby form always seemed to be covered from head to foot in grease and grime – much more so than the other fitters, even Albert Smith.

I was soon to find out why. Percy was the 'front end' man and spent his days either in smoke boxes renewing super-heater elements or their copper ferrules (washers) where they joined to the steam header, or renewing piston rings, etc. on some of our older engines with inside cylinders. Each of these jobs necessitated the liberal use of graphite paste when grinding in the seating of either the ferrules or the piston rings, and when refitting the cylinder cover gaskets. Together with the soot and ashes invariably found in smoke boxes, the mixture seemed to form a concoction from which there was no escape. I was soon as covered in this grime as Percy, especially when working in confined spaces, when his cloth cap would frequently be rubbing against my face, giving me the look of one of the black-faced minstrels who sometimes appeared at our local New Theatre.

Once I asked Percy why it was that he always had these particular jobs allocated to him. He told me that he had been a gas fitter prior to the war, but when found to be unfit for the armed services, he had been drafted on to the railway. With the limited training given, the work we were doing was about all he was qualified to do. Percy was a jolly little chap and we got on quite well – even though he swore at me even more than the other fitters when I did work that was not to his satisfaction.

Renewing super-heater elements was another heavy job, and it was as much as I could do to carry one of these from their storage place to the engine on which we were working. There was one long-wheelbase trolley at the shed, but usually, by the time I had found it, and, if not in use, dragged it to the storage place and thence to the engine, I could half-carry/half-drag the element to the engine in less time, and with about equal effort.

One job I could do alone, and was allowed to, was to renew the wooden brake blocks on the tenders of some of the old LNWR engines – 'eighteen inches' and 'coalers' for instance – although, as far as I remember, none of them were 2C engines. These brake blocks were quite light as they only had a type of metal compound inserted into holes drilled in the face of the blocks. Even I could hold one in position with a hand or knee while fitting the cotter pin in its hole. These blocks I was told were a wartime measure to save the use of iron. Later, when I became a fireman, I found it not uncommon for such brake blocks to smoke and almost catch fire when the hand brake was applied strongly while attempting to assist the driver in slowing a train of wagons on a down gradient.

Dirty though the work was, I was enjoying my time with the fitters shop crew. I had by now been accepted as one of them, and was often taken to Dick Ford's pub – just across the road from the loco shed – and treated to a half pint of beer (fourpence in those days). The shed staff (fitters, labourers, and some footplate men) had formed a Home Guard unit sometime previous to my joining the railway, and sometimes I went with them when the unit went on 'manoeuvres' to the old iron workings at Hunsbury Hill, about ¾ of a mile from the loco depot.

These so-called manoeuvres usually consisted of some semblance of marching to the workings, and then the men checking their various snares to see if any rabbits had been caught. If successful, we would later adjourn to Dick Ford's where a rabbit might be exchanged for a pint of beer, or perhaps a shilling.

However, one weekend (these outings were usually on a Sunday morning), some live grenades had been obtained, and a practice was to be done in throwing them. The majority of those present were First World War veterans, and all went well as two of the men threw their grenades, from the ditch in which we were crouching, into the old workings, where they exploded in the soft sandstone at the bottom. Then it was Percy's turn to lob a grenade. Unfortunately, Percy's position in the ditch was somewhat muddy, and as he braced himself to hurl the grenade, he slipped. The grenade hit the branch of an overhanging tree and dropped into the mud of the ditch not more than twenty feet from Percy. I had never seen so many elderly men move so quickly – even quicker than when someone offered to buy the next round – and this young person was just as quick I can tell you. Luckily for all concerned, the force of it ricocheting off the branch had sent the grenade fairly deep into the ooze in that part of the ditch, and except for a splattering of mud no-one was hurt – except for Percy's pride. He certainly took some ribbing, and not a few curses from the other men.

This rather frightening incident, of course, brought to a somewhat premature end the morning's training, and all adjourned to Dick Ford's for a calming drop of ale, where a rather protracted inquest was held into who the stupid so and so was who suggested them using live ammo!

We now had four apprentices in addition to me, including a lad named Ron ('Soss') Surridge with whom I got on well. He was a few years older than me, and had been drafted onto the railway having apparently failed his medical for the forces. Soss would always be singing, so one knew where he was most of the time, and his favourite song was 'You Are My Sunshine', which he would sing at the drop of a hat, especially when we were all in the fitters shop having our break. Soss had a most unpleasant accident one day. He came into the shop singing his usual tune, perched himself on the rim of the forge, and before anyone could warn him, put his hand on a brake block cotter pin – which was also on the rim – and which unbeknown to Soss was cooling down after having been heated and worked on. The pin was so hot it stuck to the flesh of Soss's hand. He stopped singing, and a somewhat less melodious sound emanated from his lips. Luckily, Colin Blick was present, and he plunged Soss's hand complete with pin into the cold-water bin. Soss fainted, as nearly did some of us present. He was later taken to hospital and was off work for several weeks.

Accidents at work were not uncommon. Torn skin on knuckles and fingers happened almost daily. Percy Freeman had, prior to my joining the railway, lost the top of one finger while renewing a brake block on an engine. He apparently was having difficulty in driving home the cotter pin, and felt inside the hole to ascertain if he had the block aligned correctly in the brake hanger – the block slipped and took off the top of his finger. A similar accident had apparently happened to Albert Smith some years previously.

Some injuries occur from actions that are well meant, such as the time when Charlie Watts began choking while eating his sandwiches. He left the fitters shop bent almost double, coughing and spluttering, his face puce under the grime. Colin Blick was not present this time, but one of the labourers – I think George Fidgit – was, and hit poor Charlie in the middle of his back with a labourer's shovel with such force that it knocked Charlie into a nearby engine pit, damaging his nose, false teeth, and spectacles. However, Charlie emerged from the mire of the pit, his choking fit cured, and thanked George for 'saving his life'. Such is camaraderie!

I was now approaching my fifteenth birthday, and I had made further entreaties of gaffer Breasley, pointing out there were now more apprentices than could be usually allocated with fitters, etc. Eventually. he acceded to my persistence, and I was accepted to joint the footplate grade in September. I felt a new beginning was about to unfold in my railway career.

This fence between the engine shed and the canal bank was there in my time but with no holes.
G. ONLEY

CHAPTER THREE
BAR BOY AND CLEANER

The shed in 1932 with the old ash pit and coaling stage in front of the smokebox of the engine, from which the picture was taken. This is more or less as I remember it during my time.
L. HANSON

SEPTEMBER 1943 and at last I was able to bid farewell to the fitters shop and the men with whom I had shared the past ten months. It was no big parting as obviously we would still be working in the same environment of the loco shed, except that now I would be under the supervision of the foreman cleaner, at that time a man known as 'Tex' Williams. He was a man in his late fifties with greying, ginger hair, and a drooping moustache of similar colouring, the shape of which was like one of the Mexican bandit types seen in the cowboy films at the local cinema. He was very bow legged – hence his nickname – and was unable to move about very quickly, a disability very much to the advantage of us cleaners.

His first instruction on my joining his team was that I obtain the bib-and-brace trousers and jacket type overalls as worn by footplatemen, together with a shiny-top cap. These, unfortunately, had to be ordered as there were none in my size in store, I being now nearly six feet tall, but still quite slim. However, I still had my boiler suit as worn by the fitting staff so carried on with the supply and launder system as I had previously. This caused a little consternation in the cabin (the loco men's mess room) when I joined the other cleaners for our lunch break. The fitters overalls were exchanged fortnightly by the laundry contractors (as indeed

were those of the footplatemen), but I had been wearing mine for a week, and working with Percy Freeman they were not what one might describe as just dirty! I was therefore made to either remove my overalls before sitting at the table, or find some paper to sit on, and to "keep your arms off the table". During that first week I felt just as ostracised as I had been in my brown overalls during my initial time with the fitters. However, I soon made friends with the other cleaners, such as Frank ('Digger') Digby, Terry Page, Bill Flint (a London evacuee), and two with whom I became lifelong friends – Norman Quennell and Harold Bollard.

Being now a cleaner (and on the 'footplate side' – I was given a disc with the number 266 thereon), I again naïvely thought that the job description meant I would be cleaning engines, but no; I was firstly initiated into the tasks of a 'bar boy'. When engines came on to the shed after their turn of work, they were 'disposed of', either by the footplate crew if their duty time had not expired, or more usually, by shed staff. Disposal meant being coaled – either by hand from wagons on the bank under the water tank (the coaling stage), or from tubs lifted by a small steam crane operated by one of the women labourers. The engine was then driven to the ash pit where one of the fire droppers made a hole in the fire with a paddle (a long metal rod with a spadelike end) or a clinker shovel, exposing the fire bars, and then using either long metal tongs or a pricker (again a long metal rod with a flattened hook at the end) he lifted three or four fire bars from their rack and put them to one side in the firebox. The residue of the fire and clinker (except for a small amount of fire – usually left below the fire hole door) was then deposited through the hole into the ash pan, from where it was raked into the pit below the engine by the other member of the team. A very dusty job – especially if the wind was in the wrong direction and the water spray was not available. The engine would then be driven to a water column by the shed turners (a driver and fireman detailed on disposal duties), the tank filled, and the engine placed on one of the shed roads in the order in which it would be required for the next turn of duty.

A winter scene, with the brazier glowing in order to keep the water column and bag from freezing. Note the 'modern' electric light – there was only a gas lamp in my time.   G. ONLEY

Now it was the turn of the bar boys to do their bit. Again, with either the use of tongs and/or pricker, we would attempt to manoeuvre the bars that had been removed, to a position where they could be either placed back or flipped back into their racks. Not infrequently we were unable to utilize the pricker or the tongs because of the position in which the bars had been left, or, we lads not having enough strength in our wrists, were unable to position the bars correctly. It would then be 'toss up time' to ascertain who was to be the unlucky one to go into the firebox and replace the bars by hand. This entailed removing the baffle plate with a borrowed firing shovel, and the unlucky lad going feet first into the box, lifting each bar in turn with the aid of some waste cloth, dropping the bars into their rack, and making a quick exit. One or two scorched trouser legs and boots were not uncommon during this exercise; it was invariably very hot in the box – made worse sometimes by the amount of fire left in by the fire droppers – and even more so should his 'pal' close the fire hole door while he was in the box!

The cleaning – if one could call it that – of the engines involved perhaps three or four cleaners being allocated an engine. An amount of thin oil (called long-light) that looked dirty even before cleaning began, and a quantity of cotton waste were issued for each engine. Old Fred in the stores was no more liberal with these items than he had been with the asbestos when more was requested. Being the junior hand, it fell to me to attempt to wheedle extra oil or cloth from him. My usual ploy was to try to catch the eye of Ivy while Fred was busy with other things. This was not often successful, and I would then find myself being lectured on the scarcity of oil and cotton during wartime, together with how it was in the old days before the Great War – when cleaners had to really clean engines – with less oil than we were getting, and soap and water, and the foreman cleaner would check all was properly clean by wiping his handkerchief around the motion. If the cloth was dirtied, the whole engine had to be cleaned again, etc, etc. I would just stay politely dumb, nodding and shaking my head as appropriate; he would then suddenly stop his tirade and say, "I can't stand here all day talking to you, go and see your foreman". He would then stalk off into the depths of the stores, at which point Ivy would usually appear with the items I had requested.

Old Fred was right of course. We made very little impression on the grime and grease of the engines. The cleaning consisted mainly of wiping the sides of the cab and tender so that the engine number and the LMS lettering could be seen, unless of course we had a named engine or one in maroon livery to clean, when a little more effort was usually made. Such a time was when a streamlined engine – I believe it was *City of Coventry*, which had failed because of a broken water feed pipe while on a diversion route via Northampton with a down express – was on shed. We really made a good job of cleaning her, although I remember there were arguments regarding who should have the use of the

One of our several Webb 'motor' tanks. This picture of 6641 shows it at the steam crane, with the fireman, or cleaner, having just tipped the tub and released the flap to cascade the coal into the bunker – a job which required a bit of strength and not a little dexterity to send the coal where it was required, and not onto the floor! The crane was the one operated by the female shed labourers during the war, as mentioned in the text.
H. C. CASSERLEY

two ladders that were available to enable the cleaning of the upper casing of the streamlining. The older boys obviously won.

This so-called cleaning was not the only task we cleaners were called upon to do. As well as being bar boys – as described previously – we were also detailed to do labouring jobs. Cleaning out the ashes and other spoil, etc, from the shed pits, helping in the coal stage (a very dirty, dusty job), and filling the tubs for the coaling crane, plus filling the sand bins located at various points in the ten roads of the shed. Steam raising was a job we were sometimes given. This was when an engine was 'dead' with no fire. We then had to obtain three or four firelighters, which were in the shape of a block about six inches long by four inches wide, and consisted of four pieces of thin wood forming the frame, which was filled with a mix of resin and wood chippings which bound it all together. A 'nest' of small coal was then made in the fire-box into which the firelighters were dropped, together with items of scrap wood, which used to be occasionally delivered by the wagon load from Wolverton carriage and wagon works, and the whole lot hopefully ignited by dropping a lighted piece of oily cotton waste onto it. Once burning well, more small coal was shovelled onto the blaze, the fire-hole door closed, and a retreat made from the

choking smoke which invariably enveloped the footplate, the fumes taking the easy route via the fire-hole rather than through the tubes to the chimney, until enough steam was raised to enable the blower to be operated.

Helping at the crane was considered to be something of a perk, especially if Ivy's sister, Audrey, or Mrs. 'Sniffsnoff' (a lady who unfortunately had a hair lip), was the crane driver. Either of them would often let one of us youngsters have a furtive turn at driving the crane while they slipped into their nearby females cabin for a cuppa – or whatever! However, one quickly learned not to be enticed into their cabin by any of the women labourers as some rather hair-raising 'initiation ceremonies' allegedly took place there!

During the early part of 1944 there appeared on the scene some German and Italian prisoners of war. These were mainly young men, although some of the Italians were older. They were in work parties of four in the charge of one of our soldiers – men of the Pioneer Corps. The prisoners were employed on general labouring tasks, such as cleaning pits, loading ashes into wagons, and also in loading the coal tubs at the crane. There appeared to be some competition in being allocated this latter task, because it brought them into the proximity of the women. They were also not averse to having a bit of fun with the hose pipe when supposedly

This shot of the loco is very indicative of how it was in the early fifties with the new roof. The unused and now redundant oil storage tanks are seen adjacent to the water softener plant. Although a turntable was provided, as the shed was inside the triangle of lines, we could go off the shed at either end, and, if necessary, negotiate two arms of the triangle to put the engine facing in the correct direction for its destination, which made a turntable somewhat redundant.

AIRFLOW STREAMLINES PLC

damping down the coal or ash dust, more than one of them returning to camp a little damp!

It quickly became the usual routine that the British soldiers would ensconce themselves in the mess room, reading newspapers, playing cards, and drinking copious amounts of tea, while the prisoners were given into the care of us youngsters and Tex. The Germans usually worked hard, and did what one would consider a good day's work. The Italians were generally more reluctant to put their backs into it, so to speak, especially if it was cold outside the shed. However, some of them were quite artistic, and would draw caricatures of some of the shed staff in chalk on the side of wagons or a wall. One of them made a very presentable Madonna from a broken shovel haft, which adorned the top of the engine allocation board for some time after the end of hostilities.

One day I was 'in charge' of an Italian foursome, and during the morning we had adjourned to the cabin for a cup of Camp coffee. The Italians were sitting at one of the two long tables with the soldiers, having made their drink. As I made my way to the table with my billycan of coffee for myself and Bill Flint – the other 'guard' – I inadvertently knocked the can over, and most of the contents went into the lap of one of the Italians. He leaped to his feet clutching a certain area of his trousers, screaming what I assumed was abuse directed at me. Many years later I related the story to an Italian lady who worked in the same department as me at New Scotland Yard, and repeated as near as I could remember what the Italian had uttered. She didn't translate it for me, but her eyes opened wide, she crossed herself, cried out, "Oh Mister Mutton", and beat a hasty retreat with her hands clasped over her ears. So I guess my original assumption of what the Italian prisoner had shouted was not far wrong!

Filling the sand bins around the shed was usually a good skive. The sand wagon would be positioned on one of the roads near the fitters shop, as the sand bag storage area was to the side of the shop behind the glass house, and backing on to the wall behind the forge, which gave some degree of warmth and dryness. The wagon was invariably an open one covered by a tarpaulin sheet, which would be peeled back a certain amount to allow the door to be dropped down to make it easier to unload the bags. There would usually be four of us detailed for the task, and each lad would shoulder a bag to be stacked in the appropriate place. When the wagon was about half empty, the sheet would be replaced over the wagon, and the rest of the sand bags manoeuvred to form a sort of maze, with a 'den' at one end of the wagon. Candles, or perhaps an oil lamp, would be lit, and a game of cards would commence – usually pontoon or nap. When Tex eventually became aware that the unloading had stopped part way through, he would come to the wagon shouting that he knew we were in there, and demanding that we come out. Of course, not a sound emanated from within the wagon, and after more ineffectual shouting he would attempt to clamber inside. When his grunting

informed us that he had made it into the wagon, and was beginning to crawl through the 'maze', one or more of the stacked sand bags would 'inadvertently' fall on him, usually pinning him to the floor, allowing enough time for us to escape via an already loosened part of the sheet in our corner of the wagon. Poor Tex never seemed to appreciate that it would be far easier to apprehend the miscreants if he took the sheet off the wagon himself!

Like the majority of youngsters we used to get up to various pranks in the course of each day. As mentioned previously, the boiler smiths' lamps were carbide fuelled, carbide being a rock-like substance which, when wetted, gives off an inflammable gas. We youngsters would acquire an amount of partly-used carbide from one of the men while they were cleaning out their lamp, and would store it until we had enough for our needs. Then an empty Tizer bottle (those with the clip down stopper) was obtained, and the carbide inserted. We would then go either to the cut (canal) alongside the loco shed, or over the running line into the meadow where there was a small lake, and an arm of the river. A small amount of water would be put into the bottle and the stopper sealed, the bottle then being thrown into the water. After a minute or so there would be a small depth-charge-like upsurge in the water as the bottle exploded. Sometimes a stunned fish would appear on the surface, and one time we had our biggest 'catch' – a pike – at the nearby river.

Minor accidents were not unusual in a locomotive shed – as mentioned previously – and cut hands and chafed knuckles were more or less normal daily occurrences. However, a much more serious accident happened one day while we

This picture shows the canal and towpath that ran alongside the shed and yard. The yard had a low wall surmounted by a tall wooden fence, supposedly to keep out intruders. We youngsters used to 'escape' from the confines of the shed by going to the 'top end' of the yard and thence via either a wire fence to the towpath, or the bridge of the Blisworth line over the canal and into the adjacent field and the river.
G. ONLEY

cleaners – for once working correctly – were attempting to move a wagon into which we were loading ashes. Several of us had our shoulders to the wagon, while Terry Page had his back braced against the buffer beam of an engine parked just behind the wagon, and his feet planted on the beam of the wagon in an attempt to use his leg muscles to assist in moving the wheels of the old grease-box axles of the wagon. Unbeknown to Terry, and the rest of us, someone had summoned the assistance of an engine to do the job for us.

Unfortunately, it approached too quickly and hit the wagon rather hard, compacting the buffers and fracturing Terry's thigh in doing so. Poor Terry was in hospital for some time, and later left the railway. Another enquiry was held, but it was decided that the fault was Terry's as he should not have been between the wagon and the engine.

Although I didn't realise it then, some of the engines seen on the shed were almost relics of a bygone age – the last of their line of the old LNWR regime. I remember having to

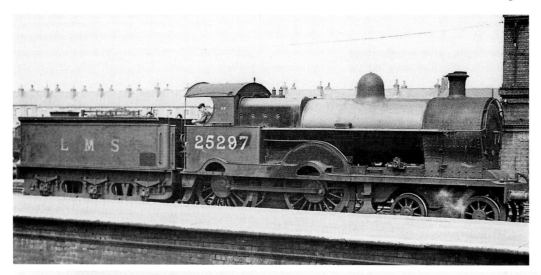

Two of the old LNWR engines which were sometimes visitors to the shed. The picture of 25648 was taken at Stafford in April 1946.
COLLECTION R. J. ESSERY and H. C. CASSERLEY

clean the tank feeds on a Prince of Wales class – No. 25648 (*Queen of the Belgians*), which had failed because of injector trouble. A passing footplateman informed me that, "there aint many of them about these days". I had a closer look around the old girl – she certainly looked much bigger than many of the other LNW engines on shed. Another old one I remember being on shed at one time was a Precursor, No. 25297 (*Sirocco*), which I believe was a Bletchley engine. Another, which I thought I remembered, was Experiment class *Lady of the Lake*, No. 25468, but I have seen in a publication that the last of the line was withdrawn in 1935, so I must be mistaken.

Another little hideaway from Tex, and later George Fidget – who was promoted from fire dropper – was in Harry the water-softening plant man's hut. There one could while away an hour or so listening to his tales of the Great War, and helping him carry the bags of water-softening agent to the mixing tank.

Later in 1944, we lads who were approaching, or had attained, our sixteenth birthday were 'requested' to do fire watching at what had obviously been a specially constructed lookout post on top of the carriage sheds, some half mile from the loco depot. This was initially rather exciting, and was my first taste of night duty, but it quickly became boring as very little enemy air activity was to be observed around Northampton. In fact, I think only four bombs were dropped in the town during the whole of the war – two in fields reasonably close to the railway, one in the Billing Road cemetery, and one on a bungalow in Duston Road not far from Bants Lane – which quickly became a local focus of interest. In fact the most damage to the town was caused when one of our own Stirling bombers crashed at the centre of town.

Another job we youngsters had to do was 'knocking up'. This we had been doing during the daytime from when I first joined the cleaning staff. Mainly, it was informing the Special Link men who, after their compulsory twelve hours rest between turns of duty, awaited the knocker-up's tap on door or window, armed with a slip of paper informing them of what time to book on, and for what sort of duty. Now, having initiated us in the delights of night duty by dint of fire-watching duties, we older cleaners were detailed for knocking up during the night. This night-time stint was not only for the Special Link men, but also for men on regular turns of duty (mainly freight trains), who requested a knock, just in case the alarm clock failed, or the "old woman didn't wake up in time"!

One somewhat amusing anecdote regarding knocking up concerned one night when Frank Digby and I were on duty, and although given two call-up slips in different directions, we had decided to ride round together. I was using my own bicycle (which I used for travel to and from home), and Frank had the loco bike, which had oil lamps. Mine were acetylene (carbide) lamps, bought while I was with the fitters and the carbide freely obtained. The lamps on the shed's old

boneshaker would frequently go out, especially when bouncing up and down kerbs at the various houses. Such was the case this particular night. The lights on Frank's bike had jolted out, but of course he continued to ride it without lights, as it was certainly not our habit to relight them, especially as they gave almost no illumination, and we knew the local roads very well – even in the blackout.

Frank was riding with one hand on the handlebars, the other holding the long piece of cane with which we tapped on bedroom windows. Our next call was to a house in a road up towards Queen Eleanor's Cross – a location neither of us knew very well. After making the call, we were just beginning the ride back to the loco when suddenly the voice of what was obviously a member of His Majesty's Constabulary boomed out – "Oi, where are your lights?". Frank, who was a little distance behind me, called back "Up near me liver", and, pedalling furiously, overtook me, swept round the next corner, and ran into one of the brick air-raid shelters built half on the pavement and half on the roadway, which itself was not illuminated. Poor Frank did his arm a bit of no good, and the bike fared even worse, the front wheel being buckled, and the handlebars twisted. The tap cane was nowhere to be seen. While we were sorting out both Frank and the bike, and searching for the cane, the long arm of the law appeared round the corner and surveyed the scene with the help of his lamp. He merely remarked, "That'll teach you young buggers not to break the law, and not to be cheeky with it", turned on his heel and disappeared into the blackness. We made our disconsolate way on foot back to the loco, where we hid the bike. It was repaired next day by one of the fitters. Frank's arm took a little longer.

Another night duty job I was 'asked' to do was tending the boiler at the carriage shed, the steam from which was used to heat the carriages prior to them being taken to the station for their respective trains next morning. The boiler was an ancient, upright one, in a lean-to building behind the shed, and fired via a large side-hinged door with wood, coke, and almost anything to hand, including bits of old carpet and seating material! The steam pressure was kept at around 80 lbs psi and the steam fed into the shed, and thence to the carriages, via a large-diameter metal pipe, over which, in the corner of the lean-to, someone (I guess the regular boiler-man) had affixed an old first-class carriage seat. This was ideal to snuggle into between bouts of stoking during the night, and certainly much better than being on the roof fire-watching!

Following my sixteenth birthday and these stints of night duty, I was informed that I would receive firing training in my progression to becoming a 'passed cleaner' – something I had looked forward to for some time. It was also known among us youngsters that because of the war, and the subsequent shortage of men, we might sometimes be employed on the main line, although not supposed to be so utilized at such a young age.

A panoramic view showing the carriage shed in the middle distance (the boiler house was at the other end). The loco shed is hidden from view by the gasometer, whilst the line to Roade is seen snaking off to the left of the council refuse incinerator towards Duston Junction West and Hunsbury Hill, where George Gee had his 'allotment' (piggery, saw bench, timber yard and stable!), and where the Home Guard did their training.
W. J. S. MEREDITH

And so, a few weeks later, I was posted with Tommy King, the driver of the Castle Yard shunt engine, for my initial firing training. Tommy had an old leg injury and was permanently engaged on shunting, and his domain was the Castle Yard sidings, shunting wagons in and out of the large goods depot at Castle Station. The engines allocated to this work were some of our loco shed's oldest – 22913 and 22916 seem to ring bells in my memory, but there were others of course, but always 0–6–0 tender engines. I remember one, I think an old MR Johnson type, which had only a steam brake operated by a brass wheel in the centre of the boiler back plate above the fire-hole, and which was practically impossible to operate with any speed by a driver craning over the side of the footplate looking for the

shunter's signal, or the proximity of wagons being backed on to. It thus became my job to operate the wheel when Tommy shouted, "Brake!". Not always an efficient operation. This engine also had an injector clack which kept sticking open when the injector was switched off, which necessitated going along the framing to give the clack housing a clout with the coal pick to make it drop into the closed position, and thus stop the noisy rush of steam which quickly enveloped the footplate and any shunters on the ground nearby.

Tommy was a very pleasant old boy, and working with him could only be classed as a doddle, as also it was with another driver permanently employed on shunting, Bill Whitlock, with whom I volunteered to work one Sunday

A shot showing part of the Castle Yard, with the well remembered shunters' cabin centrally placed and looking northwards beyond No. 2 box towards Spencer Bridge Road overbridge, with the Rugby bay to the left. No. 22913, photographed in 1950, was one of the engines frequently to be seen here and one with a more comfortable footplate as I remember.
COLLECTION R. J. ESSERY

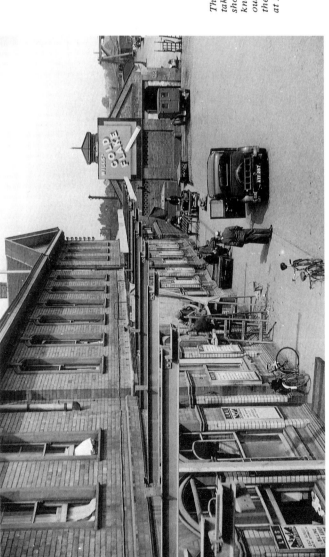

The pictures of the front of the station in 1939 were obviously taken during the construction of the new canopy. The photo showing the goods shed in the background, also shows the 'coffee knob' to the left of the Wilkins & Bedford sign, where we often had our tea cans filled, together with the purchase of a cake or two, on the trudge from the loco shed to relieve trains further along the line at No. 3 or 4 signal boxes.

W. J. S. MEREDITH

on the down side shunt. I guess one could say that all aspects of firing were learned while employed on a shunting engine: shovelling coal and guiding it to where it was wanted in the firebox; tank filling – hauling the heavy leather 'bag' on to the tender and into the tank; cleaning the fire with the clinker shovel, etc; but all at a somewhat leisurely pace – unlike what one imagined it would be when employed on main-line working!

Although I didn't know it, I was soon to be enlightened in this respect, for after my few weeks with Tommy, his regular fireman returned from sickness, and I was back in the shed on cleaning duties. However, one morning my world changed, and I found myself beginning what I thought of only as a terrific adventure, not appreciating what was ahead of me.

More views of the goods shed and yard. The father of Johnny Warden, one of our firemen, was a drayman here, and, like Johnny, was rather rotund, being shaped like one of the barrels he was so often required to transport.
W. J. S. MEREDITH
J. HARRISON

These pictures show the entrance to Castle Station, and the nearby entrance/exit of the goods shed to the station, and beyond to No. 3 and 4 signal boxes and the up and down sidings, I used this route to the shed rather than via Far Cotton, while I was living at Northwood Road and later at Brunswick Place.

Once I became a fireman and learned of the 'footpath' from the loco shed to the

W. J. S. MEREDITH

W. J. S. MEREDITH

J. HARRISON

BOOKING OFFICE

WAY OUT

STATION MASTER
OFFICE

TELEGRAPH OFFICE

BRITISH TIMKEN LTD
tapered roller
BEARINGS
for the Railways of the World

Castle Station platform 1, as I remember it, with Wymans bookstall beneath the Tele-
graph Office sign. The way to platforms 4 and 5 and to the loco shed was behind the
cameraman, who was positioned under the road of West Bridge. The handrail on the left
of the picture was on the stairway leading to the footbridge to platforms 6, 7 & 8. There
were also exit doors on the footbridge by which passengers could be let out onto West
Bridge at busy times.
R. J. F. RAWLINSON

'Cauliflower' No. 8601 seen here at Willesden in 1936. It had become 28601 by the time of my trip to Oxford.
J. P. RICHARDS

These two views of 'Cauliflower' 28614, looking rather forlorn, having lost its tender, provide a valued record of the footplate.

Right: *A view inside the cab from a position where the tender should be. Obviously, with the pile of firebars on the footplate, some work was in hand in the firebox, and the ratchet mechanism of the fire-hole door had been removed and stored beneath the fireman's seat. The ratchet type of fire-hole door was not over popular with firemen because in use it sometimes became red hot and began to droop, thus restricting the aperture of the fire-hole and consequently the amount of coal on the shovel one could direct towards the front of the box. Not too bad on the smaller engines, as this type were, but not so good on engines with longer fireboxes. The actual mechanics of the footplate were similar to those of a 'D' (see page 186), with the reversing wheel visible on the left (driver's side), and the regulator handle — with only one 'arm' — seen in the centre of the boiler, above the fire-hole. The two injectors are shown, one on either side of the boiler, with that on the fireman's side having the 'fizzle pipe' valve and pipe visible. The single boiler gauge glass can also be seen to the right of the regulator, and above the latter can be seen the brake handles, joined by the metal bar as on a 'D'. Also just visible are the steam valves for the injectors between the two brake handles. Above the fireman's seat, the handle of the 'blower' can just be seen, and on the driver's side, attached to the cabside, can be seen the cylinder lubricator. High above the boiler can just be made out the vacuum gauge (slightly on the driver's side) and whistle valve, whilst on the fireman's side are the steam gauges for boiler pressure and the carriage heating. Below the footplate can be seen the drawbar (with cotter pin and a wagon coupling chain, obviously used as a temporary device when moving the tenderless engine), plus the water feed pipes to the injectors, and the vacuum and steam heating pipes. Also to be seen are the back sander pipes descending towards the rail on either side, the sand box lids being house within the footplate floorboards.*

CHAPTER FOUR
DOUBLE TRIP OXFORD

THE 'Cauliflower' simmered gently, steam from her safety valves mingling with that from the faulty whistle cock and being lost almost immediately in the murky drizzle of the mid-December morning.

I contemplated the steam also slightly hissing and bubbling from the regulator gland, and the gland of one of the injectors, accentuating the muggy atmosphere on the footplate – closeted as we were under the protective shroud of a blackout sheet 'borrowed' from an engine on the shed – and which was proving far better than the short cab of the old LNWR engine for keeping out the rain. Didn't fitters' apprentices do any packing of footplate glands these days? Different in my day – no splashing a drop of thick oil around the glands and a quick tightening of the nuts then. Archie Harris would soon have spotted that and jumped on me.

I thought back to the day two years ago – December 1942 – when as a very green fourteen-year-old I had begun work at the nearby loco shed, and my time with the fitters before transferring to the 'footplate side'. Now, today, here I was out on the main line ! Not that it felt at the moment much different to the shunting firing turns I had done – similar type of engine, an 0–6–0 – and sitting in a shunting yard not a stone's throw from the loco shed.

All that seemed different to me was the fact that I was with a driver whom I couldn't remember ever having seen before, and that he had told me to build up the fire well, "ready for the slog up the bank". The only 'slogs' I had done so far were the relatively short runs up the shunting neck of the Down Sidings with Bill Whitlock, and then only for one Sunday.

I was jolted from my reverie by the clang of coupling chains on hooks as the guard made his way along the train towards the engine, a progress interspersed by curses every time his shunting pole became caught between wagon hook and coupling chain. I peered from under the blackout sheet at the approaching figure, who grunted his approval when he saw that the engine had already been coupled to the first wagon. "Got 'im trained I see, Bosco", he called up to the driver. "We'll no doubt find out about that a bit later on", replied Bosco (whose surname I had discovered was Kirton). "How many have we got on Harry?". Harry, huddled in his great coat with collar turned up and cap pulled down so that it appeared to be held up by his ears, and with about four days growth of stubble around his chin, consulted a scrap of damp-looking paper in his hand. "You've got twenty-three and a brake, equal to thirty", he said, "and eight of them are for Bliserth, so right away as soon as the bobby's ready for us".

Twenty-three, I thought, that's nearly as many firing turns as I've done. Now, I'm out main line for the first time, not a normal situation I was sure; but then, this was the fifth year of the war, and no doubt a great many sixteen-year-olds were doing jobs they should not really be doing at that age.

It seemed that as far as the railway was concerned, it was generally accepted that if a driver would take a chance with an unproven fireman, youngsters such as myself sometimes had the opportunity of getting away from the shed or shunting yards.

Such an occasion was today. I had booked on at 8am as usual for cleaning duties, and was engaged as such when I was called away from the Black Five I had been wiping over with the proverbial oily rag, and told to find an engine numbered 28601. I was to be the fireman on a 'double trip' to Oxford. When I queried this, I was told it entailed lodging at Oxford for the night, and working a train back to Northampton tomorrow; the call-up boy would inform my mother that I would not be home that day. I collected my bag with my sandwiches from the mess room before finding the engine in the gloomy confines of the shed, the driver already busy 'fatting up' with oil can in one hand and a flaming torch in the other.

I introduced myself to him, and learned that he had already been informed of my lack of experience, and was obviously not too happy with his lot. Where was the regular fireman? He had apparently knocked sick' again because his wife was afraid of being left alone at night in case there was an air raid. I learned later that the more likely reason for the fireman's sickness was that his wife's former boyfriend was home on leave from the army!

Having 'gonged off' the shed at the Bridge Street Junction box, the engine would move down the line for about a hundred yards, beyond the points, whistle, and when the points were set, move forward and across to the up line, to a position beyond the points for access to the yard. Another whistle and again, when the points were set, reverse into the yard, and onto the train, the guard having set the hand points for this manoeuvre.

Now here we were about to start on what I could only think of as an adventure. I reached for the water feed handle as the engine blew off steam, but before I could start the injector, Bosco turned from looking at the dolly signal – which would give the path to the running line – stopped me, and said, "Don't fill her too full, by the looks of the smoke box she's a primer". I looked round the side of the cab, and saw the telltale whitish streaks down the sides of the smoke box and front end of the boiler, and queried the cause. She's about clapped out", Bosco said, "And picks up water with the steam when she's working hard. She obviously needs a boiler washout". I knew about those from my time with Fanny Sutton, so supposed the engine would go in for an X scheme at some time in the near future at her home shed of Bletchley. "Just try and keep her at half a glass", said Bosco, "And we'll see how she goes". Just then we heard the clang of the signal and a shout from 'Dickie' Bird, the signalman. The journey was about to begin. I closed the firehole door and opened the damper as Bosco

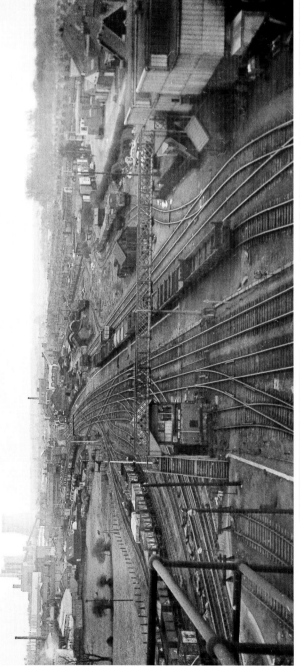

Two pictures looking towards Bridge Street station and level crossing in the distance. Note also the cooling towers of the power station. The footbridge can be seen in the upper picture, and the 'old' CMD sidings on the right (also seen in the lower picture) from where began my 'adventure'. G. ONLEY

The 'Blisworth Flyer' having just passed Duston West and making a storming approach towards the bank beyond Rothersthorpe crossing on 12th June 1948.
L. HANSON

eased the regulator open. 28601 wheezed forward, gently tightening the couplings – very different to shunting activities, when it's all snatch and clang, the wagon draw bars, couplings, and buffers often taking a terrific pounding. A slight retarding effect on our forward progress indicated that the couplings were taut all the way to the brake van, and that Harry had yet to release his hand brake.

Bosco opened the regulator a little more and the old 'eighteen inch' chuffed towards the points from the yard to the running line. Almost immediately the engine wheels began slipping on the wet rail. Bosco snatched the regulator closed with a curse. "Come on old gal, dig your toes in", he muttered as he re-opened the regulator. I yanked on the sander handle, but seemingly without much success because the wheels again began to slip. Bosco coaxed her out of the sidings, and as if she appreciated being on the main line at last, 28601 stopped slipping and chuffed strongly towards Duston West and the next signals. "Make sure you get the tip from Harry", said Bosco. I leaned from the cab, looked back, and saw the guard waving his arm from the verandah of the brake van. I acknowledged the wave by extending my arm in a similar fashion, then busied myself with the injector as the safety valves lifted as we rolled gently towards the home signal.

"Got to wait for the Blisworth Motor, I expect", said Bosco. "Don't fill her too full, just let her blow off, we're not upsetting anyone here." A few minutes later, 6754 came scudding round the curve from the direction of Castle Station, the little Webb tank engine seemingly making light work of her two-coach 'motor' train on the four-mile trip to Blisworth, where it would connect with the main Euston – Rugby line, and also with the old SMJ railway to Towcester, for the Banbury and Stratford upon Avon branches.

I smiled to myself as I watched the little passenger train disappear under the bridge of the Northampton to Roade line. Not more than two or three years ago I was one of several young 'number snatchers' who, on Saturdays, armed with a few sandwiches, a bottle of pop, and a note book and pencil, would travel on the 'Blisworth Flyer' to collect the engine numbers of the expresses as they thundered through Blisworth station. Now, here I was working a train along that very line. My thoughts were quickly returned to the present as the signal in front was raised. Bosco said, "Right, he's cleared 'Thrup' crossing, now it's our turn". Again the gentle start as Bosco eased the regulator open. I looked back to make sure the brake van was moving too. All seemed in order, smoke was curling from the stove pipe of Harry's van so he was obviously generating some heat in order to dry his damp clothing. I thankfully let the flap of the blackout sheet fall back into place as I withdrew my head. It certainly was a damp, raw morning out there.

As the train gathered momentum, Bosco opened the regulator a little wider, and wound back the reversing wheel about a turn. He then searched among the spilled coal on the footplate for a small piece, which he wedged between the regulator handle and the stop, so the handle wouldn't work itself closed because of the vibration of the engine. I knew of this practice, but thought it a little unnecessary at the speed we were going. Under the directions of Bosco, while we were in the sidings, I had broken as much as I could of the poor-looking coal and briquettes at the front of the tender into reasonably small pieces. "As big as your fist", had been Bosco's words, but I was not sure I had completely complied with that instruction. Now, having wedged the regulator open, Bosco reached for the firing shovel, opened the firehole door, and said, "Watch me. Do it the same as I do and we'll be alright". With that he began firing the engine, muttering as he did so, "Two at the front, two each side, two under the door, and one in the middle". I watched with some fascination as this 'old' man seemingly effortlessly glided the shovel into the firehole, and with a twist of the wrist sent coals to where he wanted. "There", said Bosco, "That's found her", as he closed the firehole door and looked at the plume of brown smoke mixed with the exhaust steam blasting from the chimney. "If you can do that, we'll be alright boy." I wasn't so sure, but already I was feeling more at ease with this stranger.

As we duly gained momentum, Bosco wound back the reversing gear another turn or so, and we chuffed quite briskly round the bend alongside the Blackwood Hodge repair works, the yard now seemingly full of large army-type earth-moving equipment, most of them damaged and with the white American star on the sides. I looked at the steam gauge – showing about 145 lbs pressure – and at the boiler gauge glass, where the water was bobbing at just under half full. So far there did not appear to have been any indication of the engine priming, and I decided to fill the boiler a little more. I had heard stories of what happened if the water level was allowed to fall too low – stories of fusible plugs blowing, scalded crews, and fires having to be shovelled out! I wanted none of that. I operated the injector and waited until another inch or so was indicated in the glass before turning it off. Bosco was peering round the cab side looking for the distant signal for Rothersthorpe Crossing. He eventually gave a grunt, pulled his head in and muttered, "He's got it off, so we're right away to Blisworth. Put a bit more round her, we shall soon be in to the bank". I opened the firehole door, yanking the ratchet down firmly, and began firing the engine as I had been shown.

Although we were not going very fast, I still found it very different to when shunting. Balancing on an oscillating platform, turning and thrusting a shovelful of coal into a rather small aperture, and directing the coal to where one wanted was not easy for me. I quickly learned to have less on the shovel when firing. However, I managed, only twice hitting the rim plate of the firehole – rather than bouncing the shovel on it – to give her the nine shovels of coal as Bosco had dictated. I closed the firehole door, scraped the spilled coal back into the tender, and thrust the shovel into the coal, and looked out at the chimney. Not as much smoke as Bosco had made, but it looked not bad to me. The steam gauge showed about 140 lbs, and the boiler was again only half full. I contemplated whether to wait until the engine had more steam pressure before injecting more water into the boiler, or to do it now before the water got any lower. I looked again at the chimney for an indication of how long the previous firing would last, and saw that we were almost at Rothersthorpe Crossing. I couldn't resist putting my head out of the cab – just in case anyone I knew was waiting at the gates. No-one was, and acknowledging the gate man's wave, I withdrew my head and, as quickly as I could, fired the engine again, then on with the injector to increase the water level.

Now we were in to the bank, and Bosco searched for a larger piece of coal as he opened the regulator wider. He also wound the reversing wheel forward a turn, and a much sharper bark emitted from the chimney. I turned off the injector. The boiler was only just over half full, but the steam pressure was now below 140 lbs. I fired the engine again, this time managing not to spread coal around the footplate – probably because we were now going more slowly. Almost at once Bosco began to curse, and I was conscious of a different sound from the chimney. "She's priming", shouted Bosco, "Watch your boiler level". I looked at the gauge glass and thought I could almost see the water level going down, although the boiler seemed to be nearly three-quarters full – a false impression I learned later, created by the lifting of the water as the engine primed. Bosco opened the cylinder drain cocks and the engine disappeared into a fog of her own making. Seeing my somewhat confused expression, Bosco explained, between curses, that while the engine was priming, water as well as steam was entering the cylinders, which could result in the cylinder ends being burst open – water does not compress like steam.

However, nothing so drastic occurred, and by dint of careful regulator manipulation, together with the frequent opening and closing of the drain cocks, plus the ever-decreasing water level in the boiler, the priming finally subsided. We eventually limped over the top of the bank and chugged feebly towards the outer home signal on the approach to Blisworth. The boiler gauge showed less than an inch of water, but on Bosco's instructions I had not put the injector on during the final crawl over the top of the bank. Now as we chuffed gently along the almost level stretch towards the signal, Bosco closed the regulator and then the drain cocks, and I put the blower on hard. Steam pressure was down well below 130 lbs, so I fired her again with just four shovels of coal, and as the pressure began to rise, opened the water and steam valves and got the injector singing as it added more water to the boiler. "Half a glass don't forget", chided Bosco, "We'll have to wait here till the motor goes back to town".

Some twenty minutes later, after three expresses had streaked through the station, and I had regained a full head of steam, one on the up line stopped, then shortly pulled forward some three or four coach lengths and stopped again; obviously too many coaches for the length of the platform. A minute or so later it blasted off towards London, and almost immediately we heard the shrill whistle of 6754 as it propelled its two carriages round the bend from the station on its short journey back to Northampton. I waved to the driver sitting in his compartment at the front of the train as it passed, and as I did so Bosco re-started our train as the signal was raised for us to continue into Blisworth. We chugged into the station, but then had to wait while a train of box vans rattled through before we could pull on to the main line in order for the brake van to clear the points to allow us to reverse into the sidings.

Once stationary in the sidings, Bosco reached into the driver's side metal trunk on the tender (the trunk on the fireman's side held the oil bottles and tool bucket, etc.) and lifted out his large 'double trip' basket, from which he took a triangular-shaped whisky bottle of cold tea. After taking a swig, he asked if I had anything to drink. When I replied in the negative, having thought I would be on shed duties this day, and able to get tea in the mess room, Bosco kindly gave

This shot of the north end of the station, with an unrebuilt Scot approaching provides a good view of the crossover from the down line, and the needful slow negotiation of the points, etc, round the right-hand curve to the Northampton line. The buildings on both platforms were the Ladies waiting rooms. The general waiting room and Gents toilets were at the south end of the platform, as seen in the right-hand picture.
W. MALLARD

Blisworth. A picture taken from the bridge over the SMJ line. In the foreground we can see the down loop and main lines, and the up main and loop line, with the sidings beyond. The train in the distance was on its way to Northampton having negotiated the slow manoeuvre from the down main, and headed by an LNW engine.
W. MALLARD

A general view of Blisworth with a 'Baby Scot' trundling through with a relatively light train towards Weedon and Rugby. The SMJ exchange sidings are seen on the right with that railway's station just visible on the far right. The wagons on the left were in the up exchange sidings, whilst the main station can just be seen where the signal gantry is. The line to Northampton swung off to the left beyond the leading wagons in the sidings, whilst just beyond can be seen the timber yard siding, which was behind the island platform.

W. J. S. MEREDITH

A shot taken from the island platform on a damp, miserable day, with a train thundering through northwards past the signal box.   W. MALLARD

A good shot of the junction, taken from the signal box. The line nearest to the camera was the down main (with the points set for something to go into the loop). The next was the up main, and then the up loop line, with the line from the sidings joining it. The other line joining was to Northampton for trains from the south, which would be crossed over from the down line, across the up line, and thence onto the curve towards Northampton. The line to the right of the wooden post (near right) was the line to/from the 'bay' platform and the sidings, which was also used as a shunting neck as and when necessary, depending on traffic conditions. The line beyond that led to Northampton from the bay, whilst the next one was the line from Northampton with, just visible, the line to the timber yard.   W. MALLARD

A shot taken from the south end of the island platform, later in BR days. The fencing of the down platform had been removed and the name board propped against one of the posts. However, opportunely, this enables the station entrance and the proximity of the hotel to be seen. The hotel had been extended since my first visit. Also to be seen is the shunting neck beyond the platform, with the old hand-operated crane, and the goods shed at left.
LENS OF SUTTON

The station entrance in LMS days, from where I went across the road to the hotel. The officer of the law was obviously keeping a watchful eye on the 'suspect' with the bike.
W. MALLARD

me sixpence, told me to go the hotel just outside the station, knock on the side door, and ask for a bottle of "whatever you want". I gratefully nipped across the main line, round the back of the signal box to the SMJ station, where an ex-Midland 0–6–0 with one coach was waiting to depart for Banbury, then out of the station to the pub, somewhat pretentiously named The Blisworth Hotel. At the jug and bottle hatchway, after some initial teasing regarding the strength of

my required 'liquor', I purchased a bottle of ginger beer from the landlord's daughter – a young lady whom I was to know somewhat less formally in future years! With my own money I also bought two packets of crisps, one of which I ate while making my way back to the siding. On my return, I found Bosco busy shunting off the wagons for Blisworth (probably for the SMJ branch), and collecting another eleven for attachment to our train. Harry informed us that five of

A general view of the SMJ station platform, with the hotel off to the right near the bus. Note the steps on the platform, which were in general use by the station staff for lamp repairs, etc, and were fitted with a pair of wheels at the back to aid manoeuvrability. They are similar to those used at Banbury (Chapter 12) for the release of the pigeons. Wagons can be seen on the shunting neck, so obviously there was an engine on the far end, either doing a spot of shunting or perhaps preparing to propel them into the loop for transfer to the up sidings.
                                                        J. E. NORRIS

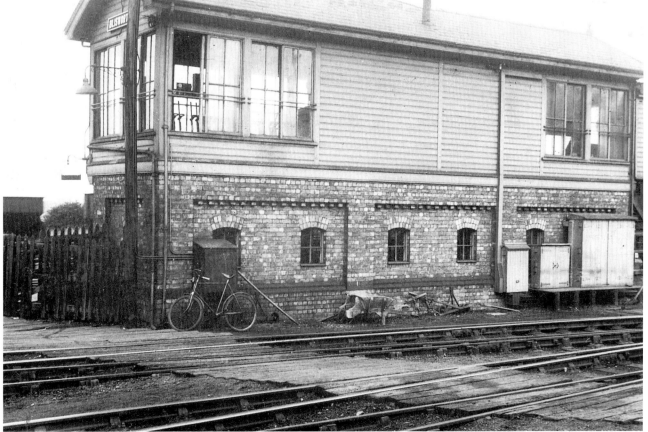

The back of the signal box, with the crossing to the SMJ station, over which I went towards the hotel.   W. MALLARD

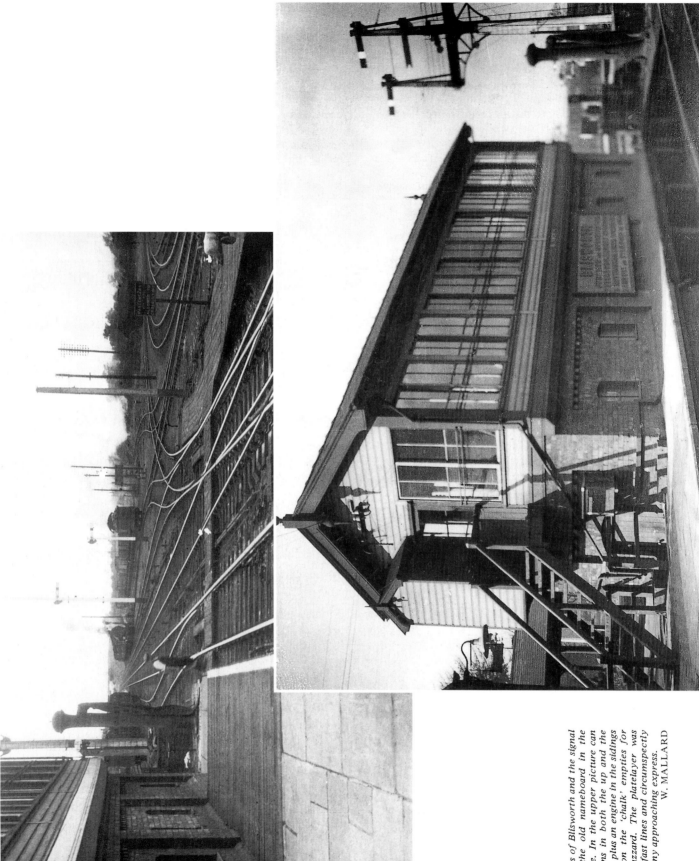

More pictures of Blisworth and the signal box. Note the old nameboard in the lower picture. In the upper picture can be seen trains in both the up and the down loops, plus an engine in the sidings — perhaps on the 'chalk' empties for Leighton Buzzard. The platelayer was crossing the fast lines and circumspectly looking for any approaching express.
W. MALLARD

these, together with two of our original train were for Bletchley, which was to be our next port of call.

I busied myself making up the fire and cleaning the footplate, while Bosco checked around the engine with the oilcan. I was glad to be back in the warmth of the engine after my excursion to the pub. Harry, still shrouded in his greatcoat, stood talking to the wheel tapper and his mate, the greaser (or gricer as they were sometimes known). The greaser's job (thought to be of fairly low status in the railway hierarchy, and usually performed by injured or partially infirm men nearing retirement age), was to check the level of lubricant in wagon axle boxes. Those on the more modern wagons were oil boxes, but most of the older wagons had 'fat boxes' which were filled with a thick yellow tallow that the greaser ladled from a container using a flat piece of metal. Although this job was rated lowly, if the greaser didn't pack the tallow into the boxes really well, the

box could soon over-heat, and a hot box could possibly cause a fire – not amusing on an ammunition or aviation fuel train. All this was related to me by Bosco as we prepared ourselves for the next stage of my adventure. However, before that Bosco decided we should fill the tank as we had no way of knowing the level of water, the gauge glass being missing from the tank gauge on the tender.

Bosco had mentioned that once we got the right of way from Blisworth, the first part of the journey would be on the main line, and we would have to "go like hell to Roade" before we could be switched to the slow line. In fact, we had to wait for well over half an hour before it was deemed there was a large enough margin between expresses and other fast trains for us to make our dash. Eventually the signal was pulled off, accompanied by a loud shout from the signal box, and we began the second part of the journey.

A view looking northwards showing the timber yard, with what could have been either No. 1218 or 1219 in the bay – although it looks a somewhat larger engine. A train is also visible in the up loop. Both were no doubt awaiting an express.
L&GRP

The island platform showing the general waiting room and gents lavatory, with the Northampton 'bay' beyond.
W. MALLARD

The waiting room and toilet block on the island platform. When we were 'number snatching', we youngsters used to hide in the waiting room to keep out of the porter's view. W. MALLARD

Looking south from the island platform. The signal gantry and the water tank can be seen in the distance. The shunting neck stop block was just short of the tank, with a drop behind it. On the other side of the neck, and hidden by the toilet block, is where the Blisworth Bacon Company sheds were. W. MALLARD

'Baby Scot' 5532 Illustrious *heading northwards through the station with what appears to be a 'senior spotter' watching from his seat on the island platform. Note the raft of wagons on the shunting neck awaiting marshalling.*
W. MALLARD

An older shot of the water tank, with the door to the pump room open at the top of the steps. The stops of the shunting neck are just visible through the fence, midway between the tank and the gantry. Note the bantam in the bit of waste ground.
W. MALLARD

The water tank, with repairs obviously being done, hence the scaffolding, etc. The picture also shows the exit from the Northampton bay to the up line, and the end of the shunting neck on the right by the platelayers hut.
NATIONAL RAILWAY MUSEUM

BLETCHLEY (eventually)

The dash towards Roade was uneventful. The little engine seemed to revel in the importance of being on the 'premier' main line, and behaved herself. Even though it seemed to me that Bosco was blasting her along, with hardly any winding back of the reversing gears, she showed no sign of resuming priming. This was all new territory to me, and I was enjoying the day – so far. I had tied back the side portion of the blackout sheet at Blisworth as the drizzle seemed to have abated somewhat, and I was looking out as we progressed past the BBC (the Blisworth Bacon Company) factory, a large corrugated iron shed (where sometime in the future, I would witness a disturbing incident – but that's another story), and we were soon passing over the Grand Union Canal. A pair of narrow boats loaded with coal were heading towards the tunnel on the way to Stoke Bruerne, the towing one obviously diesel powered as there was no horse to be seen, although I couldn't hear the boat's exhaust because of the noise we were making. Again my mind drifted back some three years or so, when, together with a couple of school friends, we had made our way to the canal bank to eat our picnic. We sometimes did this if number-taking at the station became a little tedious, or, as was more likely, we were told to leave the station by a porter because too many of us were occupying the island platform. From the canal bank we could still see the trains go by, albeit only fleetingly, but long enough to 'cop' the number, and possibly the name.

Sometimes as a diversion from train-spotting, one could earn a ha'penny by walking a boatman's horse over the hill, while he and his wife footed the boats through the tunnel below. I vividly remembered one such day when I had been 'smooth talked' by a boatman's wife into helping to do the footing (or legging as they called it) while she walked the horse over the top – she being pregnant again! I couldn't recall anything more painful or scary. My back felt as if it had been rubbed raw by the planking on which I had to lie, and I had visions of falling into the blackness of the water below me as I attempted to find some footholds on the slippery unseen surface of the tunnel wall in order to propel the boat along. The end of the tunnel came not a moment too soon for me. To make matters worse, I didn't get my ha'penny from the disgruntled boatman, who complained, "It took twice as long as when missus does it, and t'bloody boat was rubbing along the wall all through y'skinny legs aint strong enough". With that he threw a rope to his wife, who was sitting contentedly on a bollard, and ordered her to "hook up t'bloody nag and get on board and get some grub goin'." Away they went, while I lay on the towpath, my leg

The tank – still with scaffolding in position – taken from the towpath of the Grand Union Canal. As young trainspotters, should we be sent from the station by one of the porters, we had two options – either go along the road to Gayton loop or go the other way to the road bridge over the canal, and thence to the towpath where we had a good view of trains on the embankment.
NATIONAL RAILWAY MUSEUM

The diverging lines, looking towards Blisworth (left) and Northampton (right).

W. J. S. MEREDITH

The support girders on the Northampton line through the deepest length of the cutting.

W. J. S. MEREDITH

muscles still trembling from the effort, and I still had to walk back over the hill to Blisworth!

Again I came back from my reverie, hearing Bosco shouting, "Put a bit more round her". A quick check of the water and steam levels, and I fired her again. Soon I saw we were approaching Roade Cutting with its walls of blue brick rising high above us, the exhaust from the chimney creating a staccato echo sound as we blasted into the cutting. Then, just as suddenly, all was quiet as Bosco closed the regulator.

We were over the slight incline from Blisworth, and were drifting towards Roade station, and the crossover to the slow line. I took advantage of the respite to put the blower on – steam pressure had fallen by more than 10 lbs – and, as she made steam, I put on the injector to increase the water level in the glass, which was again showing only about an inch.

As we trundled through the station and over the crossover to the slow line, Bosco began gently to open up again, and wound the reversing wheel back a couple of turns, but

A 'Baby Scot' heading its train southwards through Roade station on the up main line. There used to be a bay to the left of this platform for SMJ trains which apparently had a small branch from the overhead line.

W. J. S. MEREDITH

South of Roade the SMJ line between Towcester and Ravenstone crossed over the top of the main lines.   C. R. H. SIMPSON

Claughton No. 6004 on the down slow line near Ashton on 9th April 1938. This engine became the longest surviving of its class.

L. HANSON

almost immediately he cursed and closed the regulator as he saw the distant signal for Ashton was at amber. This was the first time I had seen other than semaphore signals. These distant signals were two-aspect electric lamps. The one for the slow line was on what appeared to be a ten foot pole at the track side, whilst that for the fast line was about as high as a shunting dolly signal, and positioned in the 'six foot' between the up fast and down slow lines. In response to my query, Bosco explained that most of the distant signals on the way to and from London were now colour light signals. We rounded the slight curve and under the road bridge towards the home signal at Ashton, and I could see the signalman standing at the top of his stairs. As we came nearly to a stop, the bobby shouted something neither of us could hear, disappeared into his box, and pulled off the signal for us to go into the loop line (the infamous Hanslope Loop – as I was to learn).

He re-appeared some seconds later holding a green flag. Bosco really let loose a string of curses on seeing this, and ordered me to – "Go and tell that ****** bobby that we're for Oxford and not a ****** coal train to be pushed in the loop behind about four others". I walked to the box and relayed Bosco's message – though not in so many words – and was told by the signalman that he required us to go in the loop to let the 1.30pm local from Northampton to go by. We could then reverse out of the loop and continue on our way, bypassing the trains already in the loop. I returned to Bosco with this explanation. He grunted his satisfaction and started the train again. On Bosco's direction I looked back and told him when the brake van was clear of the

points, and he stopped the train. Harry was by this time on his verandah, obviously anxious to discover what was happening. While this had been going on I had noticed that a fast 'box van' train had passed on the up fast line, indicating how little time to spare we had on the run from Blisworth, and why Bosco had thrashed the old girl along.

Now we had a few minutes peace while waiting for the local passenger train, Rugby to Bletchley, to pass by. This gave me a chance both to make up the fire without spilling coal around the footplate, and to increase the water level in the boiler. Bosco had said it was more or less level most of the way to Bletchley, so I should have few problems on the coming leg of the journey. The local – a Black Five heading eight coaches – duly barked its way past and almost immediately we heard Harry blowing his whistle and signalling us with his arm for us to reverse. Once back behind the home signal, the bobby re-set the points, pulled off the signal, and we re-commenced our journey. I was intrigued on looking out as we passed the trains in the loop. The first two had no-one on the footplate. In answer to my query, Bosco said he guessed that each crew was in the brake van of the train in front of their engine – probably playing cards – where it would be much warmer than on their footplate.

By the time we approached Hanslope box, the signal was off, indicating that the passenger train had cleared Castlethorpe. Bosco began to accelerate the train a little more. As we chugged past the leading train in the loop, we acknowledged the driver and fireman who were looking out, obviously wondering what sort of train was passing them. I did not recognise them, and Bosco said they were

'Bletchley Wills'. which meant nothing to me at that time. He completed his acknowledgement by giving a long and a short toot on the whistle (railway language for a non-polite two-fingered gesture), which was responded to in a like manner by the Bletchley men.

The rest of the journey to Bletchley was uninterrupted, and more or less uneventful. I managed to keep water and steam at reasonable levels, and Bosco's legs mostly free of misdirected shovels of coal. As we trundled along the water troughs between Castlethorpe and Wolverton, Bosco explained how, had we had a different engine and been going faster, we could have picked up water as an alternative to using the water column at Bletchley. However, our engine not only had no tender water gauge, it also had no scoop pan fitted. "Probably taken off and fitted to an engine more likely to need it," Bosco had said. It made me realise

Heading south through Castlethorpe and then Wolverton stations.   H. C. CASSERLEY

An aerial view of Bletchley, looking more or less southwards. No. 2 signal box can be seen in the left foreground, with what appears to be a train in the up loop, to the left of which is possibly a shunt engine in the sidings in which we disposed of our wagons, and collected others. The station can be seen in the centre, with the Bedford line 'bays', on the left (Platforms 8 & 7), then the up and down slow lines (Platforms 6 & 5), then the up and down fast lines (Platforms 4 & 3), and the Oxford 'bays' (Platforms 2 & 1). Our route from the sidings to the Oxford branch was via the up slow line through the station and then a rather protracted manoeuvre across the down slow line and the up and down fast lines adjacent to No. 1 box, and thence round the curve on to the branch beyond the carriage shed, which can be seen top right. Note the loco shed with turntable and coaling stage in the middle foreground. On the right is the 'secret' Bletchley Park.

SIMMONS AEROFILMS

The Oxford 'bay', with No. 1 box in the distance.

how dilapidated the railway was becoming after four years of war. However, as Bosco pointed out, getting water at Bletchley would give us a chance to mash a can of tea.

By the time we had passed Loughton and Denbigh Hall, and slowed for the points into the Bletchley yard, it seemed to be almost dark. The drizzle had only abated for short periods throughout the day, and the cold air certainly grabbed at your nose if it was inadvertently exposed for too long beyond the cab side. As we crawled round the back of the sidings, a shunter emerged from his cabin and called up to Bosco, greeting him by name, and asking where we had been until this late in the day, suggesting that our somewhat belated arrival was to assist the collation of overtime pay. Bosco gave him a suitable one-word reply and informed the shunter, whom Bosco called Jacko, that we had seven wagons for him, and asked how many we had to pick up. Jacko replied that twelve wagons were awaiting our collection, and four of them were for "dropping off at Verney for the Met".

The re-assembly of the train duly completed, and a few ribald comments exchanged with Jacko and Harry, we pulled up to the water column. I clambered over the tender and, after hauling up the bag and putting it in the tank, took Bosco's billy can, and following his directions found the way to the 'coffee knob' on platform three. There, again with Bosco's money, I had the can filled with tea. I also managed to 'acquire' a cup from the platform, so that on return to the engine we both enjoyed our first warm drink since leaving home that morning. I also opened my bag of sandwiches, and having replied to Bosco's query regarding their content, he delved in his basket and withdrew a wire homemade toasting fork. He impaled one of my sandwiches, thrust it into the mouth of the open firehole, and quickly toasted it. I gratefully accepted the slightly burnt offering, and almost as

quickly devoured it. I hadn't realised how hungry I was until the smell of the toast awoke my taste buds. Even powdered egg flapjack tasted good at that moment.

Two sandwiches later, Bosco, who had only turned on the water at the column at a slow trickle, announced that the tank must be full by now. I climbed over the coals and peered into the tank, to find that the water level was less than a foot from the top. Bosco increased the water flow, and in next to no time the tank was full. As usual I had to struggle to get the heavy bag – still with water in it – over the side of the tender so that the residue of water in it pulled it with a sploosh into its position beside the column. Drivers, of course, beat a hasty retreat from the vicinity of the columns while firemen were doing this, and Bosco was no exception. When we were both back on the footplate, he pointed out a telephone cupboard beside the shunters' cabin, and told me to lift the receiver, crank the handle, and when the signalman answered inform him that the Oxford tripper was ready for right o'way.

That done, I began to busy myself with the fire, but Bosco told me not to be too eager as we would probably have to wait some time because we had to cross over the four main lines to get to the Oxford branch. However, his prediction was not quite correct as within ten minutes our signal from the yard to the up slow line was pulled off, and after shouting to Harry, who was in the shunters' cabin – having no doubt cadged a cuppa and a cigarette – Bosco eased the train forward once more out of the sidings and into the station. There we had to wait for nearly fifteen minutes while trains sped by on the up and down fast lines, and an empty wagon train trundled through the station on the down slow line. Then suddenly the right-hand signal on the gantry was raised, and we began the next stage of our journey.

VERNEY JUNCTION (wearily)

I looked back as we made our way across the junction on to the branch to make sure the brake van was following, and was just in time to see Harry signalling to us – this time with his hand lamp – which was being waved from side to side indicating all was well, and which was just about visible through the murk of the December evening. I used the whistle in acknowledgement, and began firing again. Bosco had indicated there was something of a climb after leaving Bletchley, more or less all the way to Swanbourne, and then it was fairly easy to Oxford. He had also said that we would probably have shunting to do, not only at Verney Junction, but also at Bicester and Islip. But before that we had to surmount this incline to Swanbourne, in which endeavour Bosco was certainly making her bark again.

I looked in the firebox. Just my luck, I thought, we've got our heaviest train – thirty-one wagons Harry had said – and the fire's beginning to look not as bright as earlier in the day. I began to wonder if I should have spent the time at Bletchley, loosening the clinker on the fire bars rather than eating my sandwiches. Too late now, I realised, I just hoped the old girl behaved herself for the next few miles. I had hardly finished firing again when the dreaded sound of priming began. Bosco, of course, began to curse, and went through the now familiar routine of juggling with the regulator and drain cocks. Fortunately, we were now well clear of the main-line junction, and the local passenger train to Oxford had left Bletchley while we were pulling out of the sidings there. That gave us about three quarters of an hour to get to Verney Junction before the next local – this one for Banbury – arrived there. All this I learned from Bosco as he tried to ease the priming and I was nursing the water level in the boiler, which seemed to be lowering at an alarming rate.

We also were going more and more slowly as Bosco eased back the regulator and had the drain cocks open. Between his cursing he was muttering something about hoping we didn't come to a stand-still as it would be unlikely that we could start the train again, and would have to halve it. I wasn't quite sure what was meant by this, but it sounded ominous. But again, once the water level in the boiler had decreased to well below a third of a glass, the priming subsided. I had the feeling Bosco was not too pleased with me for my persistence in trying to keep the water level above halfway up the glass, but he said nothing. Now, with the cocks closed, and a sharper note from the chimney, the old engine began to lift the train again – but only at what seemed a little more than walking pace. However, I was not happy; the water level was low, and the steam pressure nearly down to 130 lbs. Although I had been firing 'little and often' as Bosco had advised, I appeared to be making no improvement to the engine's steaming. In fact, as I once again popped the injector on for a couple of minutes to keep the water level visible in the glass, the steam pressure dropped to near the 120 lbs mark.

This is worse than the approach to Blisworth, I thought, what price on us dropping a plug soon? I pondered on what I could do to improve the situation. Bosco must have seen my worried expression because he said, "Don't worry, boy, we've already passed Newton so we should make Swanbourne alright. Once we get there, we'll be over the top and you can try to run the fire down a bit so we can get the dart in it at Verney". I had no idea where we were, but presumed Newton and Swanbourne were signal boxes en-route to Verney Junction, where I knew we had some wagons to deposit. I would certainly be glad of a few minutes respite in order to attain what I considered a comfortable level of steam and water.

So we continued our slow progress, with me fighting a losing battle with the steam pressure, but keeping the water level in view – just. Suddenly I was conscious of a different sound, and looking out from under the blackout sheet saw we were passing through a station – almost as black as the night itself, being illuminated only by a glimmering oil lamp positioned near a door of a building under the platform canopy. I crossed to the driver's side of the footplate and looked out. Again I could see only one oil lamp, but was unable to read what had pre-war obviously been the station name, now mostly blacked out. Bosco shouted, "Swanbourne, we're okay now. Only got Winslow to go through and then it's Verney". I let the flap of the sheet fall back into place and picked up the shovel, using it to deflect air into various parts of the firebox, attempting to see how deep the fire was. I was disappointed with what I saw – a thick fire, and looking rather a dead red, not bright orange as it should be. Well, there wasn't much I could do about it until we were stationary, the fire irons being at the back of

Swanbourne (opposite) and Winslow (right) – stations along the Oxford branch which we passed before we got to the sanctuary of Verney Junction.
LENS OF SUTTON

the tender, where I had put them while cracking up the coal at Northampton.

That really seemed a long time ago, I thought. Here we are at well beyond five o'clock, and only just over half the journey done, according to what Bosco had been saying earlier. I was conscious of feeling just a little bit weary. What had been my big adventure was now becoming something of a trial. Just then Bosco shut off steam, flicking the blower on as he did so. I immediately put the injector on as the water in the gauge glass disappeared into the bottom nut. "She should roll to Verney", Bosco said, "And that should give us a chance to get her round a bit". I was certainly glad of any respite. I had been trying to release some coal jammed behind the tender doors, and in doing so was hoping that my struggles didn't break my shovel. Finally I was able to prise the coal loose – although perhaps the word coal was something of a misnomer, as what had jammed were several briquettes, each about the size of four house bricks. Once these had been released, a cascade of ovals (also made of coal dust and cement), and even some coke slid under the doors, together with some yellow-streaked coal. Certainly one didn't get best steam coal on such engines, or on such working as a local tripper on branch lines. Bosco turned as he heard the falling coal and grunted. "Looks like best Desford", he said with a grin. "They let 'em smoke down that pit, the coal's so bad there's no fear of an explosion".

While I was breaking the briquettes with the coal pick, I was aware of us trundling through another station, which I guessed would be Winslow. Sometime afterwards, Bosco began braking the train while we peered into the gloom ahead looking for the light of the signal as we approached Verney Junction. The distant signal was on, which was to be expected, and as we crawled towards the outer home signal Bosco blew the whistle. I thought to myself, well, we've got enough steam for that – just! Within a few seconds the signal

was pulled off, and we trundled slowly into the station and to the home signals at the end of the platform. Bosco said, "The box is on your side. The bobby will call us past the signal as we have to back down the old Met branch and drop the wagons for here in the dead road. They're probably for Quainton Road or Aylesbury". I lifted the sheet and looked out. Sure enough, from the box a short distance in front of us the signalman was waving a green light in our direction. I acknowledged with a toot on the whistle, and told Bosco it

This picture of Verney Junction shows the box and the line off to the right towards Brackley and Banbury.

This picture more easily shows the layout at Verney, with the entrance to the Metropolitan line off to the left behind the station buildings.

was alright to go forward. As we did so, Bosco told me to "Drop off at the box and get the staff from the bobby, you and Harry will need it for the ground frame". This of course was completely new to me. I had no idea what a ground frame was, but guessed it was something I had to help Harry with. From the signal box I collected the staff (a metal rod about an inch in diameter and a foot long which had four raised rings along part of its length, and a mortise-type key shape at one end). Bosco had pulled the train forward clear of the crossover points, and Harry was on his verandah waving a red signal to Bosco with his hand lamp. I began making my way towards the train, stumbling over point rods and signal wires in the dark, and uttering oaths not quite in keeping with a sixteen year old! Harry chuckled as I groped towards the brake van. "'ow yer doin' lad? Are yer knackered yet ?" he called, but I wasn't feeling in a very conversational mood, and I merely replied, "Yes, and the ******* engine is as well". Harry asked for the key, saying he didn't need any help. I gratefully handed it to him and carried on my uncertain way towards the engine.

As I clambered on the footplate I could see Harry calling us back with his hand lamp, and relayed this to Bosco, who was looking in the firebox. I, too, looked in the box as Bosco began to reverse the train. The fire was certainly no brighter than before, but at least it had burned down a little. As we slowly reversed, I made as if to climb on the tender to get the dart, but Bosco stopped me with a shout. "Don't go up there yet, there's a footbridge a bit further back, and a loading gauge somewhere beyond that; wait 'til we've gone past those, then you'll be alright". What a pity I had to do my first trip over this line in the dark, I thought. I haven't a clue where we are or what it all looks like. Just then I was conscious of the sound of us going by buildings and, looking out, saw the vague outline of a platform canopy and a building on my side of the engine. Then we were under the footbridge and moving gently back into what I guessed were sidings. I hadn't seen the loading gauge, but as Bosco had shouted "Okay now", I unhooked the blackout sheet, after closing the firehole door. To attract a stray German bomb would just about make our day complete. Then I climbed onto the tender, scrambled over the coal, and felt around for the dart. Having located it, I returned to the footplate, re-secured the sheet, opened the firehole door, and thrust the dart into the fire as hard as I could to try to break through the clinker on the bars.

By this time we had stopped, and I heard Harry shouting for us to ease up. Bosco buffered up gently and I heard the coupling chain clang as Harry unhooked behind the wagons we were to deposit. I was aware of this going on while I was still lunging with the dart. Suddenly I had success – a portion of clinker about two feet long and a foot wide was forced up on end, and I managed to manoeuvre it to the side of the box. Now that I had made a hole in the clinker, I was able to get the dart under the rest of it more easily. By the time Bosco had put off the four wagons, re-coupled to the train, and pulled forward to the signal, I had about ten pieces of clinker of varying sizes leaning against the sides of the firebox. Bosco looked in and voiced his approval. "Nip up and get the clinker shovel", he said, "We've got to wait for the Brackley local to go, so we may as well get rid of that lot".

With the shovel obtained in similar manner to the dart, Bosco told me to "have a blow", and with very little fuss was soon tossing the still-glowing pieces of clinker onto the slight embankment next to the engine. "Don't think they will do much harm there", he said as he looked down at the already cooling clinkers. "The drizzle will soon damp them down". However, he put the injector on and used the fizzle pipe to complete the job. I returned the fire irons to the back of the tender, and again re-secured the sheet. The fire was looking much brighter now, and on Bosco's advice I shovelled the broken briquettes, etc, very thinly all over the firebox. With the blower on, the old girl began to regain steam pressure once more.

OXFORD (thankfully)

While we had been busy on the footplate, the local had called at the station and gone on its way. Shortly the signal was heard to clang into its off position, and we pulled forward and stopped to allow Harry to do the necessary at the ground frame. He eventually came up to the engine, handed me the key, and told us there were ten wagons of 'Yankee stuff' to put off at Bicester, then, as far as he was aware, we were next stop Oxford. Although I had not managed to get a full head of steam, Bosco said, "Let's go anyway, we're losing drinking time". He set the train in motion, and while I was looking back to make sure Harry was in his van, Bosco reminded me to drop the key off to the bobby at the box. As we approached the box, I saw the dim glow of the signalman's hand lamp bobbing across the lines towards our line. He held the lamp so it illuminated his other hand, which was raised above his head, and as we passed I leaned from the cab and slapped the smooth end of the key into his hand so that his fingers automatically closed around it, just as Bosco had instructed. With a shouted cheery "Good night", the bobby disappeared into the night, back to the presumed warmth of his box, and I thankfully lowered the flap of the blackout sheet.

So we were on our way again, eventually passing through another station that, Bosco shouted, was Claydon. Not long afterwards he drew my attention to the fact that we were about to go under a bridge, over which could just be discerned a wagon train heading off to our right, which I guessed was northwards. The usual long and short whistled greetings were exchanged as Bosco enlightened me to the fact that we had just gone under the old Great Central line, now part of the LNER. The going now was easy – steam and water in good order – for which I was thankful, and Bosco had the train 'tiddly bumping' along at what seemed quite a brisk pace, or at least it was compared with our pre-

The quiet little station of Claydon and the level crossing. Note the wooden platform on the left.

The stations of Marsh Gibbon (top left), Launton (top right), Bicester (bottom left) and Islip (bottom right), through which we trundled on the way to Oxford, only stopping at Bicester to shunt off wagons. All were unseen until the return journey!
H. C. CASSERLEY and LENS OF SUTTON

G2A class 0−8−0 No. 49339 approaching Oxford.

vious efforts on this branch. Bosco introduced me in turn to Marsh Gibbon and Launton stations, before he later shut off steam and we drifted towards what I guessed would be Bicester.

Sure enough, he shortly said, "We're just going under the Great Western, and then we'll be in Bicester". There were no trains to be seen or heard on the line overhead, and to my comment that it looked a bit dead, he said with a grin, "Probably all in bed by now. It's a boys' railway, full of branch lines". Considering that we were on one too, I thought the remark to be a bit caustic, but I was already aware of the feelings one company's men had for those of another company. Even on the LMS there was a general air of 'we are better than you' between ex-LNWR men and ex-MR men. As we drew into the station, the engine safety valves blew – the first time since we had been standing at Bletchley. I put a drop more water in the boiler just to keep her quiet, while Harry was heard to be busy with the couplings along the train. He shortly appeared, climbing the steps onto the footplate, and said, "Right, let's get rid of these few and get going, I've got a thirst on". The ten wagons were soon deposited in a siding somewhere behind the station, and in very short time we were re-coupled to the rest of the train. After Harry had ascertained via the signal box that there were no other stops to be made prior to Oxford, we were quickly on our way. I had begun to make up the fire while we were shunting off the wagons, but Bosco had stopped me, explaining there was only a slight incline on the way to Islip, and then it was downhill to our

destination, a distance of about twelve miles. The train was much lighter now, and Bosco trundled it along without any fuss, the priming all forgotten. I too felt lighter in spirit as I was able to cope quite well with steam and water levels while the engine was working more economically, and of course we had a brighter fire. Also it seemed that I was getting more adept at firing on a moving platform, so not spilling coal so frequently as earlier in the day.

Now we were nearing the end of our journey I was somewhat intrigued as to where we would stay that night. All that Bosco had said in reply to my questioning was, "It's private digs, you'll be alright boy". Which really didn't tell me much at all. However, I did surmise from conversation between Harry and Bosco at Bicester that a pub was nearby, to which we would venture after a wash and brush up, and before retiring for the night. Soon I heard Bosco calling the word 'Islip' and, on looking out, was aware of us passing through yet another station, completely blacked out, with just a faint glow visible in the signal box window; obviously the bobby had got his stove red hot and was enjoying the warmth of his isolated cocoon.

In what seemed a very short time, we passed over a level crossing and then a junction, the wheels clickety-clacking over the points. Soon afterwards, Bosco shut off steam and remarked, "Right, we should coast in from here. Don't put any more round her, we don't want to be too long in bedding her down for the night". I peered into the box and was pleased to see that the fire was quite thin. It wouldn't take long to dispose of her once we got on shed. I had

Rewley Road station on 1st May 1940, with the loco shed in the distance. The canal was over there somewhere to the right.

NATIONAL RAILWAY MUSEUM

already been informed by Bosco that it was our job to do it as there were no coalers or fire-droppers at the small Oxford depot.

We were slowing down now. I was conscious of trundling over metal bridges over water, and then we came to a stand. Bosco came across the footplate, lifted the black-out sheet, and shouted into the darkness, "Where do you want them?". Back came a reply, "In the goods shed road". Bosco told me to uncouple the engine, and once I was back on the footplate, he drew forward. After receiving a signal from the now just discernible signal box, we ran round the train, and propelled it into a siding. The brake van was then shunted into another siding, and Harry, loaded with his bags and lamp, clambered onto the footplate, grinned at the two of us and said, "That's not too bad, we shall have time for a wash and a pint before supper. Well done, lad, we didn't have to stop for a blow up". Before I could think of a suit-able reply to what I thought was a somewhat back-handed compliment, Bosco said, "No, but it was a near thing

coming up to Swanny. Still the kid's worked hard, and we got here okay, so no complaints". I wasn't quite sure what to say, so busied myself giving the footplate a last tidy-up with my hand brush.

Then it was off to the loco shed. Harry helped by turning the water column on and off for me while I was on the tender as the tank was filled. Bosco had found an ashpan rake, and busied himself in pulling the fire to the back of the box, while he had the injector on to fill the boiler – "Up to the whistle", as he put it. He decided not to turn the engine in the dark because it had to be balanced precisely on the turntable in order to be pushed round with any degree of ease. It would perhaps be better to do it when fresh, and hopefully in daylight next morning. Likewise, should it be considered we required more coal – they might have some better fuel than we had – that could be obtained at the same time. With the engine stabled for the night, to be looked after by the night duty steam raiser, we booked off at the cabin and made our way towards our lodgings.

Oxford shed on 3rd October 1948 and the canal which we had to cross, somewhere left of the picture. MILLBROOK HOUSE

This aerial view of Oxford, taken in 1935, shows the LNWR station terminus alongside the GWR station. As far as I can judge, I think our digs were somewhere off the bottom of this picture — somewhere near to Nelson Street, I think.
SIMMONS AEROFILMS LTD.

LODGINGS AND REST (gratefully)

I was aware of us walking along the line for a short distance towards what I guessed was the station, crossing a small bridge over water (the cut or canal Bosco indicated), then through an alley into a street of terraced houses, our way vaguely illuminated by the hand lamps of Harry and Bosco as they trudged along chatting to each other. I brought up the rear, carrying one of Harry's two bags as well as my own. A corner was turned, and I caught a glimpse of a name plate – Nelson Street. Shortly they stopped at a door and Bosco knocked. A woman answered, then stepped back inside for us to enter. I closed the door behind us, and she then parted the blackout curtain hanging a yard or so along the passage. In the light from the bulb hanging from the ceiling, I saw a small, elderly lady, with a wrap-round pinafore that seemed to reach almost to the floor. Her hair was pulled back in a bun, and she had what appeared to be large felt slippers on her feet. "You're late tonight, Mr. Kirton", she said, as she stepped aside for us to pass. Then, on seeing me, she said, "Blimey, are you taking 'em straight from school now?". Bosco grinned, explained about his regular mate, and introduced me to her, and her to me – as Mrs. Lock (it might have been Luck but sounded like Lock).

Our outer clothes and overalls deposited on hooks under the stairs, together with our boots, we entered a small scullery, where we washed in a large stone sink with water scooped from a brick-encased copper, under which a small fire burned, then dried ourselves on a roller towel affixed behind the door. I of course was last with the water, and the towel! That done, Bosco and Harry took small packages from their basket and bag respectively. These were their supper and breakfast meals; Bosco had a piece of homemade pie and some potatoes to be warmed for his supper. When Mrs. Lock asked what I had, I explained that I had been given this trip at short notice, and only had two of my sandwiches left. She showed some concern, but explained that she could only let me have some soup and bread, but, "If you're going to the Swan, you might find the faggot man there. If you bring some back, I'll warm them up with Mr. Kirton's pie". I was in luck, there were homemade faggots at the pub – and they were warm – so I decided to eat them while drinking my pint of beer, kindly paid for by Harry (and later, a second by Bosco). Life wasn't so bad after all, I thought, although the faggots had very little meat in them – mostly bread, potatoes, and onions by the taste of them. While I was eating, Bosco and Harry played dominoes. When Harry won and challenged me, I quickly declined; after two pints and a long day, I was feeling a little the worse for wear and, although chivvied by Harry, I still made my excuses. Bosco came to the rescue, indicating that he wanted his supper, it being alright for guards not to feel tired or hungry because "they were sitting on their backsides in the dry and warm most of the day, and really were only required on trains because of a Board of Trade regulation". Harry flung back that he had been out in the rain and cold more

than Bosco that day, and he had been doing all the brain-work! This was typical of the banter between them as we made our way back to Mrs. Lock's. There, Bosco ate his supper, while Harry opened his package of bread and cheese, plus a really strong-smelling raw onion, which made my eyes water just sitting at the same table. Mrs. Lock queried whether they'd had faggots at the pub. I nodded , but admitted I had eaten them there. However, I quickly said, "Yes please" when she asked if I would like some 'bread and soup for afters, as I was a growing lad'.

Soon it was time for bed – in fact it was well after 11 o'clock. It was then that I had my biggest surprise of the day. The two men led the way upstairs to what I guessed was the main bedroom in the two-up-two-down house. Harry struck a match and lit the mantle of the gas bracket on the wall (downstairs there had been electric light). The only furniture in the room was the bed – if bed it could be called. It was, in fact, a large wooden bench-type structure. The mattress, which it soon became apparent, was filled with flock (a sort of wool and cotton waste), was nearly three feet from the floor, a distance that necessitated a climb onto it. There were pegs on the door to hang clothes on, and a large mirror above the mantle shelf – the fireplace itself was boarded up. The window was covered by dark velvet-type curtains, and on the bed were several blankets neatly folded in a pile. The mattress was covered with what appeared to be two sheets sewn together, and there were three pillows, also filled with flock.

Bosco, who like Harry, was by this time undressing, could obviously see my somewhat bewildered expression, grinned and said, "That's right, we all sleep in the one bed, it's warmer that way". I, still nonplussed, began to take off my jumper and shirt, by which time Harry and Bosco were down to their long johns and long-sleeved vests, and were each grabbing a couple of blankets. I followed suit, but felt somewhat naked, stripped down to my singlet and short underpants. I was certainly glad the two men were on the bed first, so I would be on the edge! Before I took the two remaining blankets, I queried the location of the toilet, to be told it was the one in the back yard we had used earlier, "but there's a bucket under the bed, and as you're the last one in, you can put the light out, and don't be too long, we've got a call at five o'clock", mumbled Harry. I turned off the gas tap and groped my way to the bed, my feet frozen from standing on the bare lino, there being only one small mat at the foot of the bed.

I found and used the bucket in the enveloping darkness, and then, once wrapped in my blankets, fatigue, a full stomach, and the two pints of beer soon lulled me into unconsciousness. The next thing of which I was aware was a banging on the door, and Mrs. Lock calling that it was "just gone five. I'll get your breakfast started". Once dressed and downstairs, we washed in the scullery, and Bosco shaved, but Harry just stroked his stubble, and muttered that he

W. A. CAMWELL

The shed at Oxford. The office was a lean-to at the far end of the building.

would shave later in the week. No wonder he was nick-named 'Blue Gillette'. Mrs. Lock cooked the egg and sausage that each of the men had brought with them, and kindly gave me three thick slices of bread and dripping for my breakfast, which went down well with a mug of steaming tea.

On the way back to the loco shed, I enquired about Mrs. Lock, and the circumstances of our lodging there. I was told she was the widow of a railway man, who now 'took in' double-trip men, and was paid by the railway for doing so, plus she was allowed a small amount of additional rations. I also learned that each crew usually gave her a shilling for doing their cooking, etc, so guessed the two men had con-tributed something on my behalf. When I queried if I owed them anything, I was told to "forget it son". I felt very grateful to them both.

At the shed we booked on, to be told that our local tripper had been cancelled, and we were to make our way to Yarnton for a special. Asked what it was, the shed-hand replied that he had no idea – Control had passed on the message via the steam raiser 'a couple of hours earlier'. Bosco surmised that we would be taking a train of empty iron ore wagons originating at Ebbw Vale in Wales back to Northampton for the quarries near Irthlingborough. He decided that obtaining more coal might be a good idea, so,

after I had spread the fire from under the firehole door all over the box, and begun to raise more steam, we moved old 28601 to the coal wagon. While Bosco went round the engine with his oilcan, I busied myself in the wagon, and I must have shovelled several hundredweight onto the tender when Bosco called a halt to my exertions. Then it was on to the turntable – with me inching her into position, while Bosco with his hand lamp illuminating the rail and leading wheel (it being still quite dark), yelled "Stop" when the engine was correctly balanced for a reasonably easy push round.

During our time of preparing the engine, Harry had not been idle. He had busied himself in the cabin and had made a can of tea, which we enjoyed – none more so than me as my twenty minutes in the coal wagon had certainly filled my mouth and nostrils with dust. We then 'gonged' off the shed and made our way towards Yarnton – a junction, I learned, with the Great Western, three or four miles north of Oxford. When we got near to Oxford Road Halt, we had to reverse onto the branch, and travel tender-first to the sidings. Although the rain had stopped during the night, the morning was still cold, and I was glad that no-one had dis-covered where I had hid the blackout sheet the previous night and 'borrowed' it for themselves.

NORTHAMPTON (expressly)

On arrival in the sidings at Yarnton, Harry went to the signal box to find out a little more about the train we were to collect. We could see many wagons in the sidings, but no brake van. He was back in less than ten minutes with the information that we had to retrace our steps as the special we were to work was in fact coming from the Didcot and Newbury branch and would be shunted on to the Bletchley branch at Oxford.

Back in Oxford, we were in time to see our train of yes-terday being shunted into the coal yard and the good shed. Both Bosco and Harry were puzzling over what sort of train this special could be, but now agreed it must be something to do with the war effort.

After some half an hour or so, a duo of whistles heralded the arrival of what at first sight appeared to be a passenger train pulling through the GW station, and headed by a 4–4–0 Southern Railway engine (not too unlike the Fowler engines of our railway I thought). It was piloted by a very old-looking GW 0–4–2 tank engine. Bosco, his eyes wide, spluttered a few expletives. "It's a ****** hospital train", he said, 'And he's got a few on as well". I began counting the coaches as the train pulled towards the crossover points – ten vehicles, two of which were large vans, the rest being a mixture of passenger carriages, painted a greenish grey, and with most of the windows seemingly boarded over. On the sides and on the roof of each vehicle was painted a large red cross on a white background. Leaning from windows at the ends of some of the coaches, could be seen men in American army uniforms, one or two wearing white helmets.

Some shouted conversation passed between the crew of the pilot engine and the GW signalman, and shortly the train drew further forward and then backed across into the exchange sidings and the LMS station. The GW engine was uncoupled and returned to its own 'parish', while the driver of the SR engine asked where he could fill his tank. Bosco climbed aboard while I uncoupled the engine from the train, and he piloted them onto the shed to the water column. With the tank filled, they returned to the train and coupled up. Bosco backed onto their engine and I coupled up, under the watchful eye of the Southern fireman, a man several years older than me. Proper greetings were exchanged, and the alien engines given a look over by each crew. The Southern men were amusingly intrigued by the wooden brake blocks on our tender. "We should get a nice smell of burnt pine when we're braking", the driver said with a chuckle. Bosco replied that we hadn't been fast enough to set fire to anything so far!

Harry appeared, together with the Southern guard whom he had relieved, carrying a large pot and a grin from ear to ear. "Have some real coffee", he said. The SR guard pro-duced mugs and we all toasted the Yanks, who had kindly donated the coffee. Harry then produced some packs of chewing gum, also given by the Americans, and shared these around. This to me was great; the only chewing gum I had had for what seemed ages had been when a neighbour's wife and her pal had been 'friendly' with some locally billeted Canadian soldiers!

Bosco gave the SR crew a rundown of the terrain over which we would be travelling, and the fact that our engine primed at times. "Don't think we're shirking if we slack off sometimes – just keep your heads in", he said. Meanwhile, I had gradually been building up my fire with the reasonably good coal I had sorted from the wagon on the shed. By the time the bobby gave us the right of way, I had a full head of steam, but only half a glass of water – Bosco's incantations were slowly sinking in! All was now ready. The signals were off. The Southern guard had disappeared in the direction of the GW station, no doubt to make his way home, and the Southern crew had sounded their whistle as an indication they were ready for their exploratory excursion over foreign metals.

Bosco had learned they were Eastleigh men, a shed, he was given to understand, near Southampton from where the train had started. They had booked on at 12.30 that morning, so had already done a day's work! They had apparently been one of several crews to be allocated trains from the docks to hospitals at various locations in the country, a ship having brought in several hundreds of wounded men from the battle zones. (I learned a long time later that these wounded men were most likely involved in the fighting in the Ardennes – the Battle of the Bulge.) The crews had been told not to exceed about 40mph, which suited me fine as, although we would be travelling faster than I had previously done as a fireman, I would hopefully be able to remain upright while firing. As it happened, I did lose balance on occasions but didn't throw coal over Bosco too many times.

In fact, the journey to Bletchley passed without any untoward incident. The Southern men really belted their engine along – it seemed to me that they were doing most of the work – but when I shouted this fact to Bosco he just grinned, and said, "What are you worrying about? It's an easier trip for us if he wants to show off". I, of course, was grateful; having less shovelling to do gave me a chance to look at the passing scene, and attempt to identify places through which we had passed in the dark yesterday evening. How different it looked in daylight to what I had imagined in the dark.

After passing Verney Junction, we were 'on the block', having apparently caught up with a train from the Brackley branch. Arriving at Bletchley eventually, we were signalled to the down slow line and halted in the station while water and other commodities were taken on board the train, and other activities done which apparently could not be done on the move. Bosco decided to take the opportunity of replenishing our tank, and while I was on the tender Harry appeared with more coffee for both crews. After the tank was filled and we had quenched our thirst, I took the opportunity to peep into one of the coaches.

There were two tiers of bunks along one side (the upper ones obviously for less seriously wounded), and a single row of bunks along the other side. Each lower bunk held an occupant – some of whom I could see were bandaged. Others, with perhaps an arm in a sling, or with crutches, sat playing cards, or even dice on the floor, or just talking to those in the bottom bunks. One end of the coach seemed to be devoted to a kitchen, or perhaps a medical closet; whatever it was, it had lots of shiny metal cupboards and utensils, and a man in a white jacket and trousers, an orderly or male nurse I presumed. All those who were active seemed quite cheerful, and chided me on the length of time it was taking to get to their destination, and on my youthful appearance, not believing, it appeared, that I was actually a fireman on the train. I had the feeling as I made my somewhat chagrined way back to the engine that they now assumed I was the reason for the journey taking so long! So, after what had been a leisurely and interesting interlude, we set off again. However, we were kept on the slow line, which rather surprised me as I thought that a hospital train would take some sort of priority.

Notwithstanding our being on the slow line, our progress was not delayed, and it was rather moving and patriotic to have overtaking expresses on the down fast line sounding their whistles in a series of blasts as they passed, and passengers (servicemen and civilians) – obviously alerted by the noise – standing at windows waving, some of the male passengers politely raising their hats to the red cross train. About as exuberant as the British get!

After a short delay at Roade, we were signalled onto the main towards Blisworth and familiar territory. Then on to the Northampton branch, down the bank past Rothersthorpe. Soon we were easing to a stop at the home signal by the loco shed, where the Southern driver indicated he needed more water, having come all the way from Oxford on the tankful he had obtained there. (I learned later that Southern tenders had larger capacity tanks than ours because there were no troughs on the Southern Railway.) I went to the box – Bridge Street Junction – where Dickie Bird was on duty again, and obtained permission for us to pull beyond the signal in order to get to the water column at the tank over the coaling stage, beside which we were standing.

Dickie informed me that we would not be leaving until after the Peterborough passenger train from Castle Station had gone, in about twenty minutes. This I relayed to both drivers, and to Harry, who had again appeared, doing his waiter act, bringing us more coffee and gum. During this respite I took the opportunity of borrowing Bosco's toasting fork, and cooked my remaining, somewhat stale two sandwiches, which went down well with the coffee. Looking back along the train, I could see several of the loco staff, including some of my cleaner colleagues, receiving titbits from the walking wounded on the train. What was completely incongruous to me was the sight of some of the Italian and German POW labourers holding up their hands to catch some of the goodies being tossed from the train. I found it hard to accept the fact of this generosity by men who had been injured by comrades of those men standing on the ground. Perhaps the Americans had not seen POWs before, and were not aware that the dark battledress type of uniform with the brightly-coloured diamond on back and

leg signified what they were. Certainly there were no British soldier guards to be seen, they, no doubt, as usual being in the warm somewhere.

Soon after the local passenger train had cruised round the curve from the canal bridge, through the junction and disappeared through Bridge Street station, we were on our way again. No hard climbing as we cruised along the Nene Valley to Wellingborough and on to Thrapston. There we were shunted into what appeared to be a recently extended siding, to which observation Bosco agreed. On the roadway, adjacent to the siding, were ten or more army ambulances, with almost, it seemed, as many jeeps, plus a group of nurses, whose appearance brought forth the inevitable chorus of whistles from the personnel on board the train.

Harry, snooping around – as was his wont – had learned that a military hospital had been instituted somewhere near Clapton (which I presumed was a village or town somewhere in the vicinity), the destination of the occupants of the train. He then went to the signal box to ascertain our next move) returning with the information that we were to leave the train in the siding and return as light engines to Northampton. I uncoupled the engines from the train while the Southern crew were receiving armfuls of goodies from the men on the train. These included the almost obligatory chewing gum, plus chocolate, cigarettes, a crate of beer (obviously smuggled onto the train at some point), and five one-gallon cans of tomato juice. These were all kindly shared between us by the Southern crew. Then after yet more coffee, and much whistle blowing from both engines, accompanied by retaliatory horn blowing from many of the road vehicles, we made our departure

As we were tender first, it meant the Southern engine was in the lead, so Harry 'volunteered' to travel on that engine to make sure the driver knew which signals to obey – not that there could be much confusion as there were no junctions in our direction. I was doubly glad of our retention of the blackout sheet as there were one or two flurries of snow! It was certainly no warmer than yesterday. Back at Northampton, the engines were uncoupled and stabled on the shed. No disposing of the engine ourselves here, I thought appreciatively; all one needed to do was wash, and book off, the driver filling in a repair card in respect of the engine, if necessary, and it was certainly necessary in respect of our old girl!

The arrival of the 'foreign' engine on shed created a bit of a stir in the foreman's office, but, after a couple of phone calls, it was ascertained that the engine would stay, and work back (probably via Willesden and Olympia) to its home territory eventually. The Southern men were to be guided to Castle Station by Harry, where he had to book off, and where they could get a meal of sorts in the coffee knob in the station forecourt. Then a ride home 'on the cushions', they having been on duty some fourteen hours, with the likelihood of it being twenty before they arrived back at Eastleigh!

We all said our farewells, agreeing it was possibly the only time Southampton and Northampton men had worked a train together. Then Harry and the two SR men began their trek along the line to the station. Bosco and I went in the opposite direction, I collecting my pedal cycle from the rack, before we both went over the footbridge over the siding from where we had set out the previous day, which now seemed so long ago!

We parted company near Dick Ford's pub, Bosco to go round the back for – as he put it – a crafty one, and me home to, I hoped, a decent meal. Mother would surely be pleased with the tomato juice, and some of the chocolate!

My first taste of main-line and double-trip working had given me quite a hunger – maybe for more of the same?

So, next day it was back to what might be described as the drudgery of being a cleaner on the shed. The only difference was that we were all chewing American gum. I, of course, was full of my 'adventure' and regaled those who would listen with my story of the two days. I was somewhat disappointed that very few of my workmates realised it was me on the hospital train's leading engine.

How different things look from the air. The aerial view of the area shows the extent of the sidings and the later development of industry and dwellings on what used to be farm land and allotments. Spencer Bridge is seen in the lower foreground, with No. 3 box visible above it, Victoria Park lower left, and No. 4 box and shunters cabin of the up sidings was opposite the entrance/exit lines of the down sidings, to the right of which can be seen what was left of the 'lido' (where I dumped the wagon in the pit), having been gradually filled with waste over the years. To the left of the shunting neck of the down sidings are industrial buildings, where Chudder's brother had his small-holding. At the far end of the neck is Kingsthorpe Mill Lane, and the bridge over the running lines, and at the very top of the picture can be seen the lines diverging – left to Rugby and right to Market Harborough. Between the bridge and the divergence can be seen No. 5 box, to the left of which, across the fields, can be seen the new housing estate where I lived with my family on their return from Leamington Spa.

NORTHAMPTON BOROUGH COUNCIL ARCHIVE

This picture appears to have been taken from Spencer Bridge and shows No. 3 box, and the 'up sidings' on the right (almost devoid of wagons), and the loop line with its exit to the up slow. Then there are the four running lines, with to the left of them the two reception lines to the 'down sidings', which were seemingly filled with stabled coaches.
W. J. S. MEREDITH

CHAPTER FIVE

CLEANER AND MORE

A 'Yankee' 2–8–0 being utlized piloting a 'D' at Berkhamsted in June 1944. Most enginemen liked them as they had a comfortable foot-plate on which to work, and were far advanced technically to our engines.
H. C. CASSERLEY

THE Southern engine was not the only 'foreign' one on shed that next day. There was also an American 2–8–0, which somehow had strayed from the normal route from Liverpool to Dover on its journey from the USA to France. I learned it had failed because of a badly leaking steam pipe in the smoke box, which could have had serious consequences for the crew, but which luckily apparently had not happened.

This engine was very intriguing to us, of course, as it had several features unknown to us at that time. The fact that most pipework and fittings were exposed made it appear ugly to British eyes, but really it made a lot of sense and it was very functional. It had a form of self-cleaning smoke box; rocker fire bars; a large sand box on top of the boiler, where the sand was kept dry by the warmth beneath it, and from where the sand was distributed to both front or rear sanders as required; a horizontal 'push/pull' regulator handle, which had a ratchet to keep it in position (not a piece of coal); and the driver was on the right side too, making it easier for the majority of firemen. The only point of real criticism was the fact that coal was retained in the tender at the shovelling point by wooden planks slotted into flanges on the tender. One could imagine it being very difficult in releasing coal jammed behind the planks, or even moving the planks themselves when there was a large amount of coal pressing against them. Of course, we didn't know at the time that American (brown) coal was mainly obtained from open-cast mining operations, and was of much smaller texture than British coal.

However, the Southern engine left the loco depot that afternoon, and I saw on the engine allocation board that she was rostered as the 6.15pm engine to Nottingham! I wondered what that could mean as it appeared to be going completely the wrong way to get back to the Southern Railway. I queried this with, I think, Bert Jennings, the acting late-turn 'running shed foreman', but he merely said, "What do you want to know for?", and disappeared into his office. A driver who had obviously heard my question told me the engine would be going on the 'empties' to Nottingham, and back with the 'Dover Mail', which also didn't mean much to me, but at least I knew Dover was in the south of the country, and I presumed was served by the SR. Little did I know then that some time later I would be firing on that train, which was also known as the 'Yankee Mail'!

After some weeks on shed duties, I was posted on the 9am to 5pm shift on the Down Side shunt with Bill Whitlock, with whom I had fired one Sunday at the same sidings some weeks previously. Bill was a likeable man who was always teasing me regarding supposed girl friends with whom he could 'fix me up'. He, like most of the drivers on permanent shunting duties, had been taken off main-line work either because of failing the strict eyesight tests, or perhaps because of some injury they had sustained, or were medically unfit. It seemed that the railway looked after its staff in that way, and was very reluctant to dispose of their services, especially should they be nearing retirement age. The fact that I was rostered on the 9 to 5 shift was also an indication that the powers that be were perhaps attempting

A view of the Down Sidings (Martin's Yard, although I don't remember it being referred to as such during my time on the railway). It was most unusual for coaches to be stored here in the forties and fifties. The train was just approaching the points, which would — had it been signalled that way — take it into one of the two arrival roads, where it would climb up the bank to a point just about visible in the distance, where the train would be left to be dealt with by the shunt engine. The people who lived on the Council estate to the left of the picture must have had very disturbed nights because of the crash and bang of the shunted wagons as they careered off the shunting bank. Added to this noise was the volume of the Tannoy system, which was used both to tell the under shunters to set the points for whichever siding was required, and to inform enginemen when their train was due to depart, the path having been signalled to the down lines. Such a call could be: '. . . right away with the 2.10 Toton. Come on Toton, dig your toes in!' On the right of the picture can be seen the Up Sidings, where a train had been left in the loop, obviously for dealing with by the up side shunter from the other end, at No. 4 box.
V. A. HATLEY

to comply with directives regarding youngsters not working night duties!

So, I did one week with Bill and the next with 'Chudder' Hillyard, another driver out to grass. Chudder was quite different to Bill, and was rather gruff until he got to know you. However, this did not stop him leaving me to do the driving and firing while he went to help his brother, who, very opportunely, had a small-holding adjacent to the quarter-mile long shunting neck along which the trains were pulled by the shunt engine, after they had been left in one of the two approach loops by the train engine, and before they were backed over the 'hump'. Chudder would sometimes spend as long as two hours with his brother, but I'll give him his due – every time I drove along the neck he would come out of whichever greenhouse he was working in and shout, asking if everything was alright. Of course, I always replied in the affirmative as I enjoyed being allowed to drive. The engine was invariably one of our D's, which are perhaps not an ideal shunting engine, but they were strong, and always managed to pull the trains up the incline from the approach loop without too much bother.

The Down Sidings (sometimes called Martins' Yard) was the largest of the Northampton shunting yards with some twenty siding roads, into which – in theory – wagons from the train being pushed gently over the hump, would be directed by the 'under shunters', operating the numerous hand points into the varying roads on the prompting of the head shunter. He would give his directions over a tannoy system as he uncoupled the wagons, regarding which road each wagon was to go to make up a train for a forward destination. Unfortunately, the hump was substandard, and necessitated shunting as in a normal yard. This frequently resulted in wagons being despatched over the hump at too great a speed, which would then have one of the under

shunters scampering after them in an effort to pin down a brake and prevent the wagon (or wagons) crashing with considerable force into wagons already in that particular siding.

Sometimes the under shunters would 'accidentally' fail to slow the flight of the wagons as they careered into the sidings, especially if the wagon was labelled as containing liquor, or perhaps grain. A heavily shunted wagon would often leak some of its contents, and men would then be seen crawling under the vehicle, attempting to catch some of the dribbling contents in a receptacle – a can or mug perhaps, or even a hat if grain was trickling between the planking frequently helped by the use of a piece of wire. Spilled grain was especially prized for feeding one's chickens, and, of course, spilled whiskey was certainly good for 'medicinal' purposes!

I had several pleasant, often hilarious, weeks with Bill and Chudder, then it was back to cleaning duties, but only for a few weeks, as within a month I was 'out main line' again, detailed to be fireman on the engineers special. This train consisted of only one coach – a sort of observation car – in which were an array of various types of instruments, and which carried the surveying/engineering team, usually three or four men. The engine was invariably one of our Midland type 4–4–0 2P class, and this day was number 412. The driver was always Arthur Watts, the very epitome of an old LNWR man, similar to old Fred the stores man, but Arthur was a large man with a big walrus moustache. He was very authoritarian, and made it known that he expected the footplate to be kept very spick and span, although he did not like over-use of the fizzle pipe as "it don't do my rheumatics much good". He told of when he was a young fireman, the drivers used to wear white corduroy trousers, and heaven help the fireman if they became soiled.

No. 412, our engine on the Engineers train for two days.
COLLECTION R. J. ESSERY

Bridge Street level crossing, looking south, with the footbridge and station on the right and signal box on the left, hidden by a building.
G. ONLEY

Arthur apparently had charge of the engineer's train on a regular basis because he had signed as knowing more of the roads within the engineer's area of supervision than any other driver at the shed. Consequently, a day out with Arthur was considered to be just that – a day out. The only drawback was that normally at least half the journey would be made tender first, with its obvious disadvantages. However, such inconveniences were lessened by the fact that Arthur had his own blackout sheet hidden away at the Central Material Depot (CMD) where the coach was stored, and which was to the east of Bridge Street level crossing. On this particular day we collected the coach, plus occupants, from the CMD and propelled it tender first along the Peterborough branch as far as Wellingborough, and round the curve to the Midland station, then engine first to Higham Ferrers, back to Wellingborough, and thence to the LNW station. From there we continued on to Peterborough East station. There the engineers left the train and walked out of the station, presumably to a local hostelry for lunch. We too had our sandwiches, and I mashed a can of tea, shared between ourselves and the guard, Jim, a man whom I did not know. After a rather extended lunch hour, the engineers returned, and we set off, this time engine first, back to Wansford, and then onto what Arthur said was the 'Harborough' branch to Seaton, and along the little branch to Uppingham. We returned to Seaton, and on to Market Harborough where another stop was made, for telephone calls, we were told by our guard, then back to Northampton

via Kelmarsh and Lamport, and a return to the CMD with the coach – all done at a speed I guessed as no more than 20 or 30mph, which, as I said, made it a pleasant day out for the fireman.

The next day I was again with Arthur, with the same engine, and this time we went over the branch to Bedford, from there along another branch to Sandy and Cambridge, where a lunch stop was made. After lunch we returned via Bedford to Bletchley, and then on the slow line to Roade, and down the bank through the tunnel to Northampton Castle station, and back to the CMD. Another trip at the relatively slow speed as the previous day, and equally as easy.

That was the end of my firing trips until after Christmas. Not that I was really disappointed – it was certainly cold on the footplate, especially when travelling tender first (as I had experienced both with Bosco, and latterly with Arthur Watts), notwithstanding the fact that we had a blackout sheet on each occasion. I had always imagined that it would be very warm on the footplate, but when the firehole door was closed, there was not much heat being given off by the well-lagged boiler.

During the period of our cleaning days, classes were organised for those of us having attained our sixteenth birthdays where we were taught certain aspects of a fireman's duties, especially those parts of the rule book relevant to those duties (Rule 55 for example, which was the instruction regarding the protection of the train when stationary at a signal). We were also taught the workings of the various types of injector and water feeds, etc. I remember at one of the classes, which were held in the mess room about twice a month, if I remember correctly, by a man from Rugby, always dressed in a perfectly clean boiler suit, I was nearly 'smooth talked' into buying two books on locomotive engineering, maintenance, and operation, by a salesman who attended the class. However, I did not succumb to his sales talk on that occasion, although I did purchase the volumes at a later date when I was studying for the 'passed fireman' exam, which unfortunately never materialised during the time I served on the railway, otherwise I might have remained in that employment. I still have the books.

These pictures show the CMD in its heyday. The one showing the electro-magnet gantry crane was looking east towards Hardingstone and Wellingborough. To the left can be seen the old Midland carriage shed. The shot with the mobile crane was looking west towards Bridge Street level crossing and station.
COLLECTION P. I. RAWLINSON

No. 8601 on the up slow at Berkhamsted on 7th February 1943.

H. C. CASSERLEY

CHAPTER SIX
LODGING AGAIN

Heading into Hunsbury Hill tunnel on the way to Roade with a coal train.   P. I. RAWLINSON

IN January I was again given occasional firing turns in our shunting yards – Down Sidings, Castle Yard, and Bridge Street. During the latter part of the winter – I think mid-February – I was again given a double trip working, this time with a driver named 'Buster' Ling, and the destination was Willesden.

It became obvious, even to us naïve youngsters, that the reason we young firemen quite frequently were given these lodging trips was because the regular firemen didn't like being away from home, for whatever reason. Some, it was rumoured, because they were not sure what the little woman was up to (as with my earlier Oxford trip), some through genuine sickness, and some because of the actual lodgings. The latter, it became apparent, was the probable reason for the non-appearance of the regular fireman on this occasion.

This time I had been warned about the job the day previously and so came prepared with extra sandwiches, although I had been informed that I could buy food at the railway lodging house at Willesden. If I remember correctly, we booked on at 10am to prepare the engine, which was a class 8 – No. 8601 – to work the 12.10pm from the Up Sidings. Pulling the 'bag' onto the tender to fill the tank during cold spells in the winter, when the bag was likely to be frozen solid unless the brazier (or 'stove') positioned by the water column had been kept burning well, could be hard

work – especially if it had not been used for some time, as was the case this morning. Once at the sidings, we learned that the train was of sixty-four wagons plus brake van, and was of mixed goods, so I was told to put our headlamp code as straight up and down.

I had been making the fire up gradually on our way from the loco shed to the sidings, a distance of about two miles, but had the front damper closed and the back one nearly so, with only half a glass of water; I didn't want a repetition of my previous double trip episode. We left the siding only about twenty minutes late and had a clear run up the bank to Roade, the engine steaming very well. In fact, she blew off in the tunnel at Hunsbury Hill, bringing down a shower of sooty particles from the tunnel roof, which caused Buster to swear – a little more than he had been about nearly everything so far that day. I had gained the impression he was not too pleased at having me as a mate, but, as the day wore on, I began to realise it was just his way of talking and he meant nothing by it. In fact he was quite amusing at times with his turn of phrase.

Our good run up the bank was to little avail, as when we passed Roade we were diverted into Hanslope Loop behind two other trains. Again I was glad of the blackout sheet I had managed to acquire at the shed, and positioned this to keep out the breeze cutting across the fields from the east. I had thought we might venture into the brake van in front, but

'On the block' — a train of coal empties awaiting the road at Roade. The bridge in the foreground was the SMJ line between Towcester and Ravenstone Wood Junction.

R. J. F. RAWLINSON

Buster sat tight, and in fact opened his sandwich tin for, as he put it, 'an afternoon snack'. Almost as soon as he did so, the train in front began to move off, which set Buster swearing again. However, he ate his sandwich as we edged along in the other train's wake, and there we stayed for an hour or so. No trains passed us on the slow line, and I queried this with Buster. He said that our delay was probably due to the shunters at Willesden having a 'go slow', as they sometimes did. Eventually, the train in front moved off, and then we were first up at the signals. Another wait there until eventually it was our turn. Buster moved off gently, saying that it was no good hurrying as we would no doubt be 'on the block' all the way. Indeed the distant signal for Castlethorpe was on, but as we drifted towards the home signal we saw that it was off. Buster immediately began to accelerate, saying that we might as well try and get water on the troughs just in case we got a run through Bletchley. We managed to get enough for the gauge to show a nearly full tank, but the signals were against us at Wolverton, though again cleared as we approached the home signal. It was similar at Loughton, but as we approached Bletchley No. 3 box, the home, and distant for No. 2, were pulled off, indicating, as Buster said, that the train in front must have gone into the loop or sidings.

Buster opened up and we galloped through the station and onwards to Leighton Buzzard, passing through the 'rat hole' tunnel just prior to that station. Then on through Cheddington and into Tring Cutting, which Buster said was our last climb before the line became mostly downhill to Willesden (Stonebridge Park sidings). As we approached Tring, the signals were on and we stopped at the home signal. Buster blew the whistle, 'to wake up the bobby' he said, as we could see that the box appeared to be in total darkness. Almost at once, a green hand signal was waved from side to side from the box, and we drew slowly forward. As we reached the box, I stood by the footplate doors on Buster's side, having some time previously folded the blackout sheet and put it on top of the tender cupboards. The signalman shouted "We're on the red, don't show any lights. You're okay down to the starter". Buster began swearing again and told me to put the sheet up again, this time covering the gap between the cab roof and tender. Having done that, I asked what was going on as this was all new to me. Buster replied that there must be an air raid in progress in London, but indicated that this was unusual as 'Jerry' seemed to have given up bombing raids lately. By this time it was nearly six o'clock and of course quite dark. We slowly made our way towards Berkhamsted, and Hemel Hempstead, all signals at caution.

At King's Langley we were stopped and informed we were "On purple. There has been one V2 and some doodle-bugs in and around London". Buster queried how long the 'raid' had been in progress, to be told, "All afternoon". He took off his greasy cloth cap he always wore in preference to the regulation uniform one, and scratched his thinning hair. "Well, Mutt", he said, "It looks like you came on the wrong trip, but what the hell, we won't know much about

it if one lands near us, will we?" With that he started the train again and drew forward so the signalman could inform the guard. So again we slowly made our way onward towards Watford. As we went through the tunnel, Buster jokingly remarked that it was a pity we couldn't stay in it all night as it would be safer than outside.

For my part, the apparent tenseness in Buster's face, and those of the signal men who had spoken to us, was alien to me. I had never been in a 'real' air raid situation. One thing that puzzled me was the fact that we had been told not to show any lights, for I knew, of course, that neither of the two flying weapons of which we had been warned were manned, and therefore could not be aware of lights. I queried this, and for the moment Buster's face lost some of its tenseness, he half smiled, and muttered that the bobbies were "quoting bloody regulations, I suppose, but there might be a plane or two photographing any damage being done". At Watford we were halted briefly, but when the signals were pulled off, Buster set off with a vengeance and I wondered why, until he informed me that there were more troughs ahead. Although we were not going very fast, we did manage to get some water, but nowhere near a full tank.

We continued our slow progress, and although passenger trains which passed in either direction were suitably dimmed, with only blue lamps showing through any gaps in blinds at windows, I was aware that an electric line was on the opposite side of the main line, and when one of those trains went by there was the occasional bright flash from the connecting shoe on the electric rail. So much for not showing lights, I thought.

We at last arrived at Wembley Central, which Buster said was where we would be switched into the sidings, and indeed the small signal on the gantry was off for us to proceed. All was very dark, and there was no sign of shunting or shunters. As we got to the end of the approach road, Buster stopped the train, told me to drop a couple of brakes on the wagons nearest to the engine and uncouple. While I was so engaged, there was an almighty flash and then an explosion some distance off to the left. I scrambled from between wagon and tender to hear Buster almost screaming at me to get back on the footplate "and let's ✱✱✱✱ off out of here". As I climbed onto the footplate I asked if we should wait for the guard. Buster used the same expletive with reference to that gentleman, indicating that he could make his way over to the electric train line for transport to Euston and home. With that we trundled off to Willesden shed, dumped the engine, and booked off to go to the lodging house. I was surprised that no-one seemed unduly concerned at the doodlebug raid in progress.

Although the lodge was not far from the shed, we were glad of the glow from Buster's hand lamp as the way was strewn with the debris gathered by most loco depots – lumps of coal, broken fire bricks, discarded fire-irons, and nearly buried rails. As we entered the double doors there was one blue bulb giving a modicum of illumination of the interior, but as the doors closed behind us, another lamp was illuminated. The walls were a dirty-looking yellow, and in one corner of the entrance lobby the steward sat in a small cubicle. Buster signed in and completed details of our wake-up call time and breakfast. Asked which cubicles we were allotted, the steward replied that there were no beds available at present, but he would have vacancies after ten o'clock when two crews were due to depart. He suggested we have a wash and brush-up and a meal, and there were books and newspapers in the 'lounge'. He issued us with a railway cloth towel (a little like a large tea-towel) so we took his initial advice, and went for a wash in the ground-floor ablutions room. There were about eight washbasins, with toilet cubicles on the other side of the room, and one open shower in the corner. The basins were filthy with residues of grease and coal dust. No soap or cleaning material was to be seen, and no plugs in the basins. Luckily, I had the little tin of soap I normally carried and washed in the running water from the taps – the hot one being very much so. I made some effort in cleaning the basin but without proper cleaning materials it was a losing battle. We made the state of the washing facilities known to the steward, but he replied that nothing would be done until the cleaners came on duty next morning. The dining room was little better; most of the enamel-topped tables were stained with spillages, especially those at what was obviously the most used end of the room – near to the kitchen-range type fireplace in which a cheery fire burned, seemingly the only warmth in the room. The kitchen was serving spam fritters and mash for supper, but we both declined, instead eating our own sandwiches and mashed our own tea from the big iron kettle sitting on the fire hob.

After our meal Bosco suggested we went for a walk to find a pub. Although there had been no further sounds of explosions, I was somewhat dubious. Enquiry of the steward revealed that an 'all clear' had indeed sounded, but "you never know when a big V is coming at you". Not a cheery thought, but, as Buster said, "if your number's up it don't matter where you are". With that sort of logic in my head, we stepped out of Stephenson Street into Old Oak Lane and turned right as Buster said he knew of a pub "the Wessie men use in Common Lane". As we crossed over the canal, there was a gate in the wall, just discernible in the darkness, from which suddenly emerged an apparition seemingly all in black, demanding in what was obviously a female voice, "D'ya worn a bamp ap?". Both of us took a couple of quick sideways steps, I nearly falling off the kerb. Buster yelled back, "**** off, you bloody hag", and was already walking on. For a second or two I was transfixed, it was the first time I had been propositioned by a prostitute – which I supposed she was – but I had always imagined them to be a little more decorous than this old-looking crone. Recovering my composure, I stumbled after Buster, whilst she mouthed blasphemous obscenities after us.

At the pub, Buster related our encounter to a couple of men who were obviously shed staff from the nearby WR shed. They apparently knew the 'lady' as she apparently operated in that area, and they volunteered the information that she had probably just had a client along the towpath of

the canal prior to offering her services to us! We chatted awhile, drinking a couple of pints each, before making our way back to the lodge. No sign of 'Sophie', as we were told she called herself and we regained the 'sanctuary' of the hostel without further incident. Once inside, we were informed that two cubicles were now vacant should we wish to make use of them. I was by this time quite ready for my bed as our call for the morning was to be at four o'clock. Buster said that he might enjoy a 'pipe' before retiring, but as I went to make my way to the first floor he warned me to "have a big game hunt before you get into bed". This I learned meant search for fleas, etc, as the sheets would not be fresh and probably used by at least two other persons that day. I made my way rather dubiously to my cubicle to find it lit by a gas jet on the wall (no mantle), the yellowish flame from which was about six inches high, with the wall and ceiling above it blackened by the smoke. In the room, in addition to the bed, were just a chair and a small mirror on another wall. There was no knob or lock on the door, so I placed the chair against it. I stripped the sheets and pillow from the bed and looked for any offensive 'wild life', but in the gloom could find nothing. So, remaking the bed, and stripping down to my underwear, I fell into bed and a deep sleep.

I was awakened by a loud banging on the door and the chair scraping across the floor as the door was pushed open. In the light of the still-burning gas jet (it was the only heating as well as lighting in the cubicle) Buster stood there in his shirt sleeves, and as I sat up rubbing my eyes, he said, "Come on you lazy sod, it's nearly half past four". A quick wash in the still-dirty basins, and it was to the canteen for breakfast. Having now been made aware of the state of the hostel, I was somewhat dubious of eating the meal provided, but Buster said we should give it a go. The breakfast was corn flakes – which we assumed could not be spoilt – followed by steamed haddock, which we saw was lying in a shallow tin of water simmering on a gas stove. When served, it looked as if it had been in the pan for hours as the top was quite hard and yellow whilst the bottom was soggy and crumbling on the plate. Quite revolting, especially at that time of the morning. However, with a couple of thick slices of bread and scrape, we got it down somehow. It's surprising what one will eat when hungry. This time we chose a table away from the old range, for although there was a decent fire in the grate, there was also a little thin old woman who frequently would wipe the range with a paraffin rag, which created wafts of smelly, oily smoke within the room. I wondered to myself if this could be Sophie's day job!

After breakfast we collected our bags from the locker room and went to the loco shed to book on, and find out what engine we had for our return journey. We saw on the engine board that we had a 'D', No. 9344 I think. Having found it on one of the outside roads, we set about preparing it. Buster swore when we saw it had what was colloquially known as a single man's tender, the shovelling plate being at footplate level, and the oil and clothing compartments being in two trunks either side of the coal bunker. Most crews

This picture of 9344 at Watford in 1947 shows her with the standard type of tender, so either my memory of her being our engine on the return from Willesden is at fault, or she had been coupled with a different tender since that time.
H. C. CASSERLEY

apparently disliked this type of tender because of coal dust getting into the clothing/bag trunk, and because of the extra bending the fireman had to do to shovel coal. However, I was not too bothered, and after spreading the fire over the box, collected some broken firebrick, which I also spread over the fire grate. This, I had learned, kept the clinker from sticking to the bars, thus creating holes for air to pass through the fire.

Following our 'fatting up', we filled the tank, obtained a little more coal, and gonged off the shed. Then it was tender first – no sheet this time, I had forgotten to hide it yesterday evening following the excitement of the 'bombing'. However, Buster had indicated that we had not far to go — just down the branch on the way to White City was how he described it. I, of course, had no idea what this meant, but in what I estimated was less than half a mile, we were backing on to a train in some sidings. Again I heard the clang of couplings as the guard made his way towards the engine. When he had hooked up we learned that again we had a mixed train, of only fifty wagons. I put the lamps into the appropriate head code formation, straight up and down, and in a very short time we set off for home. It was only a little after seven o'clock.

Buster, like the majority of LNW drivers, while we were in the sidings bled the vacuum brake reservoir by removing the 'rose' in the pipe to the gauge; now as we wheezed our way gently out of the sidings back towards Willesden Junction, he was keeping a sharp lookout for signals so that he had plenty of time for stopping should we have to. As it happened, we had a clear road round the bend adjacent to the loco shed, across the main line, and on to the slow line. While I was firing I was aware of Buster acknowledging the guard's signal with his own hand lamp and a shrill toot of the whistle. We had a clear run to Bourne End where we were held at the outer home while one of the early commuter trains was crossed from the up fast to up slow line. Then it was off again until we reached Leighton Buzzard; then we were on the block all the way to Ashton, where we were held for almost half an hour. Buster surmised that it was a train of chalk from the Dunstable branch in front, which had

held us up all the way from Leighton Buzzard, and was now awaiting a path on the main line to Blisworth and beyond. His assumption was most likely correct as once our signal was pulled off we had a clear run down the bank through Hunsbury Hill tunnel and into the Down Sidings at Northampton. There we left the train in the approach loop to the tender mercies of the shunt engine, and, once more tender first, made our way to the loco shed.

There, as we had only been on duty some six hours, we had to make a start on the disposal routine. We filled the tank, got coal via the crane tubs, and drove the engine to the ash pit. There Buster called a halt, and we made our way to the office, explained to 'Cloggy' Elliot, the booking on clerk, what job we had been on, and he signed us off.

Mother was surprised to see me home at lunchtime, but got me a meal while I related our 'adventure' with the bombing in London, but I missed out the bit about 'Sophie'! I slept really well that evening – in clean sheets!

Later in that February of 1945, I was posted with 'Jockey' Smith on the Up Side shunt. This yard was on the opposite side of the main line to the Down Side yard and was much smaller with only some nine roads, but these were 'through roads'. Again trains arrived in the loop, and the shunt engine used to either pull off that part of the train labelled for Northampton, marshalled at the rear of the train (or all of the train in portions, as the shunting neck was only about the length of forty wagons). The wagons for Northampton were deposited in one of the siding roads, and others for forward destinations taken from another siding and together with the brake van were re-marshalled on the train. The wagons removed from the train would then be shunted into the appropriate roads for transfer to other local yards, or for making a train for some other destination. Conversely, the train engine might be required to collect wagons from the other end of the sidings for attachment to its train before going on to Bletchley or beyond.

Jockey Smith was not a regular shunt driver, but was in the Special Link, from which men were given jobs either where there were vacancies, or were utilised to relieve crews on overtime, or perhaps to work special trains such as excursions. Jockey was spare at this time, his fireman being off sick. I had two weeks with him on the Up Side shunt, again with our usual D's as our engine. It was my first time with a younger driver, and Jockey was full of fun, with a penchant for a spot of ventriloquism, which I later came to know well, and which frequently had guards or shunters shouting instructions to 'unseen' colleagues thought to be on the other side of trains or wagons.

During these training days, we cleaners were sometimes employed on one of the shunting turns at any of the seven yards at Northampton, either on a day-to-day basis, or as had

been my luck, a week or more at a time. The engines normally employed were ex-LNWR D's in the Up and Down sidings, an ex-MR 2F in the Castle Yard, and in the Coal Yard (this latter yard was only shunted in the late evening – 7pm to 1am or thereabouts), whilst both Bridge Street and Far Cotton yards employed 'Humpies' (sometimes known as Jinties). The CMD – both the main depot east of the level crossing at Bridge Street, and the small yard west of the crossing – used mainly for storage of old used materials for disposal (from where I had set off on my Oxford adventure), were shunted by Harry Noakes with whatever engine he

A view from Bridge Street level crossing, looking eastwards towards the CMD, the gantry crane of which can be seen in the middle distance. The train, headed by a 'foreigner' – a Southern engine – was somewhat unusual even for wartime working, although, of course, one had accompanied us on the return journey of my Oxford adventure.
MILEPOST 92½

This picture shows Bridge Street level crossing and box in 1934, the building on the left being the one featured on the left of the previous picture. It looks as if the tram lines were still in situ in the roadway.
W. J. S. MEREDITH

Cotton End at Northampton with an engine backing onto the shed towards the coal stage. This picture provides a good view of the footbridge over which I carried my pedal cycle a few hundred times during my time on the railway, and on which I hit my head while I was standing on the tender of an engine backing under it. It appears that the exit from the right-hand end of the bridge – where the cyclists are seen – had been altered over the years. It used to be via an enclosed footpath which turned right by the end of the fencing and led out on to Main Road by the side of an old chapel, and opposite the working men's club. This picture was apparently taken in 1964 and one can see that there was still a lot of freight working around Northampton.

BRIAN BIBB

was allotted each day, usually a D or a Midland type class 4 0–6–0. Harry was a similar man to Arthur Watts, again an ex-LNW man, in his sixties, and not on the main line because of an injury, although the trip he had to make at the end of each day from the CMD to the Down Sidings entailed a couple of miles 'main line' running.

This final run of the day was a highlight for any of us novice firemen who happened to be Harry's mate for the day. Frequently the train was over ninety wagon lengths – many of them being bogie-bolsters loaded with rail lengths, or completed units of track – which meant the train being made up from two of the sidings at the depot. This then necessitated the front of the train occupying the level crossing while it pulled out of one siding and then reversed into the next to collect the rear portion. Although road traffic was not considerable in those days, there were a great many cyclists on their way home from the local factories at that time of the day (around 5.30) and obviously there were many disgruntled people waiting at the gates. Sometimes the delay was made worse when Harry couldn't get the train started immediately, either because it was so heavy, or the rails were wet and the engine slipping, necessitating a rever-

Bridge Street station, looking east to the level crossing and footbridge in June 1955. The architecture of the station is worthy of note.
H. C. CASSERLEY

Bridge Street station, taken from the footbridge, with the Wellingborough train just departing. P. I. RAWLINSON

sal to buffer up the wagons, and then a lunge forwards, hoping the snatch didn't break any couplings. 'Noakes's Tripper' was always guaranteed a clear run on its two-mile dash, otherwise the length of the train meant that wherever the train was held at signals the rear of the train would be blocking one or more of the junctions behind it. The engine really had to work hard, both in starting the train and in getting it over the one in thirty-five gradient of the canal bridge adjacent to the loco shed. After that it was fairly level until the climb up the arrival road at the Down Sidings. Once there, the engine was uncoupled and returned light to the shed. For many it was the nearest experience to mainline working before actually being given a chance at the real thing.

It was while I was with Harry one day that I had my first really painful accident. I was on the tender of our engine – a Midland class 3 0–6–0 – trying to move or break up a very large lump of coal which was wedged behind the front of the tender. Harry was moving wagons, again in the yard opposite the loco and Bridge Street Junction signal box. As he moved the engine forward, I happened to stand up, and the smoke plate of the footbridge caught me in the back, knocking me over so that I fell against the rails on the side of the tender, causing a sharp pain in my ribs. As I fell over the

side of the tender, I managed to grab at those rails, which put me in an upright position as I continued my descent to the ground, and at least landed me feet first before I fell to the ground very winded. The outcome of that little incident – which had been my own fault as I knew the bridge was there, having travelled over it at least twice a day since I had begun work on the railway – was that I had my cracked rib strapped, and found it somewhat uncomfortable to either breathe or laugh for a couple of weeks, but I did not report sick – you didn't receive much sickness pay (club money) in those days.

Looking back, I guess it was really exploitation in using youngsters on main-line duties, especially as we discovered eventually that we should not be so employed until seventeen – but it was wartime and footplate men seemed to be always in short supply as many had been drafted into the forces, irrespective of the railway being a supposed reserved occupation. It appeared to be the case that if a driver (or passed fireman) agreed to take one of us 'under their wing', it was given the okay by the shed foreman, or perhaps by an even higher authority. Speaking for myself, I did not mind such alterations to my normal working day. It was an adventure to be firing on the main line, although I was conscious of it putting added responsibilities on the driver.

Another view of the footbridge, showing more clearly the smoke plates, one of which hit me in the back and knocked me over while I was on the tender.
R. J. ESSERY

CHAPTER SEVEN

PASSED CLEANER

SO I continued duties on the shed as cleaner through most of the spring and summer of 1945. The biggest excitement of that period was the end of the war, but any great expectations of alterations and improvements in our way of life were quickly dashed. Rationing became even more stringent, the prisoners of war were still with us at the shed most days, and the expected swift return of men from the army did not materialise, many, we learned, being retained in the Royal Engineers to drive and fire engines on the re-emerging railways of mainland Europe.

However, as autumn approached, the instruction classes having been completed, I was detailed as fireman on the Castle Yard shunt engine – again with Tommy King – and tested by the footplate inspector, a man named Fred Lacy, and so became a passed cleaner, which meant I was authorised to be fireman as necessary, but still cleaner until required. Although excited by this 'promotion', it made little difference to the daily routine, except that I did get 'requested' to do one or two Sunday turns in the two yards which operated on that day of the week, the Down Side and the Up Side, which was good for a little overtime pay – I was saving up to buy a second-hand motorcycle.

Even shunting had its moments of excitement and amusement. I was on the Up Side shunt one Sunday with Charlie Wake, a passed fireman, and I had been winning at 'stop the bus', a card game played in the shunters' cabin with Gus Bellamy and his mate during our break time. A 'phone call from No.4 box informed Gus that a train was approaching that had a wagon with a hot axlebox which would need to be deposited in the sidings for attention by the wheel tapper and mate. As I had been winning the pennies, I was detailed to do the deed. Our D's boiler had been somewhat overfilled so that she would stand without attention during our usual protracted lunch break; I was cognisant of the possibility of her priming, so kept the cylinder drain cocks open as I eased her on to the rear of the train. The hot box was fortunately only about ten wagons from the brake van, the possible reason why the guard had heard the squealing of the axle as the train moved along. He hooked off at the hot-box wagon and came back to ask where we were going, then hooked the brake van to the engine, and I hissed and wheezed gently along the shunting neck, having been told by Gus to deposit the offending wagon into the 'lido'. This was a short siding temporarily laid over quite uneven ground, and used by permanent way staff to dump waste ballast, etc. into the lido, which was in fact a disused gravel pit, now full of water, and of unknown depth. This short 100 yard long line terminated in a 'stop block' made of an old sleeper complete with rail chairs inverted across the track. The guard unhooked the wagon and switched the points into the lido. I opened the regulator to shunt the wagon in there, but unfortunately the engine picked up the water from the overfilled boiler and charged into the siding. I managed to bring the engine under control by use of brakes

and reversing gear, but the shunted-off wagon hit a solitary ballast wagon so hard that the vehicle careered to the end of the siding, pushing the stop block to one side, and disappearing with an almighty splash into the murky depths below. Fortunately, the other wagon did not follow it, the guard managing to scramble after it and pin a brake down.

I was obviously somewhat concerned at what had happened, but I saw that the guard – after he had recovered his composure – and the signalman in the nearby box were both grinning broadly. I returned the brake van and wagons to their train, re-stabled the engine, heaved the somewhat damaged sleeper back on the rails, and returned to the cabin, to the only comment, "Been having fun out there?" No one said any more about the incident, but I often wondered what the platelayers thought had happened to their wagon!

I continued to volunteer for the odd Sunday duty, and one such weekend I was given a seven o'clock booking-on time to partner George Carter, a driver in the Special Link, on what I thought was possibly shed duties. However, when we booked on, we were told to report to 'Control' at Castle Station. From there we were directed to the Up Side loop at No. 3 box to relieve a set of Leicester men on a coal train which had apparently left Toton sometime the previous day, and was destined for Willesden. The Leicester men, on overtime, had already been waiting some two hours for relief. On the way from the station to the loop, George casually asked how long I had been firing, and when I truthfully told him that I had only recently been posted into the shunting link, but had done two double trips, he looked at me a little quizzically as if weighing in his mind what he had been lumbered with. As we approached No. 3 box, we could see a train in the loop headed by a Black 8, which, as we got closer, I could see was 8273.

The Leicester men had very worthily cleaned the fire, filled the tank, and made some effort in bringing some coal forward, so that was a good start for me. After due exchanges of greetings and information regarding wagon numbers, and how good or bad the engine was, the Midland men wandered off to the station, no doubt to catch a train to their home depot, 'riding on the cushions'. George checked around the engine, and climbed on the tender to look in the tank, "just in case the gauge is wrong". I later learned from many other trips with George that he never passed a water column without topping up the tank, a precaution that had its annoying moments, but as it turned out had been quite wise in this instance.

George gave a toot on the whistle to let the bobby know we were ready to go, but he came to the door of the box and made an unintelligible gesture to us. I was sent to find out what the gesture meant, and was informed that everything was on the block as the shunters at Stonebridge Park were again on a 'work to rule' session because of some labour dispute, and we would probably not move for an hour or so. And so we sat, dampers closed, but the fire well

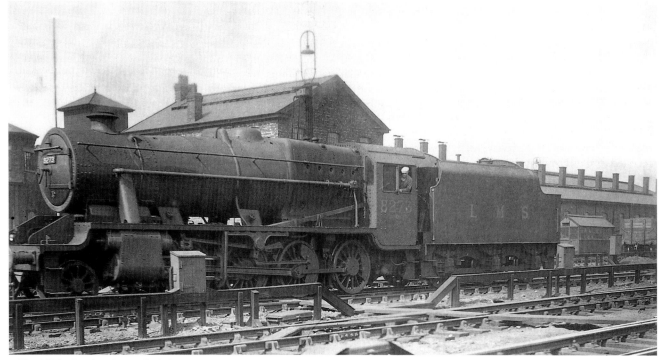

No. 8273, the class 8 on which I partnered George Carter — an engine in 'good nick' but found to have no water scoop, much to George's chagrin.
A. C. ROBERTS

made up just in case our turn came more quickly than the signalman had indicated. I was quite liking the situation of sitting on a relatively comfortable seat watching the passenger trains going by. There were more than on a usual Sunday, so I guessed trains were being diverted from the old main line because of permanent-way work. Very different to standing most of the day on shunting engines, or trying to get more than half of my posterior on the semi-circle of seat on a 'D'.

Mid-day came and went, and still no move. Eventually, shortly after 1.30, a shout from the signal box alerted us to the fact that the signal was off – we were on our way. As we pulled out of the loop and thence on to the through road approaching No. 2 box, the distant signal for No. 1 box was lowered, and George said, "Here we go then, don't forget your damper" – which I had done. I opened the back one as George opened the regulator even more, and we blasted through Castle Station awakening the echoes on this hitherto quiet Sunday afternoon, and disturbing the pigeons who were strutting along the platforms. George gradually accelerated our train of 69 wagons plus brake van (the occupant of which had exchanged hand waves as we left the loop) round the bend and into the long drag up the bank to Roade.

I fired the engine as we approached Duston Junction West and, after putting on the exhaust injector, went over to George's side of the footplate and looked towards the loco shed. I wondered who was watching us, just as I had watched scores of trains during my months on the shed. Certainly no cleaners, it being Sunday – in fact there appeared to be little activity at all. George, having found the

almost mandatory piece of coal for the regulator stop, picked up the shovel and said, "Try and do it this way if you can", and began firing the engine. I sat on my seat and watched as he stroked three shovels of coal along each side of the firebox and then four more at the back of the box. He half closed the firehole door, put the shovel in the tender, and looked out at the chimney, where a slight discolouring of the exhaust steam was all the smoke there was. He closed the firehole door further, and then there was a definite brown colour to the exhaust. He grinned and nodded with obvious satisfaction as he said, "If you can make as little smoke as that, you know you have good combustion. Real black smoke means wasted fuel as the gases are not being burned before they are blown out of the chimney".

Those words were remembered all through my firing days, and I tried hard to emulate George on our journey south, and also on future firing turns – not always with complete success I may add. Firing a Stanier Black 8 ,with plenty of room on the footplate, an engine in good order, as this one was, and at a relatively slow speed up this bank was not too difficult, even for a relative novice like me. With the exhaust injector on for most of the time, she held steam pressure at over the 200lbs mark on the gauge through Hunsbury Hill Tunnel and on towards Roade. Blasting through the chasm-like brick walls of Roade Cutting under the support girders, made me realise the power being generated just by heating water. I've always marvelled at the seeming simplicity of it.

As we trundled through Roade Station, the distant signal for Ashton was on, and George remarked that we were no doubt destined for Hanslope Loop. His assumption was correct, for, as we approached the home signal, the bobby went through the now familiar routine of pulling off the signal and appearing on his verandah with a green flag. As we slowly passed him he called, "Still on the block; there are three in there". We drifted into the loop, keeping a sharp lookout for the brake van of the train in front. This we soon saw, and George brought our train to a stop, almost touching the buffers of the van.

I had already closed the dampers and opened the firehole door so as not to make too much steam and waste water. Luckily, on George's suggestion, I had filled my billy can with water before we left Northampton, and now I placed it on the shovel, and rested the heel of the shovel on the lip plate. It was not long before the water boiled, and I dropped in the 'makings', from a little packet of tea and sugar, to brew a cup of tea. George, who like most of the Special Link men, had a bottle of cold tea, or Camp coffee, which had been placed on the shelf over the firehole, had gone to the brake van in front to ascertain how long the train had been in the loop. When, however, I shouted "Mash ho!" in the direction of the van, he returned, accompanied by the guard – complete with billy-can lid – who I learned was a Rugby man, and who had been in the loop for well over an hour, and moved up one place during that time.

We enjoyed a convivial cuppa, and the guard invited us to share the warmth of his van, but George declined, explaining to me, after the departure of the guard, that the stove in there was red hot, and the temperature so high that all one wanted to do was sleep. That seemed a good idea to me, but I said nothing. Another boring hour went by with nothing to do except dwell on our own thoughts. George and I had spasmodic periods of conversation, but after explaining our background, and reasons for becoming a railway man, there was little to talk about.

Darkness came, and I trimmed and lit the lamps. I had already utilized this static time to scrape and shovel quite an amount of coal forward in the tender, although George had said we would no doubt be relieved at Bletchley. I had also eaten some of my sandwiches with the tea I made, although on George's advice I had saved some for 'the twelfth hour', which seemed to be the minimum period of duty one expected to do when the situation was on the block! The fire was by now well damped down, and, with a cool breeze blowing across the fields, we were glad of being able to close the sliding side windows (made of plywood actually, the glass no doubt having long since disappeared), and utilize the piece of a blackout sheet we had found in the fire-iron cubby hole in the tender to keep out some of the wind.

So time dragged on, until some time after 7pm (by George's watch) when a shout from in front alerted us to the fact that the train in front was moving, and we followed gently after it. We had been passed by two passenger trains, a parcels train, and a fitted freight train on the up slow while we had been stationary in the loop, the second passenger train not long before we began to move forward. This train must have been the one we were all awaiting, because

within a quarter of an hour of us stopping again, the van in front began to move, quickly followed by the guard's yell to warn us. Again we followed slowly behind it, but keeping a safe distance – seventy wagons of coal could not be stopped on a sixpence. Again, within fifteen to twenty minutes after stopping, the van in front moved off, with a cheery shout from the guard to the effect he would no doubt see us at Bletchley. We now rolled along to the signal at the end of the loop, almost opposite Hanslope box, and there we stayed.

By this time I was getting somewhat thirsty, having sipped the last of the stewed brew I had made earlier. George mentioned there was a spring in the field near the signal post which sometimes gurgled water, so after swilling out the can with the fizzle pipe, I borrowed his hand lamp and went to investigate. Sure enough, I found a trickle of water running from what appeared to be a clay pipe, from which, by use of the lid of my can, I was able to half fill the can within a few minutes, and quench my thirst at the same time. Back on the footplate, George also had a drink of the water, he having almost finished his bottle of lukewarm tea. I asked if the water was really from a spring or from a drain of some sort. He replied, "Who cares, it tastes sweet enough to me, and a good many men have swallowed it before us".

By this time it was after 8.30, and we had been on duty more than thirteen hours. I decided to eat the rest of my sandwiches, the water having refreshed my mouth enough to enable me to chew satisfactorily. Shortly after finishing them, a fitted freight went past on the up slow, and we guessed that was what we had been waiting for, because within what seemed only a few minutes we heard the points snap open and the signal pulled off. I had put coal on the fire when we became the first train in the loop, and now I opened the back damper and put the blower on to liven up the fire as George eased the regulator open, tightening the couplings as we once more continued our journey.

The signals were off for Castlethorpe and, as we went through the station, I unchained the scoop handle ready for the troughs. George had accelerated well on seeing the green signals, and we were going at an adequate speed to pick up some water, but when I lowered the scoop as we came to the trough, there was no movement of the tank gauge. George attempted to wind the gear down even more, but it was obvious I had wound it to its full extent. With seemingly no water obtained, I wound up the gear until the indicator was at the up position. I could sense George was a little agitated, but we had something over a quarter of a tank full – according to the gauge – so knowing we were less than ten miles from Bletchley, I thought we had plenty for the journey.

We had green signals through Wolverton, but we were checked at Loughton, before stopping at Bletchley No. 3, and then signalled in to the loop. As we stopped at the south end of the loop, George took his hand lamp and went to look under the tender at the scoop. He yelled for me to follow his example, and saw there was no blade on the scoop mechanism. George cursed the Leicester men for not

A 'D' chugging along Castlethorpe troughs on the down slow with her load of coal empties. There is no sign of her picking up water – perhaps another one with no scoop?

Bletchley, looking from the north end of the station towards the Bedford line and the coal yard, etc. Note the water column and the clinker pile, which appear to be alongside the up loop where George and I were relieved.   COLLECTION MIKE WILLIAMS

informing us of the defect, but then modified his language, saying that they had possibly not known of it as they would have had no cause to use the scoop. While we were talking we were approached by a set of men who said they were our relief. After the usual formalities, including the information about the scoop, we walked to the loco-men's cabin at the station and reported to 'Control'. As expected, we were told to make our way home on the next available train.

George said we had two options: we could ride in the brake van of the first wagon train to trundle through on the down slow, and which was going to or via Northampton, or await the midnight express from Euston, which stopped at both Bletchley and Northampton. Before I could voice an opinion (not that I really had one), he said we'd opt for the latter alternative. In view of what he had said earlier about being in brake vans, I was not surprised. I followed him as he went out of the station where we found that a WVS all-night tea trolley was still operational, manned by two senior ladies, where we were able to buy a cuppa and a couple of

potted meat sandwiches. When I queried why there should be a tea stall at such a 'dead hole' as Bletchley at this time of night, George indicated there was an army establishment almost opposite, with a lot of coming and going at all hours – though I saw no activity during the few minutes we were drinking our tea. I learned many years later that this establishment was in fact Bletchley Park, of Enigma fame.

We adjourned to the loco-men's cabin to await the train home, which arrived some twenty minutes late. It was nearly 3.00a.m. before we booked off. So ended my initiation into the very slow running of many wagon trains. Nearly nineteen hours to travel twenty miles and return. My aunt, with whom I was lodging at this time (I had moved out of my parents' home to allow mother to take in two lodgers, who paid her more than I did, Father still being in an army hospital having been injured some months previously), had apparently been worried at my non-arrival home at the normal time, and had instructed uncle, who was barman at Franklins Gardens Hotel, to make enquiries at the station as he cycled to work for his evening duties. Having ascertained I was still at work, he had telephoned from the hotel to the 'corner shop' near his home, and the young son of the shopkeeper had delivered the message to my aunt. Luckily, I had a key to the door and, having cycled home, I washed and fell into bed. I slept until teatime that day.

As mentioned above, having been taken in as a lodger at my uncle and aunt's home, I soon found there to be one big shortcoming. They lived in a small terraced house next door to an equally small factory in a cul-de-sac off the Kettering Road, opposite the school of that name. The house – long since demolished – had an outside toilet, and no bathroom; the tin bath, which normally hung on a wall in the back yard, had to be dragged into the kitchen and water ladled from the fire-heated copper for baths. Not too bad when one was on the right shift to enable this to be done in the late evening when everyone else was in bed, but otherwise very unsatisfactory. So together with pal Norman Quennell, who lived in a similar type of house in an area called Semilong, we investigated the public baths in town. We found that for sixpence you could have a very cleansing and refreshing bath – with towel provided for an extra two pence – and we began attending this establishment at least twice each week. However, what we also discovered some weeks after first attending, was the wonder of Turkish baths. Although you thought yourself clean after a normal bath, coming out of the steam room of the Turkish bath you frequently resembled a black man. It certainly demonstrated how much railway dirt and grime became ingrained in one's pores. This type of bath cost us a shilling, but was worth it once or twice a month.

Pure nostalgia for me, this picture shows the closed end of Brunswick Place, Northampton. The last house on the right before the small factory is where I was born in 1928, the home of my maternal grandparents, and where eventually I lodged when it was the home of my uncle (Mother's brother) and his wife and family. The factory, at the time of my lodging, manufactured beds and settees. Just beyond the factory was a gate by the wall which led to an alley into Dover Street, where at the exit of the alley was a bakehouse to which many of the local housewives took the Sunday roast and potatoes to be cooked. One could see them making their way to the alley carrying the metal baking dish covered with a clean tea towel. Although I say the housewives did this, in fact quite a few of the husbands volunteered for this chore, as it provided them with an excuse to drop into the adjacent Dover Arms for a pint or two while their joint was cooking. At a shilling a time, it was quite lucrative for the baker and it kept his oven hot over the weekend. It was even more lucrative at Christmas time when he charged two shillings and more customers attended.
CTY. NORTHAMPTON BOROUGH COUNCIL

CHAPTER EIGHT

REGULAR FIRING

IT was shortly after the long shift with George that I was informed by the shed foreman that I was to be posted into the shunting link as a permanency. This meant I renewed my association with Chudder Hillyard and Bill Whitlock at the Down Sidings, plus getting to know men such as Frank Copnal on the Bridge Street humpy, and George Harris on the similar engine at Far Cotton. There were also the two trip engines, Harry Noakes at the CMD, previously mentioned, and Fred Linnel who shunted the south end of the Up Sidings and flitted between all the yards – except the CMD – with various amount of wagons during his shift, always ending at Far Cotton before returning to the shed. The two-shift Up Sidings shunter appeared to be short of regular drivers, and the vacancies were filled on a weekly basis by Special Link drivers, as was the Coal Yard shunt. The yard shunt engines operated daytime shifts systems, as did the 'trippers' (the coal yard being shunted in the late evening), whilst the trip engines did any necessary ancillary shunting at the yards during the late afternoon/early evening. The Down Sidings operated throughout the twenty-four hours, again with a special link driver on the night shift as required. As the Far Cotton, Bridge Street, Castle Yard, and the trip engines had their regular 'off main line duty' crews, it was only occasionally that one was detailed on those jobs, as had been my lot with Tommy King.

I was in this link until approaching my eighteenth birthday. Then, at the end of July, I was posted to the Special Link, with a driver named Harry 'Big Adge' Stockwin. He was in his thirties and, as one can imagine from his nickname, was a large man. We got on well from the beginning. Our main work function was to relieve crews on overtime on wagon trains, and our usual area of operation was to Rugby in the west, Leicester in the north, and Bletchley in the south. We did manage sometimes to get through Bletchley to Willesden, which usually meant making good overtime money. Adge needed that as he and his wife Lilly had at that time, I believe, five young sons. After about a month together, he began to let me drive on occasions, and subsequently I drove on alternate days. We were rostered together through the winter, but of course on several occasions one of us would be posted with a different mate, when only a driver or a fireman was required for an engine. Usually we would be given duties for the following day when we booked off but if this was not the case, because I lived well outside the knocking-up area, I would attend the depot after the compulsory twelve hours off, and would frequently be given a job with another driver before the time that Adge had been knocked for; the fireman, who should have partnered the driver I was now with, would likewise be knocked to book on with Adge. Somewhat confusing perhaps, but the office staff seemed to have it worked out okay.

Some of these other drivers were men such as Fred and Jack Pettit (brothers who were passed firemen), Ted Fell, Joe Hasdell, Walt Gardner, Bill Tarry, and Albert 'Punch' Pointer. Punch was what might be termed as a 'character', and did the odd singing/story-telling turn at the local working men's club, where he was known by his 'stage' name, Ted Edwards! He was always good company, especially when in a cabin full of appreciative footplate men.

I can remember nothing extraordinary happening during my time with Adge, except that on one trip on a class 8 with a coal train to London, I shovelled the last scrap of coal from the tender just after passing Watford. Luckily, after passing Bushey troughs, it was all downhill to Wembley, but we had to stop in that station before entering Stonebridge Park sidings so that I could steal enough coal from the wagons behind the engine to maintain enough fire and steam to enable us to get to Willesden loco shed.

One night I booked on at 12.15am. This was classed as a day turn of duty, and we had frequent job allocations beginning at 12.01am (especially on a Sunday night/Monday morning) to avoid it being classed as a Sunday duty with the consequent increase in pay. Most of the freight links were of twelve-week duties, and if you had three of those weeks with nights in bed, it was lucky indeed. However, on this particular night I was detailed to ride on a 'dead' engine (a D) from the shed to Crewe Works. Obviously it had failed for some reason, which could not be rectified at our depot. I suspected it involved either cylinders and/or valve gear as the connecting rods had been removed and placed in the tender. I was told that lubrication had been done, and that the engine was to be attached to the 1.20am Manchester from the Down Sidings, the engine of which was on the shed. I found this engine – another D – and introduced myself to the crew, George Quartermain and Fred Pettit. They, of course, already knew of their extra load, but seemed unconcerned about it. Coupled up, we arrived at the sidings and backed on to the train, which was of mixed freight and of only some forty wagons, so the loading was not severe. Fred suggested that I ride on their engine as it would be warmer on this bitterly cold night, but I had been instructed by the shed foreman that I was in charge of the dead engine and should be on it at all times, not only to make sure everything stayed in place, but also to assist by use of the hand brake should it be needed.

I was still naïve enough to believe one should follow orders, so I declined Fred's offer and sat tight on the very cold footplate. It was somewhat eerie being alone on the footplate with no life in the engine. However, wrapped in my greatcoat, I made the best of it, although soon wishing I had taken the sensible option of riding with the two in front of me. We seemed to make good time on the climb through Althorpe Park and up to Long Buckby and, being on a silent footplate, I was able to hear the somewhat wheezy bark of

This engine was my Nemesis in one direction, and Aphrodite on the return.
COLLECTION
R. J. ESSERY

the lead engine quite clearly. Down the hill through Kilsby and Crick and the tunnels – where the dankness seemed to be extra cold – and I was beginning to really wish I was on the front engine. I thought I might be able to make such a move at Rugby, but we had greens all the way and we trundled through and on to the Trent Valley Line.

Luck was eventually with me as we were stopped short of Nuneaton. I quickly grabbed my bag, gave a shout to George that I was joining them, and scrambled along the 'six foot' and on to their engine. Fred indicated that he had wondered how long I would stick it in the cold, and expected to see me appearing over the tender before this moment. We were soon on our way again, and I began to thaw out a little, but kept my big coat on. However, there is not much room on a D's footplate, so whenever Fred was firing I had to stand by the hand rail in the gap between engine and tender – which again was very cold – but at least I was able to warm up between firings, and also helped by cracking up coal.

George said that on this Manchester double trip run they were usually routed via Stoke, but as the dead engine was for Crewe works an alteration would no doubt be made, but he would find out by the time we got to Rugeley. As it happened, we were diverted into the loop at that station, and George took the opportunity of ringing control to clarify the matter. He returned with the information that he was to drop the dead engine at Stafford and take his normal route via Norton Bridge to Stoke. He explained that he was unable to find out if there was a train or engine at Stafford to take me forward to Crewe. At Stafford I was shunted into a siding and I bade farewell to George and Fred who continued their journey to Manchester. I stayed with the engine for some twenty minutes, but nothing appeared to be happening, so I went to the signal box to enquire. I was told that an engine was coming off the shed for the dead engine. Within four or five minutes another 'D' appeared and we hooked on, but instead of heading forward to Crewe I was told we were to drop the engine on the shed "for the time

being". After doing so, I found the foreman's office and enquired what was to happen to the engine, and what I should do. I was told that the engine was to stay on shed to await another engine due for the works, coming from Shrewsbury, and that I should make my way home. As it was now nearing seven o'clock, I mashed my can of tea, and ate my sandwiches in the mess room before making my way to the station and a return to Northampton 'on the cushions'.

It was during this early period of being in the special link that I had the worst experience of my relatively short firing career. I was detailed to be mate to a driver I did not know named Ernie Smith, booking on at about eight in the evening to relieve a passenger train at Castle Station for forward progress to Euston. On the walk to the station, I learned from Ernie that this was a regular job in one of our passenger links, and was known as the 'Barrow' up and the 'News' down. I gathered that the train originated at Barrow-in-Furness, and was due to depart from Northampton at 9.10pm. On arrival at the station, we discovered that the train was nearly an hour late.

When it did arrive, it had at its head an ex-Midland-type compound engine, number 1159 (indelibly printed on my mind), with a set of Stafford men on board. They had faces as long as fiddles, and indicated they had had a rough trip. "She's a cow" said the driver. "The fire's knackered, and we've had a job to keep her going". I looked in the firebox and saw a dull red mass nearly up to the brick arch. The coal in the tender was some way back, and didn't look like good steam coal. While Ernie and the other driver were talking on the platform, I had the injector on to fill the boiler – thinking that at least we would have a reasonable start and while the boiler was filling I got the dart from the tender and attempted to get some air through the fire. The fire was too thick for my efforts to have much effect, and before I had really prepared myself, or the engine, I heard whistles blowing and Ernie climbed on the footplate, and we were off, signalled via Blisworth, with our eight coaches.

I switched off the injector with the glass nearly full, but the steam pressure down below 180 psi. I knew nothing of Ernie, or his prowess as an engineman, but I had heard that compounds were somewhat alien to NW men, and needed to be worked properly. However, once we had cleared the curves round to Duston West, Ernie opened her up with a vengeance, and almost immediately she began to prime, which was the last thing I wanted. Ernie began cursing, but did nothing to try to alleviate our problem. I had been firing little and often to try to get some life in the fire, but the steam pressure was going down almost as quickly as the water in the boiler. The priming eventually subsided when the water was down to about a quarter of the glass, but our troubles were not over, as we were losing headway up the bank. Eventually, with the steam pressure down below 130 psi, the brakes began to drag. Ernie opened the large ejector but it made little difference, and we gradually came to a standstill part way up the bank to Blisworth! What ignominy – and with a so-called express too.

Ernie seemed to be jumping up and down with frustration, calling me a 'long Peruvian ponce' (which I later learned was his favourite expression of chastisement), and demanding me to get more steam in the boiler. I again tried with the dart, and this time did eventually make a hole through the clinker, but it was obviously too little too late. Gradually we gained steam and water in the boiler and, after pacifying the guard, who had made his way through the train to ascertain the possible length of time we would be stationary, thinking no doubt of his responsibility of protecting the rear of the train, we made another start. Our first scheduled stop was Bletchley, and as we approached Blisworth the signals were green for us. We limped through the curves of the bay platform and on to the main line, when Ernie again opened her up, apparently with no thought of nursing the engine (or me).

We made it to Roade okay, and began the slight descent to Castlethorpe and the troughs, but with the reversing wheel hardly wound back more than a turn or two, and with the regulator still nearly fully open, I was again losing the battle with steam and water. I managed to get water on the troughs, but, as we swept through the curve of Wolverton station, the brakes began rubbing again, and we eventually came to a stand. Again the cursing and gesticulating from Ernie, but there was little either of us could do except wait for the pressure to rise enough for the brakes to be released. And so we limped to Bletchley where quite shrewdly we were switched to the slow line. Once in the station, I made a real attack on the fire with the dart, and eventually managed to prise several pieces of clinker from the bars, getting the fire in a far healthier condition, and the steam and water levels in the best condition than they had been since we left Northampton.

After some twenty minutes more than the supposed allotted time of two minutes at the station, we decided to make a move. Next stop was to be Watford, but I was not optimistic about making it. Ernie set off again with fire in his

belly, his walrus moustache sticking out belligerently as if daring me to lose steam again. It was a misty winter night, and every time that Ernie pulled his head in from looking at the road ahead he had dew on his moustache, which seemed to accentuate his look of a walrus, and of course amused me, but did little to improve Ernie's temper, and I was frequently labelled 'you long Peruvian' etc. during the journey.

I was pleased to note that my disturbing of the clinker seemed to have had a remarkable effect on the fire which was now burning much brighter, and although the steam pressure was still falling, it was nowhere near as severe as it had been before Bletchley. So we ploughed our way through Leighton Buzzard and up to Tring. I was sure that Ernie had not had the engine compounding at any stage of the journey, but now that we were over the top, he did close the regulator a little, and wound the gears back a couple more turns. We now began to pick up speed, and in fact I had some difficulty in firing, not being used to such speed and oscillation while attempting to shovel coal into the firebox.

However, no more disasters on the way to Watford. Ernie pulled his head in and grinned, giving me a flash of his brown teeth in the firelight, which I took to mean that our performance met with his approval. We were quickly away and over Bushey troughs where I managed to fill the tank, then it was down hill most of the way to Euston, where we arrived some two hours late! No cheerful "goodnight" from the detraining passengers, most of whom appeared to be service personnel. No doubt many of them would have missed their connections to wherever they were hoping to get at that time of the night. I busied myself in unhooking the engine from the train, ready for the pilot engine to pull the coaches into what I guessed would be a siding, to enable us to get to the turntable and water column, which Ernie had described as being adjacent to platform fifteen. The guard, a Rugby man, came to the engine and commiserated with us, saying that the previous enginemen had stopped near Kilsby and Crick station for a blow-up, which made me feel a little bit better about our performance. This was my first time of firing a train into Euston, and I hoped that if I ever did again it would be under much different circumstances!

Once at the service point, Ernie pointed out that because of our late arrival we had a relatively quick turn-around. The engine was turned, the tank topped up, while I cleaned the fire with the help of the fire irons, and Ernie began to shovel coal forward ready for the journey back, having pointed out the way to the 'cat walk' which went at roof level from the side of the train shed adjacent to platform 15 across to platform 6 where there was a staff canteen, and where I could have my billy can filled with tea (or mash my own brew should I wish). On my return, Ernie had kindly completed his work in the tender, and we washed our hands in the bucket with water from the fizzle pipe (very hot) and had our sandwiches, with what I considered a well-deserved cuppa.

Our return train, I learned, was the 2.15am newspaper train, which apparently usually had about three long parcel-type vans, plus a passenger/brake carriage used mostly by returning loco men and guards, but also for the public, although the facility was not advertised. In fact, when we backed on to the train in platform seven, it consisted of only two carriage-length vans plus the brake-van coach, so I was optimistic about a possible comfortable trip home. The scheduled stops were due to be Watford, Hemel Hempstead, Leighton Buzzard, Bletchley and Northampton, which meant that even if things were not good on the footplate, there would be several recovery points along the route. As it happened, having banked up the fire after my refreshments, the firing of the engine was relatively easy, even though we were speeding along between stops! Our arrival at Northampton was more or less on time, and after the train was unloaded of the rest of the newspapers and shunted into a siding, we left the engine on the shed and went home, me hoping I never had another trip on a passenger train like the first half of that one. Fortunately, I never did.

Remembering my cold ride on the dead engine, strangely enough, some months later I partnered George Quartermain on the double trip Manchester. I believe his mate Fred Pettit was 'sick' because his wife was due to give birth. This time, for a pleasant change, we had a 'Crab' (2858) – which gave more room on the footplate than on a D, albeit the pedestal seat was not overly comfortable as it was loose on its mounting. On this occasion, too, we had a reasonably light train and made good progress until reaching the Potteries area where we were either on the block or 'sprinting' between the early-morning passenger trains. Finally, we reached our destination, left the train in the sidings and made our way to Longsight shed, the home of our engine, where we booked off, and cadged a lift on a passing light engine to the lodging house; quite smart compared to Willesden. There, after breakfast (or supper), I went to bed in a clean little cubicle, which had white tiled walls; the only offputting aspect was it reminded me of a gents toilet! However, I slept soundly until I was awoken by a sound I didn't recognise, which turned out to be the sea-lions barking at the nearby Belle View Zoo during their afternoon feeding time!

Our booking-on time for our return journey to Northampton was not until seven o'clock, so I was none too pleased at being awoken early. George had warned me to keep my window closed because of noise, but I hadn't because it was lovely warm weather. Anyway, I got up and showered – a luxury indeed – and went for a walk to buy a local newspaper, which I sat reading until George appeared and we had our evening meal. Then it was a trudge back to the shed to prepare our engine for our return trip. This time we had a class 8 (8648), so again we were lucky – according to George. When we backed onto the train, the guard told us we had six braked vans next to the engine (fruit wagons, George said), so with better braking we should be able to run more quickly than normal, if we got a clear road.

In fact, we had a super run with only slight checking through the Stoke area. Once on the Trent Valley line, we galloped along on the up slow and didn't stop until we arrived at Rugby. There we were held for about half an hour, obviously to await the departure of a passenger train, before we set off again for Northampton. Arriving there just after one o'clock, we had to wait in the loop at No. 3 box for our relief, the train being destined for Willesden. Eventually relieved by Bletchley men, we made our way to the shed and home – and I still had two sandwiches left in my tin!

I always liked the 'Crabs'. They were usually good steamers, although not always good riders, and they had a somewhat pugnacious look about them — as though to give the impression that 'we can do anything', which, of course, they did.
H. C. CASSERLEY

CHAPTER NINE

PASSENGER AND FREIGHT

AFTER several months rostered with Adge Stockwin, I was promoted into the Motor Link with Freddy Ping as my driver. Fred was a jolly, somewhat rotund man, who had a liking for jellied eels (not often available at the places we visited) and raw onions – which were! He often boasted that he ate a raw onion every day – "Just like an apple" he would say. I certainly came to know the smell of those onions, cocooned as we were within the confines of

our little 2–4–2 Webb tank engines. These, if I remember correctly, were numbered 6604, 6616, 6666, and 6754. Not very comfortable engines to work on, either for firing or sitting; in fact, one could not really sit, as the so-called seat was affixed on top of that part of the tank which protruded into the cab, and if you sat on it, your head was jammed against the roof. Okay for midgets I suppose. Fred talked proudly of his son who drove a "giant ten-wheeled lorry"

No. 6754 looking pristine – fresh from shops I would think. There was not much room on the foot-plate in which to operate.

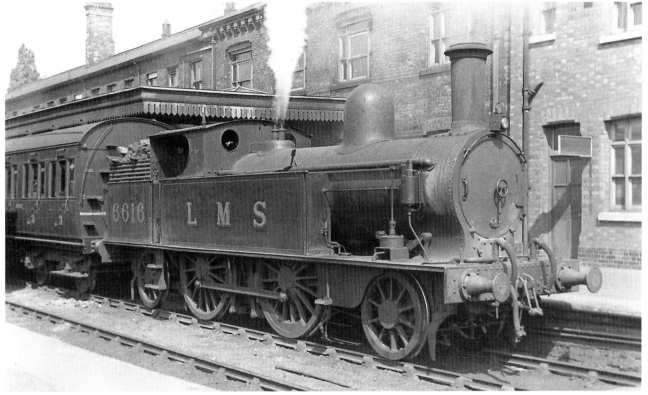

Another of our Webb 'tankies', all of which I fired at one time or another. No. 6616, seen here in 1937, was renumbered 26616 at the end of the war, for some reason, but none of the others was given a '2' prefix, and we thought it had been a mistake at Rugby shops. However, she carried the number until the general renumbering after nationalisation.

L. HANSON

95

More pictures of Blisworth. A Webb tank approaching the station after its 4-mile, 10-minute journey from Castle station. The porter was obviously walking across the line from the signal box to intercept it, and any parcels that might be on board.
R. K. BLENCOWE

The station was looking rather run down in this 1950s view, with paintwork in need of renewing, weeds growing on the platforms and the waiting rooms had lost their rounded roofs. LENS OF SUTTON

for a local haulage firm, and often related to me the long journeys his son did, Manchester, and Newcastle, etc., which, in later years would be more or less classed as fairly local trips in the haulage business.

However, the majority of *our* journeys were short – ten-minute trips to Blisworth and back with the motor train to connect with expresses on the old London-Birmingham line, and with the odd one or two trains from the SMJ branch. I enjoyed being on the footplate on my own while Fred was in the driving compartment at the other end of the two-coach train. Communication between us was via a bell code affixed to the cab on the driver's side, but unless any-

thing untoward occurred, Fred controlled the regulator and brake from his compartment by means of vacuum controls.

Our longest trip with the motor train was an afternoon run to Leamington Spa, via Blisworth, engine first, then via the main line, propelling the two coaches, to Weedon, on to the single line, reverse into the platform, then after disgorging passengers (mostly school children) collect the staff (token) and up the bank to Daventry, Braunston, Flecknoe, Southam, Marton Junction (double track from here), where we joined the branch from Rugby, and on to Leamington, where we had time for a sandwich and a cuppa before setting off on the return journey.

The Leamington Spa motor train heading back towards Blisworth, near Gayton, in 1937. I only remember the format of four coaches, with the engine in the middle being implemented on rare occasions, such as during racing at Warwick, or a festival at Leamington Spa. On such occasions, the fireman would be on the footplate alone in both directions. I must say that I enjoyed being alone during the 'push' part of our journeys because I had more room in which to operate in the cramped confines of the Webb tank footplate, and I could regulate steam and water levels as I thought fit, without any 'helpful' looks, gestures, or words from my mate. L. HANSON

Weedon station in 1958. Up the bank from Weedon was quite a climb, especially with a heavy train of chalk for Southam, but with our two-coach motor trains, it was not over-strenuous for the engine or fireman. Once at Daventry, it was fairly plain sailing to Leamington, via the stations at Braunston, Flecknoe, Napton & Stockton, and Southam & Long Itchington. Then to Marton Junction and onto the Rugby—Leamington line to our destination.

P. I. RAWLINSON

The 'bobby', who would be a porter/signalman, on the platform at Daventry ready to exchange the 'staff' with the fireman.

H. F. WHEELLER

A deserted Daventry station, although the door of the signal cabin was open, indicating some form of life was present.

J. H. RUSSELL

Braunston was one of the few stations that had what might be termed a 'proper' signal box. Most had a small cabin incorporated within the station buildings, very similar to that shown with the door open at Daventry on the opposite page. H. F. WHEELLER

Two photos at Napton & Stockton, showing the engine propelling the train on its outward journey from Weedon and Blisworth. H. F. WHEELLER

*Two views of Southam & Long Itchington
station.   H. J. STRETTON WARD*

*Marton Junction, with the motor
train on the branch line, either
coming or going.   H. F. WHEELER*

The eastern approach to Leamington with the GWR on the left.   P. KINGSTON

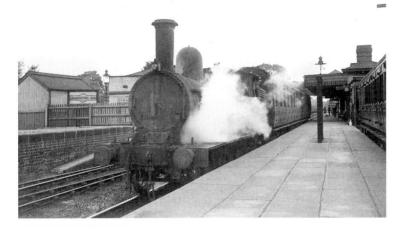

Leamington station with the motor train about to depart for Weedon. We never saw much of the GW side, but heard plenty of activity while we sat eating our sandwiches, after filling our tank at the column.

Leamington Spa station forecourt via which my mother used to trudge with her bottles of beer for Tommy and me.   R. KING

Also in the motor link we had conventional trains to and from Wellingborough (Midland) throughout the day. These were worked with one of our 2–4–0 Midland-type 2P engines, 412 or 421 usually, although there were six such engines at Northampton at this time. These trains, of three coaches, not being motor, necessitated a visit to Wellingborough shed to turn the engine, and my first trip there with Freddy Ping was somewhat nostalgic as I remembered visiting the shed several times prior to the war, when I was about eight or nine years old, with an uncle who was at that time a driver at that loco depot.

I was only in the motor link for a few months, then back in the special link, this time with Harry Stevens. He was a great character, always laughing about something or other, and full of 'dus-tha knows' and 'ba-gums', coming as he did from Hellifield in Yorkshire, at the southern end of the Settle to Carlisle line of the old Midland main line. He was a cracking chap to work with, and although quite old (by my youthful standards), being in his forties, he too would give me a turn on the regulator on occasions.

One such occasion was when we were working an empty wagon train towards Toton near Nottingham. We had relieved Willesden men at Northampton, and had traversed the line to Market Harborough, and on to the Midland main line there. Now approaching Leicester London Road we had had a clear run through Wigston and were hopefully anticipating that we would get past Leicester and on to

Toton in order for a little overtime. I was driving this day and, in the enthusiasm of doing so, was obviously approaching Leicester at too fast a speed (possibly about 15 to 20 mph), just letting the train drift down the incline without very much buffering up of the wagons. It was only Harry's shout of "Get a hold of them, the peg's on", which alerted me to the fact of my indiscretion. Our engine, a class 8, had a steam brake as well as the more normal vacuum one, and I yanked down the handle of the former, which had an immediate retarding effect on the engine, but as the 70 wagons, although empty, began to buffer up behind us, there was a constant nudging forward of the engine as it slowed in its forward progression. Finally, there was an almighty thump from the train as all the buffers were impacted, and the guard's van bore the brunt of my rough handling of the brakes. A pall of coal dust hung over the train, shaken from the many old wooden wagons by the impact. However, I was successful in stopping the train at the signal, with only the nose of the engine protruding beyond the post. I did later have to apologise to the guard who alleged that the 'rough shunt' had dislodged the stovepipe in his van and filled the van with dust, necessitating him having to wash before daring to board a passenger train home.

No, we did not get beyond Leicester that trip, as there were Toton men awaiting our arrival in the nearby signal box. In fact, we had to work a coal train back to Northampton, with Harry driving this time. This was fairly

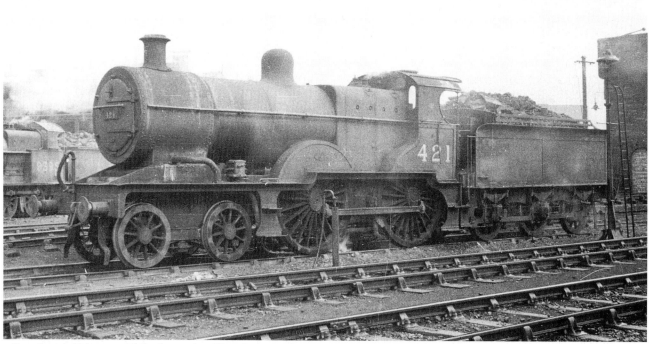

One of our half-dozen ex-Midland type class 2Ps – decent engines to work on, except for the ash dust flying around the footplate.
H. F. WHEELLER

Wellingborough loco depot was much larger than Northampton's and, having so much room, never seemed overloaded with engines. It didn't seem to change much from the time that I, as a wondering 8-year-old, accompanied my uncle to collect his pay, and have the ride on a 'Jinty', and the few weeks I spent there during my service about twenty years later. R. J. F. RAWLINSON

uneventful except that as we had a full load (69 plus brake van) behind the engine – again a class 8 – we had to whistle (two crows) for a banker as we passed Great Bowden box. The shed at Market Harborough was a small sub-shed of Rugby and only housed a few engines, mainly used for shunting locally at Welham sidings which were on the line to Peterborough about five miles from 'Harborough. However, the shed also housed the banker for the Northampton line. The engine was invariably a D, and usually one with a tender cab, as the banker travelled tender first when banking. This was because there were two 'rat-hole' tunnels, one at Oxendon and one at Kelmarsh, on a gradient of about 1 in 100 until the exit of the latter tunnel; it must have been bad enough to have the choking smoke and fumes lingering from the train engine, without having to suffer an added concentration from your own banking engine. These two tunnels were built when engines were much smaller that those of the present day, and certainly engines such as our class 8 nearly filled the aperture, thus the smoke, steam, and heat blasting from the chimney soon filled the cab, making it very difficult to breathe. Men frequently wet their handkerchiefs and held them over their nose and mouth while making the slow journey through these tunnels. You obviously endeavoured not to fire the engine during this time, and to breathe shallowly with mouth closed. Conditions were made worse should the

engine slip within the tunnel, a not infrequent occurrence because of the rails being wet with constant dripping of water from the roof.

Nothing untoward happened, neither of us being asthmatically inclined – a condition which caused some crew men to collapse while negotiating those infamous tunnels. Once 'over the top' at the exit from Kelmarsh Tunnel, the next problem was stopping the train on its downward progression towards Lamport, where there was a level crossing with gates on the A508 road, and drivers usually shut off steam before leaving the tunnel in order to get control of the train, and to let the banker engine 'do a bit of work' over the final few hundred yards. On this day, as normal, the distant signal for Lamport was on when I first saw it from my side of the footplate, but giving the usual two long blasts on the whistle, we saw that it was pulled off before we had got to it, and we sailed through the station, giving a wave to the signalman as we did so. Soon we were nosing our way into the loop at No. 3 box at Northampton and relief by Bletchley men. Another day done.

While rostered with Harry, I was on one occasion posted with driver Steve Powell, a man I knew marginally as he had introduced himself to me some time previously as a former boyfriend (a distant cousin) of my mother when they were teenagers, he apparently being aware of her married name. We were to be on the 'Yankee mail', which had a sort of

Nottingham Victoria was the station to which we ran with the local passenger trains from Northampton. On the Yankee Mail train, we used the old low-level station, which was downgraded to a parcels-only station sometime in 1944, I think.   H. C. CASSERLEY

Engine No. 534 piloting a 'Baby Scot' on an express on what looks like the up fast line at Road in 1938.   L. HANSON

aura about it, as it only ran at night and consisted of about twenty to thirty sealed box vans. It was in fact just what its title indicated, the mail destined for the American forces on the Continent, and originated at Nottingham for travel to Dover where the mail was shipped across the Channel. The train was worked by Northampton men as far as Olympia where a Southern engine and crew took over. Sometimes, so I had been told, box vans were taken to Nottingham, and on other occasions the engine went light. This evening we had fifteen vans to take with us, and our engine was 534, a Midland 4–4–0 2P. When we started from Castle Yard, I knew where we were until we got to Market Harborough, but instead of joining the Midland main line there we went underneath it. When I queried this with Steve, he said we were going by the old GN route via Melton Mowbray, 'over the Alps', which meant little to me. However, with such a light train we bowled easily along, and I hardly noticed whether we were going uphill or down.

On arrival at Nottingham we were routed into what appeared to be carriage siding, where we left our train. Then it was on to a turntable somewhere near a station as I could see vaguely illuminated platforms, and the occasional voice of an announcer over the Tannoy. I darted the fire, but there was not much clinker to bother about, so we just filled the tank at a nearby column. While I had been busy with the fire, Steve had disappeared with his billy-can, and shortly re-appeared with a brew of tea with which we slaked our thirst while eating some of our sandwiches. Then it was off to a loading bay or perhaps a cattle dock somewhere behind what looked like a goods shed, where we backed onto our train, and I hooked on, screw couplings and vacuum hose. The guard appeared, stating we had twenty-six box vans and a brake van, another relatively light train. We left shortly after ten o'clock, retracing our route via Market Harborough (where Steve took the precaution of filling the tank), to Northampton, where we ran through the middle road and up the bank to Roade, and so onwards to Willesden where it seemed we were routed through some sidings or loop line before crossing the main lines and heading down the branch to what Steve said was Olympia and the engine change-over point.

There, I began uncoupling the engine, only to be halted by a shout from somewhere in the darkness. Two figures appeared out of the gloom, who turned out to be a driver and guard; the former volunteered the information that there was no engine or crew at Nine Elms, a shed covering that area, I was given to understand, and he was here to pilot us as far as Hither Green depot where the change-over would be made. I recoupled the engine, and off we went, our guard electing to stay with us to enable him to get home again. Of course, neither Steve nor I had much idea where we were heading once we were over the Thames, but I did see a signal box with a Loughborough Junction name board, just after the Southern man had shouted that we were at Brixton. I suppose I associated it with the Loughborough on the Midland main line north of Leicester. It was not long

before the pilotman shouted "Lewisham over there", which again meant nothing to me, but when he continued, "We're nearly there", I knew not to fire the engine again. We were signalled into a loop line, and the Southern man went to find out what was to happen. He returned shortly with the information that an engine and crew were waiting for us, so we could hook off and either return tender-first to Willesden, or he would take us on the shed so we could use the turntable. As might be expected, Steve opted for the latter, and while we were on the table the Southern driver went off with Steve's billy-can and shortly reappeared with a brew which we three plus our guard enjoyed. I still had a couple of sandwiches, so ate those too, and my bottle of Camp coffee was still half full and lying on the plate over the firehole door keeping warm. All in all it had been quite a night, and we still had to return to Northampton. This was done as light engine, we dropping the pilotman and our guard at Willesden, the Southern man indicating that it would be easier for him to get a lift to his own metals from there rather than at Olympia, and the guard opting to go into Euston for a ride home on the cushions rather than with us on the footplate.

The journey home was done in good time, and we booked off with less than ten hours duty performed, which seemed remarkable when one considered the mileage we had done. As Steve said, "We will be due for mileage money as we have done well over the 140 on our travels". (I think I remember that for every fifteen miles over 140 that one did during a shift one received an hour's pay). Quite lucrative!.

In the summer of 1946, having completed the statutory 313 firing turns, I was to be tested for qualification for being a fully-fledged fireman, again under the supervision of the footplate inspector, Fred Lacy. For this day I was to be fireman with a man whom I hardly knew, William (Cock) Allen, but with whom I developed a great bond of friendship over the years, even standing as witness at his eventual wedding to May. Our engine for this day was 2538, one of the 2–6–4 Stanier Tanks, and the train was of six coaches – empty stock to Uppingham, a special to Euston, and empty

The engine on which I was 'passed' as a fully-fledged fireman, on what was quite an eventful trip. This engine and her sister, 2604, were used mainly on our morning commuter trains, 7.5 a.m. and 8.5 a.m. to Euston, to very good effect. As more class 5s were allocated to our shed, they were transferred, I believe, to Aston and Walsall respectively.
                                                        H. C. CASSERLEY

Seaton station looking quite busy! What would presumably be a Peterborough train was at the right-hand platform, with, in the bay, firstly a Stamford train, and behind it the push-pull to Uppingham.

F. J. SAUNDERS

stock return to Northampton, not seemingly an expected onerous task. We set off bunker first to Seaton via Market Harborough, and up the branch to Uppingham, where we ran round the train and backed into the station.

We were to be the Uppingham School vacation train to London, and although we didn't know it then, we were in for troublesome times ahead. The train was of non-corridor stock, and we were scheduled to stop at Northampton for toilets. It appeared to be well filled with these boisterous-sounding young 'gentlemen' from this quite well-known public school, and there was much raucous shouting of farewells as we pulled from the station. As we had run round the train, most of the windows were down along the train, and the boys were attempting to urinate at the engine – and one presumes us – as we passed them. Fred Lacy had been all for turning the fizzle pipe on them, but I desisted, and we were soon coupled up and on our way to Euston.

Through Market Harborough, up the bank and through Clipston tunnel. However, we were stopped by the signals at Kelmarsh, then called forward to the box, where the signalman shouted that the bobby at Clipston and Oxendon had seen carriage doors open and boys hanging out, apparently trying to whip each other with what looked like lengths of cloth! I walked back along the length of the train, on the

offside of the down line, but all the doors were closed. I explained to the guard what the bobby had related, and returned to the engine by the same route. I could see that several of the boys had knotted their ties together, and had them dangling from the windows. The guard walked up the other side of the train – brave/foolish man. When he arrived at the engine, it was with several globules of spittle on his uniform. Fred Lacy was really irate, left the engine and went about halfway along the train, taking the route I had done. Once there, he yelled at the top of his voice to the effect that should there be any more trouble we would take the train back to Uppingham and leave them there.

Our journey continued to Northampton without further interruptions, but as soon as we arrived for the 'toilet' stop there was a general exodus in all directions, mainly towards the refreshment room. It was nearly a quarter of an hour before all were rounded up and shepherded back on the train. Fred had in the meantime had words with Control, and on his return the guard was instructed to lock all the doors of the carriages, on both sides of the train. So we set off again. Bill, at the start of the day, had told Fred not to sit on my seat, but stand out of the way; however, I found him to be more 'out of my way' sitting down, so we agreed on that policy. Fred was dressed in his usual boiler suit with black beret headwear, so did look a little like a militia man, and probably why the schoolboys had appeared more subdued when herded onto the train at Northampton.

All went well on the climb to Blisworth, and on to the main line, although we could occasionally see one or two heads appearing out of windows, and could see that they were now spitting at those lads daring to put their heads out of compartments behind the spitters. As we tore towards Castlethorpe troughs, Fred suggested that I should leave the scoop down as long as possible, to "drown the little sods", but, of course, being a tank engine with the tank vents in front of the footplate, I think we got most of the excess water cascading over the cab before it hit the train.

We had a good run through Bletchley, up through Tring, and really rattled down through Berkhamsted, Bill and Fred constantly looking back checking on the behaviour of our passengers. It was during one of these neck-craning moments that Bill lost his uniform cap, blown off by the speed we were going. He thereupon opened his bag and donned a red beret, which caused me to remark that I felt I was in the company of a tank commander, and a red devil from the war years. Neither was amused. We continued our speedy run towards London, but were stopped by signals at Harrow and Wealdstone, where we were again informed that passengers were hanging out of windows trailing lengths of rope (their ties, of course). After due chastisement of those who showed their faces, we continued into Euston where there seemed to be a fleet of Rolls Royce, Bentley, and other expensive cars awaiting our somewhat late arrival. Fred and the guard went along the train from opposite ends unlocking the doors, which brought forth queries from some of the parents as to why it had been necessary to lock their beloved sons in like so many prisoners. I didn't hear all that Fred or Bill (who had joined Fred on the platform) had to say, but I did hear what sounded like "the little bastards home" from Fred.

I don't think any official complaints were made by either side, and after Fred had left us, having said he had seen enough of me and "this zoo train, so I'm going home on the cushions", we reversed the stock into the carriage sidings, and I uncoupled. From there we went to the servicing area to turn and water our engine, and to mash a can of tea to drink with our sandwiches. When eventually I telephoned the bobby to 'book off shed' to pick up our stock, it was to be told that we were to go light engine back to Northampton, which was an even better end to the day than trundling our train back. A few days later I was informed that I was now a fully-fledged fireman, with a slight rise in pay!

A couple of months later I was detailed once again with Bosco Kirton, not double trip this time, but a chalk train from sidings near Leighton Buzzard to Southam Cement works on the Weedon to Marton Junction line. We booked on before 5am, prepared our engine (one of our Ds – I think 9321) and went light engine to Blisworth, picked up a train of chalk empties and eventually trundled to Bletchley, where we left the train in the loop while we went on shed and turned on the shed table. Then it was tender first to Leighton Buzzard, and into sidings a short way along the Dunstable branch. There, while waiting for the guard to arrive and marshal the train, I enjoyed a sandwich and a sip or two from my bottle of coffee. We were in a cutting, and had noticed hens pecking in the grass at the top of the cutting. Bosco opened his basket, and took out a couple of currant buns, which I thought he was going to eat, but instead he began to break them into small pieces. When he saw me looking quizzically at him, he said, "It's okay, they're stale, I'm going to feed the chickens". With that he left the engine and clambered up the bank towards where the hens were. Once there, he sat down and began throwing pieces of his buns towards the birds, enticing them ever nearer to him. As soon as one came within arm's length he

No. 9321, one of the ex-LNWR ubiquitous 'Ds', with which Bosco and I worked the Leighton Buzzard to Southam chalk train. R. K. BLENCOWE

grabbed it, wrung its neck, and stuffed it under his jacket as he hurriedly descended the embankment and back to the engine. The bird was quickly stuffed into his basket which was returned to the locker, and he just turned to me and tapped the side of his nose with his finger and winked. It had all been done so surreptitiously that all I could do was laugh.

Shortly afterwards, the guard appeared and gave us the loading – 43 and a brake – and we were soon off to the down slow line and our trundle back towards Roade. There we were held for about twenty minutes before being let out main line for a blast to Blisworth and into the loop to Gayton. Another wait there before an equally hectic blast to Weedon and on to the single-line branch and the climb up the bank towards Daventry. Here Bosco surprised me again. As our speed became slower and slower, he shouted "Come on, she'll be alright like this", dropped down onto the six-foot and over a gate into a field where he began picking mushrooms. Not to appear a ditherer, I followed suit and soon had a hat full of good large field mushrooms. Then it was out through the gate and a quick scramble after the retreating engine, where once again on the footplate our spoils were put in Bosco's basket (which I think was his double trip one), and I put on the injector just as she began to blow off. I suppose we were away from the engine for less then ten minutes, but when I thought about it later, it was a risky thing to do, but somehow indicative of branch line working.

Southam was reached without further incident, and once the train had been backed into the sidings and the engine uncoupled, we drew up to the yard foreman's cabin, where-upon Bosco began shovelling coal onto the ground until there was quite a pile. Then he disappeared into the cabin, to reappear a few moments later with his hat in his hand in which were half a dozen eggs. Back on the footplate he washed out the shovel with the fizzle pipe, opened his basket, took out most of the mushrooms, a knife, and from under the chicken some rashers of bacon, together with a bit of lard, all wrapped in greaseproof paper. These went into the shovel, later followed by two of the eggs, and all were cooked by resting the shovel on the lip plate of the firehole. Bosco, as might be guessed, had his own cutlery and plate in his basket, on which he placed his half of the feast. I had to make do with the shovel, but I did have bread (my sand-wiches) with which to mop up the juices. Delicious! The only thing one could find fault with was the fact that we would be tender first on the return to Blisworth where we were due to leave the thirty or so wagons we had for the return trip, and I didn't have a blackout sheet on this occa-sion. However, trundling along the branch at a relatively slow speed, it was no hardship, fortified as we were with our substantial breakfast. We did have to 'give her a bash' once we were on the main line at Weedon, but once in the shelter of Gayton loop it only meant that we had to shunt the train into the sidings at Blisworth, and return to Northampton (engine first) and off duty. All in all a most entertaining and enlightening day! I don't remember ever firing for Bosco again, but my two trips with him are certainly imprinted in my memory

Southam station, looking through the bridge towards the Rugby Portland 'Blue Circle' cement works on the right.   H. F. WHEELLER

CHAPTER TEN

DOUBLE TRIP AGAIN

Toton sidings, looking from the 'hump', which was a proper one, not like the substandard one at our down sidings.

NATIONAL RAILWAY MUSEUM

IT was while I was still rostered with Harry that I was posted for a week with Cyril Millward on a double trip to Toton. Cyril was a big man – both in stature and in personality – jovially boisterous one might describe him. He was quite fun to be with, and a good engineman, though he did give the engine 'some stick' at times. My three trips to Toton that week were not without incident. The first day we took an engine from the shed, a tapered-boiler Crab, after preparing her, and made our way to the Down Sidings. Our train was of mixed goods of some fifty wagons, so was not over heavy, and we had a good run to Market Harborough, although I was somewhat nonplussed at Cyril 'hanging on the whistle' as we approached Little Bowden crossing. He explained that it was dinner time at the local factories and men would probably be using the pedestrian gates, pushing their bicycles over the crossing, taking no notice of the main gates being closed against them. Sure enough, as the crossing came in to view, there were pedestrians scuttling across, not wanting to waste precious minutes of their dinner hour waiting at the barrier for a fairly slow-moving goods train to pass.

The rest of the journey passed relatively smoothly, although we had many stoppages at signals, obviously being on the block. I was especially interested in that part of the trip beyond Leicester, as I had only been as far as Toton on one previous occasion, and that in the dark. Now in the daylight of a summer's evening it was interesting to see our surroundings as we trundled through such places as Barrow-on-Soar & Quorn, Loughborough, and Long Eaton before

arriving at Toton Yard. Here I could see what a properly constructed shunting yard and hump looked like. After unhooking our train, and while awaiting a road to the shed, I watched as the shunt engine slowly pushed the train to be shunted onto the hump. The shunter unhooked wagons at the appropriate places, which, when propelled over the top of the hump, ran away into a predetermined siding, the speed of the wagons being controlled by electrically-driven retarders on either side of the rail, operated from a nearby box, which gripped the bottom edge of the wheels just enough to slow the wagons sufficiently for a relatively smooth buffering-up to other wagons already in the siding.

By the time we had taken the engine to the shed and booked off, it was dusk, and we began the walk to the lodging house, a railway hostel, Cyril had told me. I hoped it was not like Willesden. But before we got to the lodge we had to walk past the sewerage farm, which one could smell in advance of getting to it. Cyril stopped, placed his double trip basket on the ground and tucked his uniform trousers into his socks, advising me to do the same. I complied, but queried the action, to be told that I would soon find out. I certainly did. In the gloom one could make out literally scores of rats scampering to and fro across the pathway, seemingly taking no notice of us, and in fact bumping against our legs as we shuffled through them. Quite an eye opener.

However, the lodge was a pleasant surprise, very spick and span, with friendly staff and very reasonable food. The washing and sleeping facilities were also fine. The steward

109

Toton 'roundhouse', with a mixed bag of engines present in July 1948.
H. C. CASSERLEY

also sold bottles of beer, which obviated the hike to a pub, which I was told was some distance away. After our ablutions, supper, and a few games of darts with some Sheffield men, we adjourned to our cubicles (with clean sheets) and a good night's sleep. Our wake-up call was not until five-thirty, luxury indeed!

We breakfasted next morning on the canteen food – beans with everything, and the spam and egg were very good, served together with warm bread! The walk to the loco shed was uneventful. No rats appeared as it was daylight. Our engine was an 'Austerity' (a WD 2–8–0). Although these engines had a reasonable footplate to work on, they were not noted for smooth running. This one, No. 90339, had the shed code 25A on the smokebox, but I hadn't a clue where that was, but guessed it was somewhere up north. Once I had spread the fire and increased the steam pressure, I filled the cylinder lubricator – located on the footplate on the fireman's side – with the thick black oil, and turned on the steam valve to begin the lubricator working. These lubricators were reminiscent of those on many of our older engines, and you had to adjust the flow of oil blobs to suit the likely speed of the engine. Our 'fatting up' finished, and coal cracked to suit, we filled the tank and booked off the shed to travel to the sidings to collect our train. We were told we had the normal sixty-nine wagons of coal, plus brake van, and were away shortly after eight o-clock.

This WD engine appeared to be relatively recently refurbished, and rode quite well, if one ignored the tell-tale clank of the motion. The journey southwards was uneventful as we trundled along the slow line, but after Leicester we became slowed by signals, and when the track became just two running lines we were routed into the loop at Kibworth, where we stayed for nearly an hour while the early-morning expresses thundered past. Those Midland

men certainly thrashed their 'Jubilees' up the bank at that location, the regulator 'in the roof', and the 'rockets' blasting from the chimney. I wondered how the fireman kept any fire in the box at that rate!

Eventually we got the signal to proceed, and Cyril set off as if he meant to catch up with the express that had just passed us. But I knew he just wanted to get a good start on the down grade to 'Harborough. Once there and off the main line, having whistled for the banker as we passed Great Bowden, we filled the tank, and awaited the banker's whistle indicating that he was on the rear of the train. I also took the opportunity of mashing a can of tea, as we had finished the one we had made at Toton shed before leaving. Cyril, who seemed to know practically everyone we saw at 'Harborough, was his usual jovial self, shouting jocular abuse at some of the platform staff, who he revealed were 'fishing' mates of his at some waters not far from the town. We had waited about half an hour when we saw what was obviously the banking engine drifting into the station on the down line, obviously having just banked an earlier train. They slowed as the engine passed us and asked if we required their services. When Cyril replied in the affirmative, they shouted that they needed water and were going on the shed. So we sat for about another twenty minutes before hearing the tell-tale shrill 'two crows' whistle of the old D. No doubt the 'Harborough men had made tea too.

The signal off, Cyril set sail with a vengeance and I was soon shovelling enthusiastically as we blasted into the bank. Some drivers with a banker on behind used to 'hang fire' a little, and let the banker do a lot of the work, but not Cyril, he really set the sheep scurrying across the fields as the exhaust from the chimney echoed across the landscape. There is something magical about an engine working really hard, especially when one is able to keep a good head of steam, and this engine, as I mentioned earlier, was in good nick as far as steaming went, although she rolled a bit, which was indicative of her class. So we eventually blasted through Oxendon Tunnel (usual handkerchief over the mouth and nose while in there) and then a slight increase in speed on the more level stretch to Kelmarsh box where I fired her for the final time, before the climb became more severe on the approach to the tunnel (hankies out again) as we blasted into the 'rat hole'. Again, unlike other drivers I had been with, Cyril did not shut off or reduce steam before emerging from the other end of the tunnel, in fact he kept steam on until we felt a snatch on the couplings indicating that the banker had dropped away, and all our couplings were tight.

Drivers I had been with previously always shut off steam some way through the tunnel, allowing the banker to buffer up the wagons so that braking could safely begin as soon as the train was on the down grade. Cyril obviously had other ideas. He let the train drift along after he eventually closed the regulator, then shouted to me to wind on the tender hand brake. This I did as hard as I could, and we could feel the wagons buffering up, although there was little retarding of our speed – in fact we were accelerating! I was looking for the distant signal, which, when it came in to view, was on. I shouted this to Cyril, and gave the customary two long blasts on the whistle, and Cyril then began to use the steam brake and, after making sure that all the wagons were well buffered up, applied the brake fully. The signal remained in the on position as we passed it, and we didn't appear to be slowing very much. I played with the sanders, attempting to make sure she didn't pick the wheels up and slide down the hill. Cyril was by this time hanging on the whistle, giving long hoots as we headed towards the station and the crossing gates some 500 yards ahead, which were closed against us.

As we entered the station, still travelling at some fifteen miles per hour, I could see the bobby standing by the operating wheel in his box, and then saw with relief that he began opening the gates for us, because I realised there was no hope of us being able to stop before reaching the crossing. As we slithered beyond the home signal (still against us) and over the crossing just as the gates were swung open for us, Cyril came to my side of the footplate, doffed his cap to the bobby as we passed his box, and shouted, "Saved again, Cyril", with a big grin on his rather reddened face. I, for my part, was almost trembling with the thought that if the signalman had not been fully aware of the situation we would have crashed through the gates and into any traffic that might have been travelling over the crossing at the time. Finally, Cyril had the train under control, and we came to a stop just about the train length beyond the crossing; in fact Cyril asked me to look back to judge when the brake van was clear of the gates. This I did and saw the gates being closed behind us. Cyril stopped the train, and I began the trudge back to make our peace with the signalman.

On arrival at the box I was met by both the bobby and the guard, who were grinning from ear to ear, probably at the forlorn expression on my face. "He did it again",

laughed the guard, and the signalman joined in with, "I guessed you were in trouble when I heard you whistling like hell, and then when I saw who the driver was I knew the reason why. He's always doing it". I learned from the signalman, whose name was Ken Musson (a name very nearly spelt like mine), that Cyril was somewhat prone to over exuberant descending of the bank at times. However, I carried out rule 55, signed the log book (which is how I knew the bobby's name, he having queried my signature on a previous occasion), and waited at the box until Ken received the appropriate bell code to signify that our road ahead was clear for us to proceed, whereupon both the guard and I made our way to our respective ends of the train.

Back at the engine, Cyril was sitting on some old sleepers at the lineside talking to a platelayer. I heard him say, "Okay, we'll do that", and with a cheery acknowledgement climbed on the footplate, grinned at me, asked, "Did you square him up?", and restarted the train. I told him that nothing was to be booked about our indiscretion as it appeared the bobby was used to it. He guffawed, and mumbled something about "Good lad", and no more was said about the incident. Some half mile along the line, Cyril opened the footplate doors on his side of the engine and shovelled some large lumps of coal over the side in the proximity of a platelayers hut – which was obviously to what his remark to the platelayer referred.

I am happy to relate that nothing untoward occurred on the other two trips to and from Toton that week, and, as you might imagine, Cyril was a most congenial man with whom to work. I had many more trips with him over the years, all entertaining. I remember that when travelling on the up slow line on the way to London with a coal train, and we were passed by a 'fitted freight' on the fast line, he would invariably say, "There goes the fish – they'll want this coal to cook it with", and would yank the regulator open wider, to increase speed, if our road was clear. Whether or not it was a fish train passing us didn't seem to matter much.

He was also an avid angler, and I remember one weekend while I was with Big Adge – who also enjoyed dangling a float into water – several of us railway men caught the early train to Wolverton and traipsed across the fields to the river Ouse. It was quite a warm day, and several of the men (one of whom was Cyril) being well loaded with their equipment, were perspiring somewhat by the time we reached the fishing area. Cyril, in addition to his rods and basket, etc., also had a bag of dried blood bait draped around the back of his neck. When he came to unload all his paraphernalia, the canvas bag of blood had absorbed some of his sweat, dissolving some of the blood, and he looked as if his throat had been cut, much to his annoyance and the amusement of the rest of the party. He washed most of it away with some river water, but it did cause the landlord of the canalside pub, which was inevitably found at lunch time, to ask if Cyril had been fishing or swimming, because of his very wet shirt.

After the Toton week I had a few more months with Harry, plus odd days with other drivers, before I again had a change of driver.

This picture was taken from the SMJ platform at Blisworth, looking towards the signal box and the line curving away towards Towcester in the distance. It shows an engine in the slip road, and what looks like a marshalled train in No. 1 siding next to it, awaiting motive power. Note the two water columns and, on the left, what used to be the cattle dock, dismantled and overgrown.   J. E. NORRIS

No. 3816 on shed at Northampton. Like many of her class (3F), she was a strong little engine, and a type probably better liked by LNW men than the class 4s. It looks from the photo as if the driver of the 'D' was trying to push her up the shed yard.   H. F. WHEELLER

CHAPTER ELEVEN
MORE OF THE SAME

AFTER my eighteenth birthday, I was still in the special link, but now with Bill Placket, again a man in his forties, quite slightly built, and with somewhat sunken cheeks. He rolled his own cigarettes – if you could call them that. They consisted of about two strands of shag tobacco rolled not very tightly in the paper, so that when ignited, the paper would frequently flare up, causing Bill to quickly remove the 'fag' from his lips before it set fire to his rather bushy eyebrows. He would smoke this somewhat slim cigarette, holding it in his lips until it went out, which it did quite often, but which he regularly failed to notice. When he did, he would relight it, and in due course it would be smoked right down to its end, which had caused him, I think, to have his permanently rather protruding lips, as if he was ready for a kiss. I often remarked that he used more matches than tobacco.

Again, Bill was very easy to get on with, and we had good companionship together. It was with him that I had my first trip over the old SMJ branch to Stratford-on-Avon.

This was, I remember, a winter's afternoon, light engine off the shed at Northampton, tender first to Blisworth (blackout sheet obtained) with a Midland class three 0–6–0, which had right-hand drive, which suited me as I still was not very adept at firing left-handed. This engine also had a stick reversing lever rather than a wheel, which I noticed made it hard for Bill to 'notch back' a little when we had gained suitable speed. However, when we arrived at Blisworth and had crossed the main lines on to the SMJ side, we found that we had only sixteen wagons, all of them for Broom junction. As Bill was apparently only qualified for (knowing the road to) Stratford, he went to the signal box and informed Control of that fact. He was informed that either a pilot-man would be provided at that location, or the train would be terminated there. Apparently this working was a Blisworth crew job, but for some reason none was available.

We eventually set off in the gloom of the winter's late afternoon, and I leaned from the cab to collect the staff from the bobby who was standing on the boardwalk near his box.

Blisworth SMJ box with the SMJ line on the left and main lines on the right. The turntable used to be just to the right and beyond the box. As can be seen, trains from the sidings could exit northwards to the down loop line to Gayton.   W. MALLARD

The staff or key, was quite small, only about ten inches long and slim, so therefore lighter than others I had handled. I gave it to Bill who lodged it in his trouser pocket for safe-keeping, and we began the accent to Tiffield, which was quite steep. With such a short train our engine was not unduly troubled by the climb. After breasting the top of the bank, we drifted down towards Towcester, where I knew we had to exchange the staff. On the approach the distant signal was on, but we could see the home signal was off for us, so Bill trundled towards the station at about 20mph. He handed me the staff and said the bobby would be on the platform on my side of the engine. I positioned myself by the handrail and leaned out, twisting my right arm so that my hand was ready to catch the new staff, while dangling the other staff loosely from my left hand some two feet behind my right hand, so that the bobby could catch it in his same hand from which I would take the new staff. What I didn't know, and could not see in the darkness, was that the new staff was much larger than the other, being some two feet long, thicker, and much heavier. As it slapped into my hand,

A good shot of the tall signal box at Towcester and of the exchanging of staffs at the foot of the box. Note the differing sizes of the staff from Blisworth and the one being received from the bobby. No wonder I received the bang on the nose by the large one on my first trip over the route in the dark.

W. J. S. MEREDITH

The turntable at Stratford, looking larger than I remember it!   R. C. RILEY

Stratford-upon-Avon, looking rather desolate in the mid-fifties, but still with the odd freight train running through.   R. C. RILEY

the force plus weight caused my arm to recoil in my surprise, and the tail of the staff swung round, catching me a hefty clip on the nose. I'm not sure what happened to the other staff but I heard a yell from where the bobby had been standing, so I hoped he had caught it okay, or at least found it on the platform. Bill laughed at my discomfort, saying he didn't think my nose was broken. I was just glad that I hadn't a nose bleed, as I'd had several of those lately. From then on I was very wary, but the staffs were all of the current size and nothing untoward happened during the rest of the journey. I again was sorry that it was not daylight so that I could see our surroundings.

Bill pointed out such locations as Woodford & Hinton where there was a junction with the GCR, and Burton Dassett, an army equipment centre with its own sidings. On arrival at Stratford, there was no pilot-man so the train was

left in the sidings, and we went on the loco shed to turn and get water. The turntable was one of those that had to be pushed round, so I manoeuvred the engine while Bill set the positioning for balancing the engine. Then a mash of tea and a sandwich while the guard was finding out about our return working. He eventually appeared with the information that there were only four wagons here at Stratford for Blisworth or beyond, and we would have to use the brake van we had brought with us, our 'proper' train being at Broom Junction. This, of course, pleased our guard as he had got the van nice and warm on the journey down and didn't want to start afresh. So, as you might imagine, with only four and a brake, the journey back to Blisworth was a doddle. Once there, having shunted the train into the exchange sidings, the three of us adjourned to the Blisworth Hotel (no sign of the land-lord's daughter on this occasion), for a pint to while away a little time, before returning light engine to Northampton and disposing of the engine.

One of the 'perks' of being a railway employee was being able to travel at reduced fare on trains. We were allowed four free passes per year, and as many 'quarter fares' as one wished. Friend Norman Quennell and I used to travel as far as we could with our free passes. We had been to Scotland a couple of times, which was quite an adventure, but now, although the war was over, rationing was still with us, so we used our free passes to travel to Dublin, via Holyhead and the railway ferry ship, *The Hibernia*. All it cost us for the journey was six shillings and four pence each way for a berth on the overnight ferry. We would take a large suitcase each with just our pyjamas, toiletries and towel, plus a couple of shirts, and return with it filled with such things as sugar, butter, bacon and ham, even clothing, and anything else which was either rationed or in short supply back home. We also had enjoyable weekends in the fair city sampling the 'dark stuff' some four times a year until rationing finally came to an end, and indeed continued at least once or twice a year until I left the railway.

My aunt, at whose home I was lodging initially, and Mrs Gee, where I lodged later, were of course very grateful for these supplements to their food stocks, as were my parents while living in Northampton, and later at their pub (The Prince of Wales) in Leamington Spa. I remember an incident following one of my visits to them during one of my infrequent weekends off. Although I had travelled to Leamington via the usual route (Blisworth – Daventry etc.), there were no trains on Sundays for the return journey, and I had to travel via Coventry and Rugby, there being one train in the evening at about 5.30. Arriving at Coventry about 6pm, I had only some ten minutes to wait for the Northampton train, a semi-fast from Birmingham. Within a few minutes a train headed by a Jubilee, blowing off steam, came noisily into the station just as the loudspeaker announced what I thought was 'Wolston next stop'. That's okay, thought I, Brandon and Wolston being the next station, he's stopping there because of Sunday working.

The train did not stop at that station. In fact it tore through at a fair rate of knots, and I began to realise I was probably in for a long journey home. Just then the ticket inspector came along the coach, and showing him my ticket I explained my predicament and how I had made my mistake. He appeared sympathetic, took my ticket, and said that although the train was not due to stop until Willesden he would have words with the guard. However, not knowing what sort of idea he had in mind, as we approached Rugby, I went into the corridor and lowered the window of the door. As luck would have it, I could see that although on the through road, the driver had yellow signals as we drifted towards, and then alongside, the station, and he slowed to about 20mph. I thought 'now or never', and as the driver, having obviously seen a green signal, opened up again, I opened the door, dropped my suitcase onto the six-foot, swung out onto the running board while holding the handle, closed the door, and dropped onto the ground at a fast run.

Luckily, I did not trip over or hit any of the station roof supports which bordered the line here, although I did grab hold of one to stop my headlong flight beside the train. I found my old cardboard case, somewhat the worse for its bouncing over the uneven ground, and made my way to the locomen's cabin at the end of the platform, being thankful that it was dark and no-one had seen my antics.

When the correct Northampton train came in, I boarded it, thankfully finding an empty compartment, and looked at my somewhat dishevelled appearance in the light. Deft use of my handkerchief and a little water from the washbasin in the toilet removed most of the grime on self and clothes, but my cardboard suitcase gave the appearance of 'long service with abuse', and I guessed I would soon have to acquire another! At Northampton I was lucky as the ticket examiner at the exit door was Ted, a former shunter who had lost a foot while crossing the line between wagons, and who obviously assumed I had one of our concessionary tickets. After passing the time of day with him I made my way out of the station yard and on to a bus to my digs.

It was while I was posted with Bill that I had what I later realised was one of the highlights of my time on the railway, although I didn't really appreciate it at the time. I had the somewhat awesome task of firing one of *the* crack engines – No. 6201 *Princess Elizabeth* – on her way home to Liverpool. I say 'home' as I believe she was an 8A engine at that time. I am more than a little happy to say as I write these words that this famous engine is still 'alive and kicking' in preservation, and on the main line, some fifty-five years later!

It happened like this: Bill and I had booked on at Northampton sometime prior to 4am to go to Blisworth and take a train of cattle from there to Cannonbury, which I was told was somewhere in north London. The train had originated at Towcester late the previous evening. We had a Midland class 4 0–6–0 engine, and with this we went via the Castle Station to collect the guard, and then to Blisworth where we backed onto the train of twenty-four and a brake van. With such a load it was not a hard trip to London, and with a train of livestock there were not many signalling delays. Two or three times we were routed via sections of the up fast line, bypassing wagon trains, held up no doubt by the not infrequent working to rule by the shunters at Stonebridge Park sidings.

When we arrived at those sidings we were routed into the loop line and so to Harlesden where a set of Willesden men were waiting to relieve us to take the train onwards. After reporting to Control and being told to make our way home, we made our way to the nearby station and caught an electric train into Euston, anticipating we could catch the 10.35am train for Crewe, which would stop at Blisworth for our connection with the motor train and thus back home. Both Bill and I were congratulating ourselves on what had been a pleasant non-hard-working morning out, but this was soon to change – at least for one of us.

On arrival at Euston we made our way towards the coffee knob near platforms six/seven for our breakfast, when we heard Bill's name being called on the Tannoy system, asking

A grubby-looking Princess Beatrice *(6209) awaiting the 'off' in platform 14 at Euston in 1962. My memorable trip on her sister engine –*
6201 Princess Elizabeth *– began from the platform on the right.*   P. I. RAWLINSON

him to report to Control. Finding a 'phone and doing so, we found it was me to whom they wanted to speak. Apparently, the fireman of the 10.20am to Liverpool had hit his head on some scaffolding while on the tender breaking up coal as the engine backed down from Camden to its train. He had been taken to hospital with a head wound and was not likely to be back before train departure time. No relief fireman was available so they asked if I would work the train as far as Rugby, where a special stop would be made in order to relieve me there.

Having only completed some six hours duty, I could hardly refuse, so after a quick cup of tea I bade Bill farewell and made my way to platform 15. Walking the length of the train I noted the banking tank engine, and counted sixteen coaches before reaching the engine, which was beyond the end of the platform, and which was of a type I had never set foot on, let alone fired. It was 6201, a 4–6–2, a 'namer' as we used to say in my youthful 'number-snatching' days, and I saw the grimy *Princess Elizabeth* on the nameplate. The driver, whose name I learned was Albert, was I think not too impressed when I informed him of my antecedents as a fireman, but it was nearly time for the off so with a curt,

"Just make sure you keep the back of the box filled, especially the corners", he busied himself with looking towards the rear of the train, presumably awaiting the tip from the guard, but I wondered if he was hopefully looking for the return of his mate from his appointment with the doctor!

I noted the water level in the boiler as three-quarters full – perfect – and the steam pressure hovering around the 250psi mark, she was in fact simmering at the safety valves. A look in the firebox rather shook me, it was full up to the baffle plate, and looking rather black. There must have been more than two tons of coal in there. I then noticed the dampers were closed, so hopefully the fire would brighten up once we were under way and a damper opened. A glance at the tender showed it to be full, with good Nottinghamshire steam coal, the tender obviously having been topped up after the firebox had been filled on the shed.

Then we were off. A smooth start except for a little slipping as we negotiated the points under the bridge, and then we were into Camden Bank. Back damper open, and firehole door half closed, we blasted up the hill. A light brown colouring of the exhaust showed good combustion, and I noticed that Albert grunted his approval. Looking back, I could see the banking engine working hard. I put the exhaust injector on as we approached Camden shed as the glass showed half full, which I thought would be perfect. I didn't want the possibility of her priming. I guessed I needn't have worried on that score; despite her rather unkempt appearance, there was hardly a wisp of steam from any of her glands. She was obviously much better looked after than the freight engines on which I was used to working.

Primrose Hill Tunnel loomed ahead as we gathered speed, having crested the incline. Into the tunnel with the blast from the chimney reverberating from the tunnel roof and I was conscious of Albert winding back the reversing handle a turn or two. Out of the tunnel at Queen's Park, and in a very short time we were thundering through Willesden, and then Wembley, where a relatively short time ago Bill and I had swung into the siding with our cattle train.

By this time the fire had burned through beautifully, and I began firing her for the first time since leaving Euston. I gave her the usual (for a Stanier engine) four shovels full along each side of the box and one under the door, not forgetting one in each back corner, but Albert shouted, "Give her a good barrowing, she'll take it". This I took to mean he didn't consider I had shovelled enough coal in, so I gave her another ten shovels full, plus a couple of huge pieces that had made their way onto the footplate from the tender (some the fireman had missed whilst cracking the coal).

All this time the exhaust injector had been on, and this was holding the water level at about half a glass, which was fine. We were now approaching Bushey troughs, but looking at the gauge on the tender, it appeared we had not used much since leaving London. I therefore delayed dropping the scoop until we were about halfway along the trough. Even so, at the speed we were going, the tank was quickly filled, and I had a hard job winding the scoop up against the pressure of the water in the trough. Several gallons from our over-filled tender were deposited over the first couple of coaches, but as it was wintertime I guessed there would be no windows open!

Through Watford and the tunnel beyond we sped, and with Albert's encouragement I kept to a pattern of firing fifteen or more shovels-full of coal at a time into the ever-hungry firebox – which was very much longer that those of engines I usually fired. This 'pattern' was somewhat alien to me, being used to firing mainly on ex-LNWR engines where the fire was kept fairly thin, 'little and often' being the norm.

However, soon we were at Tring and 'over the top', and from the 40 to 50mph we had been doing on the climb from London, we were now going downhill and our speed rapidly increased. Unlike many of the Black Fives I had fired, this engine was riding superbly, and I found firing her at 80mph almost no trouble at all – no coal thrown over the driver's lap, or around the footplate!

Although Albert still had her on second regulator, the regulator handle appeared almost closed, and he had the valve gear notched well back too. She was obviously in her element on this 'billiard table' railway – as ex-Midland men used to derisively call it – and I had time to relax a little. I began to look out for any Northampton colleagues trundling towards London on the up slow line, but we were travelling too quickly for anything other than a brief wave to be given.

Soon we were approaching Leighton Buzzard and time to make sure the firehole door and damper were closed, and the blower on full, ready for the impact as we thundered into the 'rat hole' tunnel at Linslade. (Here, some unwary footplate crews have been burned by the fierce blowback as modern engines filled the relatively small aperture of the single-track tunnel, and it was not unknown for the floor-boards of the footplate to be forced up by the pressure created by high speeds into the tunnel.) This day all was well, and except for the popping of our ears, the short burst through the tunnel was uneventful.

Soon we were crashing through Bletchley station, Albert hanging on the whistle as with a great crescendo of noise we thundered through those very familiar surroundings. Then it was Wolverton, round the curve and on to the troughs at Castlethorpe, where I again overfilled the tank. A slight climb to Roade before levelling out through Blisworth, Weedon, and up another climb to Hillmorton Tunnel, and so down to Rugby.

The journey had been an enlightenment to me. The engine had steamed so freely, the needle of the steam gauge deviating no more than ten or fifteen pounds during the trip, and she obviously liked a thick fire, especially at the back of the box. I closed the damper when Albert shut off steam as we coasted towards Rugby, and I began making the fire up for my relief, ready for his journey onwards.

As we approached Rugby, all the signals were off for us on the through road, and Albert said, "What's the betting there's no one here for you?". I was not unduly bothered as I had enjoyed my trip on a top link engine. Albert brought the train to a stop at No. 4 box, and I crossed to the locomen's hut at the end of the platform. It was empty, and my 'phone call to Control revealed there would be no relief for me here – "would I go on to Crewe?" Definite relief was promised there. I informed Control that I would be leaving the train there, whether or not relief was provided, and made my way back to the engine, after relieving my thirst by a drink of water from a nearby tap. Albert was grinning with an 'I told you so' look as I climbed back on the footplate. "You'll probably come right through with me", he said. I didn't reply, but knew what I was going to do at Crewe.

However, our unscheduled stop had cost about ten minutes lost time, and Albert started off with a purpose through the crossovers on to the Trent Valley line. Soon we were up to the sixties on this easy stretch of line, and I quickly filled the tank on the troughs near Brinklow – more over spilling – I wasn't judging the speed at which we were travelling very well.

Then, in what seemed quick succession, we were through Nuneaton, Tamworth, Litchfield, Rugely and

Stafford, having again filled the tank on the troughs near Whitmore. Finally, we slowed as we had a signal check on the approach to Crewe, and drifted into the station just before 1.30pm.

Albert had given the engine some stick after leaving Rugby, but she had retained her good steaming properties, and with the exhaust injector on most of the time, I had not found it hard work. In fact, I had frequently had much harder trips on wagon trains. Albert looked at his watch as we stopped, and said that we were still nearly five minutes adrift, but that we would be able to make that up before arriving at Lime Street as the timetable allowed us some recovery time. Before I had time to give him a rude reply to the effect that I would be nowhere near Liverpool that day, a

voice from the platform called an enquiry as to who wanted relief and a senior-looking fireman climbed on board.

I quickly gathered my belongings as Albert thanked me for, as he put it, "a reasonable trip". I said my goodbyes, climbed down onto the platform, and made my way to the refreshment room for what I considered a well-earned cup of tea and a sandwich. Then I caught the first train I could back to Northampton. A memorable day's work, and profitable too, as I didn't book off until nearly 6pm – a fourteen-hour day, plus some mileage allowance as I had worked over 140 miles distance.

During the rest of my railway service – some eight or nine years – I never set foot on 'Lizzie' again, and I never knowingly saw Albert again.

A lineside glimpse of a 'Princess'. This picture was taken at Victoria Park, Northampton, near Spencer Bridge.   W. J. S. MEREDITH

Platform 4 for Blisworth in March 1952. This looks like 1219, one of our two Ivatt tanks, which were superb engines to work on and a different world to our previous Webb tanks.
H. C. CASSERLEY

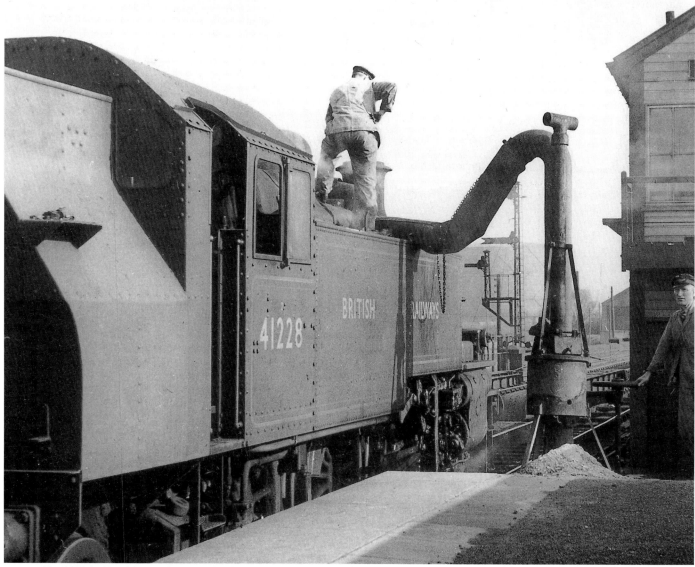

No. 1228 in No. 4 bay at Castle station having her tank filled. She was a Warwick engine initially, but obviously had been transferred by the time this photo was taken. Anyway, here she is seen with Bedford men on board, on what must have been winter time, as ashes can still be seen beneath the stove, which was used to prevent the water bag freezing during such times.
R. K. BLENCOWE

CHAPTER TWELVE
PASSENGER LINKS AGAIN

IN 1947 I was again in the motor link, this time with Tommy Collins, a man in his early sixties, who spoke with a soft country accent, and walked with a slight limp caused, I was told, by an accident some years ago. He was an easy man to get on with, and I again enjoyed the relative freedom of being alone on the footplate – it reminded me of the hours I had spent alone shunting the Down Sidings when posted with Chudder Hillyard. The pleasure of the motor link was further enhanced when we were delivered two of the new 'Ivatt designed' 2–6–2 tank engines – Nos. 1218 and 1219. What superb little engines they were, and a delight to work on. At last we had room on the footplate with comfortable seats, and everything to hand, plus 'rocker fire-bars', which made breaking up any clinker forming on the bars so much easier. We were the first Northampton crew to try out the earliest delivered engine, 1218, on the afternoon Leamington run. She certainly turned a few heads as we ran into the various stations en route, and the speed with which she handled the train had us waiting at stations for our departure time. All the crews in the link took great pride in these little engines, and the brasswork on the footplate was kept gleaming by much polishing with 'Paget's Paste', a slightly abrasive cream on sale in those days.

It was while I was with Tom that we were involved in a suicide. The engine was one of our Midland 2P 4–4–0s No. 412, and we were on our way home with the evening local from Wellingborough Midland. It was a pleasant late spring evening and after stopping at Wellingborough LNW, we were non-stop to Northampton. I had a good fire on, and had perched myself on the tender handrail near the hand-brake as we approached Castle Ashby, and was looking across the fields. Tom, on the right hand-side of the engine, suddenly said, "That old boy was a bit close wasn't he?" I looked backwards along our three-coach train, but could see no one, and we continued to Castle Station.

It was our final trip of the day, and after shunting our train into the carriage sidings, we drew back into platform four at No. 1 box to await a road to the shed, when we were approached by one of the transport police officers. Apparently, the driver of a train travelling in the opposite direction had reported seeing what looked like a body lying in the up line, and he asked if we had seen anything. We replied in the negative, then Tom remembered seeing the man near Castle Ashby, and told the officer. I then went to look at the front of the engine, and saw what looked like blood on the front coupling and buffer beam, and a further look under the engine revealed more blood and bits of clothing on the brake hanger. We were then required to go to the police room and make statements regarding what we had seen/not seen, before we at last took the engine to the shed, where I threw buckets of hot water to wash the blood away, the policeman having retained the bits of cloth from the brake hanger. An inquest was later held but neither of us had to attend.

About this time there had been rumours that the railways were to be nationalised, and I think most railwaymen were hoping something would be done. Many of our engines were just about 'clapped out', little proper maintenance having been done throughout the war, and the situation appeared not to be improving in these financially restricted days of peace. Quite a few engines had only one injector which worked, gauges were also missing or broken, brake blocks worn down so much that no more adjustment could be made, tools and equipment missing and often hard to obtain. It was very apparent that the private companies were not going to spend money if the government was about to take them over.

My time with Tommy continued through late summer, and on one of the days when we were relieved by the crew who would continue the 'late turn' push-pull Blisworth run, I had my one and only ride on the last remaining engine of the Claughton class, No. 6004, which was travelling tender first to the shed after working a wagon train to the Down Sidings and was held momentarily at No. 1 box signals.

No. 6004, the last of the Claughtons, on which I was privileged to ride to the shed one day, seen at Crewe in August 1946.
R. K. BLENCOWE

121

No. 8610, a Willesden engine, was a regular visitor to the shed and made use of by the shed foreman to work trains — not necessarily back to her home shed.

H. F. WHEELLER

No. 3098 was typical of the engines used in shunting at Castle Yard, and also on the trip trains. They were also employed on the SMJ by both Northampton and Blisworth men should there be no Stratford engines available. The 86 plate is rather intriguing, but I've no idea what it was for. The fireman is seen on the tender with the bag in the tank but apparently no water running. The driver must have handed the chain to his mate to enable him to pull up the bag, so why didn't he turn on the water before climbing back onto the footplate? Perhaps the driver had just turned the water off, but the fireman was unable to eject the bag from the tender because it had fouled some projection, and the driver was returning to the footplate in order to move the engine slightly, and so release the bag. There are sometimes several facets in a picture if one looks close enough.

H. F. WHEELLER

Tommy and I clambered aboard. I was very impressed by both the length of the footplate from coal area to firehole door, and by the length of the firebox itself. The fireman, Vic Cosford, said that a long-handled shovel was a necessity. I could quite believe it!

At the end of the summer I was moved into the middle passenger link, the majority of workings of this link being to either Peterborough or Nottingham. My driver in this link was to be Ernie 'Tojo' Smith, and my heart sank somewhat as I remembered our previous encounter on the compound engine in my early days of firing.

Ernie was known by those young firemen who had been posted with him as not being one of the world's best enginemen, in fact quite a few of the lads alleged that they burned almost twice as much coal firing for him as they did with most of the other drivers. Such information, though jokingly imparted, did nothing to alleviate my misgivings about my new posting, especially as one of his previous firemen, a fellow named Stan Baldwin, had related a somewhat bizarre story of how he was so fed up with Ernie's driving and treatment of him, that, having discovered that Ernie had a somewhat weak stomach, he secreted an item of female monthly apparel, spread with strawberry jam, on his person. On reaching Nottingham with their three-coach train, he got down to uncouple the engine while Ernie as normal began

to eat his sandwiches. Stan took slightly longer than usual in his task while Ernie was munching away, and when he finally climbed on to the footplate he was dangling the article, saying, "Look what I've found". Ernie apparently shouted at him to "throw it away, you dirty bastard". At which Stan said, "No fear, it's fresh", and proceeded to lick the jam, whereupon Ernie disappeared into the tender and relieved himself of his recently swallowed sandwiches, and most of his previously eaten lunch.

I'm not sure what Stan's actions did for his relationship with Ernie, but I would guess they did not improve the situation. Anyway, their partnership was terminated shortly afterwards when Stan was moved into the top passenger link.

My first week with Ernie saw us on the early-morning run to Peterborough East with one of our 4–4–0 2P Midland engines, with a train of three non-corridor coaches. This was a local stopping train, and I soon realised that Ernie was not too adept at controlling the speed as we approached the various stations. He blasted between stations quite efficiently, but when it came to stopping we were nearly through some of the stations before we stopped. It seemed to be the case of shutting off steam at the last moment, then slamming on the brake and hoping that the somewhat limited braking power of only three coaches would bring us to a stand within the confines of the station. This was general practice,

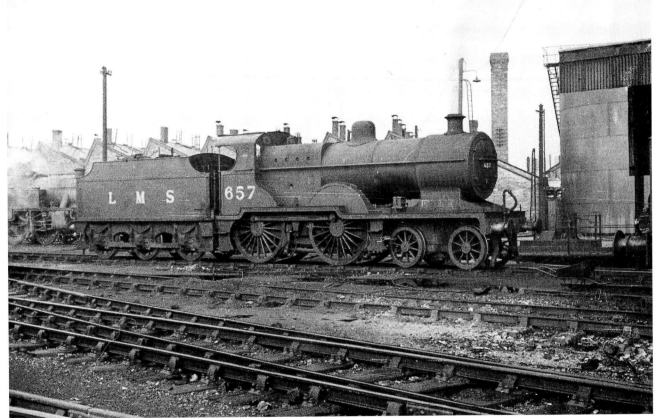

No. 657, one of our 'high steppers', on shed awaiting coaling at the crane c.1946. The water softening plant can be seen beyond the front of the engine.
H. F. WHEELLER

Peterborough East, looking west along the bay through line, towards the signal box, in June 1938.

R. F. ROBERTS

but relied on the driver's assessment of speed and distance, plus experience gained of the likely braking power of both engine and train. Ernie appeared to lack some of these skills.

However, with such a short train I had no difficulty in maintaining satisfactory steam and water levels. On arrival at Peterborough, the train was backed into the carriage road and we went onto the shed – not really a shed at this time

but there was a water column and turntable available. There I was able to clean the fire, and bring some coal forward on the tender while the tank was filling. Then it was on to the turntable, where the engine had to be positioned precisely – which took a bit of doing – to ensure a not too difficult push round. Following that it was wash-up time, followed by breakfast, before our return to Northampton.

Peterborough East station, showing the elevated signal box and with engine 62530 (LNER) nearing the end of its journey from March to the North station.
MILEPOST 92½

A Class 4 0–6–0 standing just west of the station, no doubt awaiting time to reverse onto its train (a local) to Leicester. F. J. SAUNDERS

Engine 412 on a return train from Peterborough, awaiting the 'off' at Thrapston on 9th June 1952.   COLLECTION R. J. ESSERY

I found these Peterborough runs relatively easy along the nearly level course of the river Nene (pronounced Nen), and certainly I found that Ernie was quite convivial while things were going well. Our trips on this line included one in the morning, booking on at about 5.45 m for the 7 o'clock train, arriving at Peterborough at about 9am, and departing there at, I think, about 10.45am for arrival back at Northampton about 12.30pm, train into the carriage siding, then to the shed and off duty.

The afternoon run entailed commencing duty at about 1.15pm for departure at 2.45pm, arriving at Peterborough at about 4.30pm, and returning at 6.15pm with arrival at Northampton at 7.30pm. This train did not stop at every station, so making Ernie's job a little easier. Each trip just about filled an eight-hour day.

A similar run was to Nottingham via Market Harborough and Melton Mowbray on the old Great Northern line – over the Alps as we used to call it – with a similar type of engine. Again there was a morning train, about 7am, arriving at Nottingham about 9.30am, departing again at about 10.45am and back at Northampton at 1.30pm. On this, and the afternoon turn, to obviate us working overtime, the engine was prepared for us before we booked on. The afternoon times were roughly 12.50pm from Northampton, arriving at Nottingham about 4pm, returning at 5.45pm and at Northampton by 8.30pm.

You can see that we had ample time at Nottingham to clean the fire as necessary, and turn and water the engine, plus have something to eat and drink. The only drawback

was, I soon found, Ernie's inability to judge speed and distance, again with a three-coach set, made worse by the fact that there were several gradients on this route, unlike the Peterborough run. He would frequently stop too soon at such stations as Hallaton, John O'Gaunt, and Harby & Stathern, and run through at others – Melton Mowbray for one, which was on a down gradient from either direction. I used to find it quite amusing, especially on misty mornings, when Ernie's moustache and eyebrows would be covered with a foggy dew, as he hung his head over the side of the footplate in his effort to see clearly and judge his speed of approach. Should he misjudge where he intended to stop, he would be cursing at the engine for not doing what he had hoped it would. I would invariably say to him, "They've moved the station again Ernie". This, of course, would provoke him into shouting his favourite expression, that I was a 'long Peruvian ponce' or something just as descriptive! I must say in his defence that in the dark, with only the glimmer of perhaps one oil lamp illuminating the platform, it was not always easy to see we were approaching a station, let alone stop precisely along the platform.

These 4–4–0 engines were quite fast runners, and usually good steamers, liking a good fire at the back of the box, tapering to a thin fire at the front. The worst thing about them was the dust from the ashpan, there being two holes about an inch and a half square at the back of the pan (only a front damper fitted) through which ash would be blown when travelling quickly, and which would be drawn up through the gap between the back of the boiler and the floor

SCALFORD

MELTON MOWBRAY NORTH

MELTON MOWBRAY NORTH

JOHN O' GAUNT

TILTON

EAST NORTON

Our journey from Northampton to Nottingham – over 'The Alps' – was via Pitsford & Brampton, Spratton, Brixworth, Lamport, Kelmarsh, Clipston & Oxendon, Market Harborough, Hallaton, East Norton, Tilton, John O' Gaunt, Great Dalby, Melton Mowbray (north), Scalford, Long Clawson & Hose, Barnstone, Bingham Road, Netherfield, and Nottingham Victoria. With that number of starts and stops, it was quite taxing for a driver, and for the engine too, but not so much for the fireman, who usually had ample recovery time while approaching, and at stations. Tilton and John O' Gaunt were also locations where you could be shunted out of the way of faster trains.

MILEPOST 92½ and T. J. EDGINGTON

Blisworth again, with an SMJ train in the bay. Usually the train for Banbury had one coach whilst that for Stratford would have two. Blisworth men seldom seemed to worry about running tender first; or perhaps it was because they didn't fancy the hard push round on the turntables! Note the full tender of coal – it was obviously expected that the engine would stay off shed for several days. Some budding rail enthusiasts are seen showing an interest in the engine.

W. A. CAMWELL

boards, and invariably into one's eyes. We footplate crews were always searching for suitable material with which to block this gap. A bundle of cotton waste was a favourite, but not easily obtained, so often we would dig lumps of grass, etc, from embankments and stuff those into the orifice and around the steam pipes. This measure would suffice until the grass and earth dried out, then it would gradually disintegrate, and more would need to be found.

Another of our pleasant jobs was the afternoon 'school bus' run from Blisworth to Banbury (picking up most of the children at Towcester), over the 'Dilly-Dally' line, with a one-coach train, and usually with a Midland class 2 or 3 0–6–0 , returning in the evening with a few freight wagons, plus brake van, attached behind the coach – but no passengers. At least, the train was not advertised to carry passengers,

but it was not unknown for one or two somewhat inebriated farmer types, especially at the end of market day, to present themselves on the platform, when we had marshalled our train and were standing either in platform 1, or the line next to it, and request being 'dropped off' at one of the stations – Farthinghoe, Helmdon, Wappingham, or sometimes even Towcester en route to Blisworth. We on the footplate, of course, didn't get involved, except for being informed by the guard where our 'guests' were to be deposited, but no doubt he made a shilling or two out of the deals.

Not infrequently when working trains over this branch, or that to Stratford-on-Avon, we would be confronted by a stray sheep, or even some cattle, on the line. This meant having to slow down, and often my having to get down on the track in an effort to catch the animal and force it through

The Blisworth SMJ box, showing the approach to the station and sidings. The turntable used to be just off the picture to the left of the box. Note the 'bobby' keeping an eye on the photographer who was passing on the line.   R. J. F. RAWLINSON

Banbury (Merton Street) with the Blisworth train awaiting time to go. One of the step ladders provided for use of passengers because of the low platforms can be seen. This, and the box type with wheels, was the sort utilized by the station staff for the release of pigeons from their baskets on race days.   J. E. NORRIS

The front of the station buildings.   H. J. STRETTON WARD

the fence into a field. Such antics, of course, created not a little amusement to passengers, especially schoolchildren, who would be hanging out of the windows urging me on in my 'round-up' activities as the sheep invariably scampered ahead of me along the track. I often felt very sheepish myself!

Several railway men at that time were 'pigeon fanciers', belonging to local clubs, and it was not an infrequent occurrence for the guard on these local passenger trains to be 'lumbered' with having to surreptitiously release a basket of birds at one of the wayside stations for them to have a training flight home to Northampton. Some weeks the birds would be released progressively at the next station along the line each day, especially if a competition was impending requiring release at a distant station along that route. On such occasions it was not unusual for there to be twenty or thirty baskets of birds to be released, but this was done by the station staff after all had been unloaded, and the train had gone on its way.

I did witness such an event at Banbury one day when we happened to be in the yard shunting. All the baskets were lined up on the platform. The fastenings of the lids were released, and lengths of string attached to the lids. The porter, with the lengths of string in his hand, then mounted a step ladder already positioned accordingly, and at the time scheduled for the mass release, raised the lids of the baskets by pulling the strings, and the birds, with a clattering of wings, rose in a maelstrom of birds and feathers, and headed off along the branch towards Blisworth or Bletchley, and hopefully to their respective coops.

That year – 1947 – we had a very hard winter, and I remember that on the early morning Peterborough run, as we scurried through Wansford tunnel there would be the sound of icicles being smashed from the roof of the tunnel. In fact there was invariably a huge one hanging at the mouth of the tunnel, seemingly about five or six feet in length, which was the first to be hit. It was so cold that winter that icicles would form inside the roof of the cab of engines on which steam glands were blowing, and would gradually lengthen until the vibration caused them to break off.

On another occasion that winter, while we were trundling back with the evening goods from Banbury, with I believe 3521, a class 3 0–6–0, we had something of a scare, and a somewhat miserable night. It had been snowing quite heavily since late in the morning, and the evening saw it turning into a blizzard, and once again I was certainly thankful that we had a blackout sheet positioned across the windward side (my side) of the engine, although snow was still whipping through various gaps onto the footplate, and we both had our overcoats on. The snow was getting deeper, and was over rail depth in most places. We could feel the engine running lumpily over the packed snow when we were thrashing though drifts. After stopping at Wappenham to drop off some coal for the porters-cum-ticket-office room (a request relayed to us at Banbury, with the information that the door would be 'left on the latch') and where Ernie was able to mash a can of tea while I was busy, we set off again. Thankfully, we were not going very fast, as about a quarter of a mile beyond the station we ran into a snow drift that was so deep and solid that it appeared to lift the engine and brought us to a rather undignified stop. Examination showed we were not derailed, but the snow was well above my waist, and seemed to extend for quite a way, obviously too much for me to shovel away. After several attempts at reversing and charging at the drift, it became apparent that we were fighting a losing battle. There was nothing for it but to reverse back to the station and report the incident to Control via the phone in the ticket office, the door of which, luckily, in my haste to get back into the warmth of the engine after depositing the several shovels full of coal, I had not closed properly.

Control informed us they would try to get in contact with platelayers – if they could alert the Station Master at Towcester – who would come and dig us out. We realised it

Engine 3521, with which Ernie Smith and I became stuck in a snowdrift near Wappenham.
COLLECTION R. J. ESSERY

was a rather forlorn hope, and prepared to settle down for the night. I got a shovel of fire from the engine and relit the fire in the ticket office, brought in some more coal, and ate the last of my sandwiches with the remainder of the tea we had. The guard stayed with us for a time, but as there were only two 'comfortable' chairs in the office, he elected to return to his van and bed down there. I was quite impressed at Ernie's apparent calmness. I had thought that he would be hopping from foot to foot because of our predicament, but he seemed quite resigned to the fact that we would be spending the night at this location. Perhaps it was the thought of the extra overtime pay which pacified him! I filled the boiler and dampened down the fire before retreating into the now rapidly warming room. At about 11.30pm the telephone rang, and Control informed us that nothing could be done until the morning. As it was still snowing that did not surprise us.

So, we spent a not very comfortable night, although much warmer than if we had been stranded on the footplate. By daylight next day it had stopped snowing, and when the early-turn porter/ticket man, Johnny Higgs, bravely riding his ex-WD Royal Enfield motorcycle (a similar model to the machine I had, and bought at 'Kings of Oxford') arrived at the station, complete with the makings for a brew of tea, he was more or less welcomed with open arms. More phone calls were made and received, and about 9.30am we heard an engine whistling, and shortly afterwards two platelayers and a fireman appeared on the platform. An engine and brake

van had been despatched from Blisworth, picked up a gang of platelayers at Towcester, and had travelled 'under Caution' without the staff towards Wappenham, and us. The other platelayers were already tackling the snow from the other end of the drift, so after handing the engine over to the new fireman, Ernie, the guard, and I ploughed our way through the snow to the engine and brake van, where the relief guard was sitting tight, apparently in the hope that a path would be cleared for him by the platelayers before we arrived. On arrival at the engine, after the usual exchange of greetings and information, the relief driver and guard trudged off towards the station, while we propelled the van back to Towcester and on to Blisworth – all tender first of course, and very cold!

On arrival at Blisworth we were relieved by another set of Blisworth men – who had been awaiting the engine; it theoretically should have been stabled at Northampton shed overnight and delivered to them by the night duty shed turning crew. We thankfully travelled home on the motor train from Blisworth. Another shift of almost twenty-four hours!

All in all I found my time with Ernie not too onerous – once I had got used to his somewhat erratic ways, and tantrums – and I always found him ready to help with fire cleaning or bringing the coal forward if it appeared that I would not have time for my refreshments during our time at our destinations.

Wappenham station, showing the ticket office, etc, with a train for Blisworth at the platform.
T. J. EDGINGTON

CHAPTER THIRTEEN

NATIONALISATION

No. 5021 double-heading an express at Berkhamsted in 1949.
H. C. CASSERLEY

HOWEVER, in 1948 I was transferred into the 'Euston/Birmingham' link (the top passenger link), with Charlie Earl as my driver. We were now a Nationalised industry, and were expecting great alterations to both the railway infrastructure and our engines. We were sadly disillusioned.

The somewhat disturbing regularity with which we firemen were transferred up and down the links was not only because of senior men returning from the armed forces and taking their position as their service dictated, but also because we were losing certain 'jobs'. Even as early as 1947/8 some branch lines which had been opened, or reopened, for the war years were now being closed, with the consequent loss of trains working over those branches. Luckily for us younger firemen, some of the men returning from the forces did not stay long on the railway – there was more lucrative work to be found elsewhere, especially in the motor industry at Coventry, and more locally at British Timken roller-bearing factory. It was, however, somewhat disrupting to us having to get used to a new mate seemingly every few months.

Charlie Earl was almost a complete opposite to Ernie. He was a superb engineman, who seemingly never 'put an engine about', always on first regulator, and not winding the gears back much beyond 40% cut off but always running to time. At first I found I was arriving at either Euston or Birmingham (our two usual destinations) with a too-thick fire. Charlie never seemed to burn much coal, and frequently we seemed to dawdle between stations. His adage was that he would keep time from station to station; if we lost time at stations, that was down to the station staff or the guard. When I got used to his working, we would often run into Euston with our Black 5 with so thin a fire that the fire-bars might be showing in places – depending on the type of coal of course.

Charlie, in his sixties, was a quiet somewhat reserved man, who just got on with his job, and expected others to do the same. He rarely assisted me in fire cleaning, or coal breaking, but of course did help at the water columns when we filled the tender tank. But then, I seemed to be firing less frequently with him than with many other drivers, and so classed my time with him as easy. Our engines on the Euston or Birmingham runs were usually our Black 5s – 5021, 5191, etc, or Stanier tanks – 2–6–4s 2602, 2538. These latter engines were predominantly used on the early morning Euston commuter trains (7.5 and 8.5 am), which were semi-fast, stopping at Bletchley, Leighton Buzzard, Tring, then all stations to Watford, then Euston.

Our runs to Birmingham were similarly what might be termed as semi-fast, stopping at Long Buckby, Rugby, Coventry, and then all stations to New Street. This latter station always appeared to me to be somewhat foreboding. It was so dark, soot begrimed, and seemingly below ground level. It was claustrophobic, but exciting in a strange way, with trains suddenly appearing out of the gloom of adjacent tunnels, or from the darkness of the inner station itself. It was much more murky than Nottingham London Road (the low level station), but I must admit that the intermediate stations were better illuminated than on the Nottingham branch.

133

Rebuilt 'Baby Scot' and a 'Scot' in two of the arrival platforms at Euston in 1954, with passengers making their way towards taxi, tube, car or bus, having completed their journey. Should passengers not have presented the engine crew with newspapers or magazines, those worthies would no doubt be looking in the carriages to ascertain if any had been left.

P. RICKARD

I enjoyed my time in this link. The engines, Black 5s or our Stanier tanks, gave one a comfortable footplate on which to work, and lent themselves to keeping the footplate clean by use of the fizzle pipe and my hand brush. I also enjoyed the Euston jobs. There was nothing so good as running into the 'premier station' on time, and with a dampened-down engine so as not to make either smoke or noise, especially on the morning commuter runs, when the grateful passengers would often voice their thanks and hand over a newspaper as they passed the engine. One usually had time after quickly unhooking the engine, and awaiting the train to be pulled out of the station by one of the pilot engines, to nip round

to the 'coffee knob' behind platform seven to fill our billy can for a drink before we set to work in the service area. If I had the opportunity, I also used to take a peek into the Great Hall with its marvellous stairway, and giant flat ceiling, the largest in the world, the like of which could only be seen on a smaller scale in Buckingham Palace. All this disappeared in the early 60s – thankfully long after I had left the railway – during the reconstruction of the station by vandals under the guise of architects!

I remained in this link with Charlie throughout 1948, without anything of note that I remember to write about. In the spring of the following year, there was obviously more

Euston's Doric Arch before it was vandalized. It still lies beneath the waters of the Grand Union Canal somewhere in East London.
W. J. S. MEREDITH

upheaval at our depot because I was posted back to the motor link (missing out the Notts/Peterbo' link), and renewed my companionship with Tommy Collins. Nothing much had changed, except that we now had a lion riding a unicycle emblem on tank side, or tender, and a figure four (or 40) had been added to the front of our engine numbers. Of course this change had taken place on engines while I had been with Charlie.

Tommy was now approaching retirement age, which would be at the end of the year, 1949, and was a little less agile than he had been when first I met him. However, we worked well together, and we still had our beloved 41218 and 41219 tanks for the majority of our work. The brass work on the footplates had been kept gleaming during my time in the other links, and they both looked a picture –

much admired by the young engine spotters who still invaded Blisworth station at weekends and holidays, and whom we allowed to spend a few moments on the footplate. My parents at this time were managing a pub – The Prince of Wales – at Leamington Spa, and if possible I used to let them know the week we would be on the evening train. Mother would then appear with a bottle of beer for each of us, which went down well with our sandwiches. All the time I was in that link with Tommy she continued to trudge to the station with a bottle of beer for each of us when we were on the afternoon run, and I remember that on my 21st birthday on the 6th September that year, she appeared with two bottles each, plus a Melton Mowbray pork pie for us to share! A splendid 21st 'party'!

Yours truly with Norman Quennell and Harold Bolllard, resting and enjoying the sunshine during one of our many trips around the Northamptonshire area on our motorcycles. I think, in this picture, we were overlooking the river at Bedford. The photographer was John Firkins, one of our friends, who worked in the offices at Castle station.

CHAPTER FOURTEEN
COCK ALLEN

TOWARDS the end of the year I was back in the special link, and this time rostered with the man who had been my driver on the Uppingham Schoolboys special some time ago – Bill (Cock) Allen. He was a man with a very ruddy complexion, a sharp nose, and a somewhat spiky 'Ronald Coleman' moustache. He came from the Chester area, and spoke with that Mersey twang in a rather high-pitched voice. We hit it off from the beginning, and had some memorable 'adventures' together during the several occasions I was rostered with him until my 'retirement'.

These adventures occurred in no small measure because Bill signed as knowing more roads than nearly every other driver at our depot. It was alleged that often when he went on holiday, he would hang his head out of the carriage window on a few occasions, and at appropriate locations, and then sign as knowing that route on his return from holiday. I don't know how true these allegations were, but I certainly fired to venues to which I had not been with any other driver. These included Llandudno, and Blackpool on several occasions, and once to Wigan – with a 'Cobblers' (Northampton Football Club) special when they played in a cup match. I remember on one of the excursions to Blackpool – which began for us at about 5am – we were returning in the evening after some convivial hours on the sea front. The necessary had been done to the engine on the shed before we went for our stroll, and it was not long before we met people from our excursion whom Bill knew. They, of course, were more than a little hospitable at various hostelries, and although we took time out to have a meal, I was a little the worse for wear by the time we re-mounted our steed – one of our Black 5s – 5191 (sorry – 45191, we never acknowledged the prefix 4), and returned to the station to hook on to our train. Before we left, several folk had made gifts to us of bottles of beer, with the plea – "Get us home fast and safe". We therefore had no cause to mash a can of tea, and slaked our thirst with our free beer.

However, it was nearly dusk when we set off, and as we approached Preston it became quite misty. As we swept round the curve towards the somewhat infamous large gantry, which was just visible from my side of the footplate, Bill shouted, "Can you see any greens?". I replied to the effect that I thought one signal was at green, to which he replied, "That'll do for us", and without any more slowing down we sailed towards the station, where we could see our signals were indeed off, and breathed a collective sigh of relief. It was at moments like these that I realised Bill was not completely *au fait* with some of the routes for which he had signed.

Similar 'jolly' days out were had on excursions to Llandudno, although we had no problems with signals in that area, it being Bill's back yard, so to speak. Sometimes on these excursion trains we would be lucky and have a Baby Scot or even a Jubilee should there be one on our shed at the appropriate time, but usually the engine would be one of our own Black 5s. We also had such trains to Skegness and Great Yarmouth, but even Bill had to have a pilotman once we got to Peterborough on the journey to the former, and March on the latter, as we were then on 'foreign metals' – Eastern Region.

We enjoyed many adventures both on and off the railway. I had a new motorcycle by this time, and one day we were going on this to Silverstone to see motorcycle racing, where riders like John Surtees, Geoff Duke, etc. would be taking part. The weather was not good, and when Ron Malin, a passed fireman, who was also going to the races and who had a motorcycle combination, offered Bill a lift in the sidecar, Bill chose to go with Ron. As they set off along the Towcester Road, with me bringing up the rear, Ron accelerated to a reasonable speed, then flipped the sidecar wheel off the road so that Bill was suspended in the air, and proceeded to ride like that all the way to Towcester, and once through that town did it again. I could see Bill holding his cap on with one hand, and the other clamped tightly on the side of the sidecar, whilst he was mouthing something to Ron – their heads being about level due to the tilt of the sidecar. When we got to the parking area at the race track, Bill eased himself gingerly from the 'chair', and I could see a certain pallor had diffused the normal redness of his cheeks. I won't repeat here what Bill was calling Ron as I came up to them. Suffice to say, that on our return after the racing, although the weather had deteriorated somewhat, Bill came back to Northampton on the pillion of my machine, with the stern instruction – "Don't try and keep up with that idiot Malin!".

I suppose our biggest, or worst 'adventure' was the mess we made at Sears Crossing. I suppose to most of you that remember the early sixties, the name of Sears Crossing perhaps conjures up visions of newsreel pictures concerning the 'great train robbery' executed by Buster Edwards and his gang, when they halted the night mail train at a false red colour light signal at this isolated spot and stole more than a million pounds in used bank notes.

To me Sears Crossing always brings to mind a day more than a decade before that incident, when this location was controlled by semaphore signals operated from the signal box there. It was a day which eventually culminated in the two of us standing on the red carpet at Rugby, and I consider, being unfairly accused and sanctioned.

The day began like many others. Bill and I booked on at 3.50pm – twelve hours after booking off the previous day, which was the norm – and were told to report to the Control office at Castle Station. From there we were directed to No.4 box to relieve the crew of a train from Bescot (a suburb of Birmingham) destined for Willesden, which was approaching Northampton from Rugby.

These were still the days of numerous freight trains and, all too often, industrial disputes. 'Working to rule' at

*No. 9142, obviously after nation-
alization but without the crest.
Perhaps this was after her rescue
and repair following the Sears
Crossing incident.*

COLLECTION R. J. ESSERY

Stonebridge Park sidings, the destination of the majority of
the trains we worked southwards, was not an infrequent
occurrence, and, as mentioned previously, it was often the
case of us being required to relieve men from Rugby or
Leicester who had completed their eight-hour shift in travelling the twenty or thirty miles respectively from those places.
Similarly, we would be relieved at Bletchley – twenty miles
on – having done more than our eight hours duty. Many
hours were still spent in loop lines or waiting at signals until
the next 'block' was clear.

However, on this day, after a cup of tea and a game of
cards with the shunters in their cabin near No.4 box, we
heard the wheezing of a D approaching, which we knew
was the type of engine on our train. As we approached the
engine, I noticed the headlamp code being carried – top and
middle – which meant it was a train of mixed freight, usually
implying that the load would not be as heavy as a coal train.
We clambered on to the footplate as the engine slowly
passed us and joined the men on the footplate. The usual
greetings and information were exchanged, and we learned
they were Bescot men, and the engine was of their home
shed (3A). It was numbered 9142 (or perhaps 49142 as we
were now well into the Nationalised era).

We were told, "She's a good un", that we had 63 and a
brake, and that the guard was a Rugby man. The Bescot
driver also mentioned that they had had a reasonable run,
and were hoping to sneak through, to at least Bletchley, to
make a bit of overtime. We were all at it!. As they had been
on duty for only seven hours, they would have to report to
Control, and perhaps work a train back home, or at least to
Rugby.

By this time we were at the south end of the loop and I
climbed onto the tender ready to pull up the bag in order to
fill the tank. The other fireman turned on the water before
he and his driver began the walk to the station. Having filled
the tank, I turned my attention to the fire. It looked fairly
good, but when I probed through it with the dart, I loosened several pieces of clinker, so quickly, using the clinker
shovel, I removed the largest pieces, depositing them where

others had been thrown onto the six-foot beside the engine.
Bill, in the meantime, had been round the engine with the
oil can. On his return to the footplate, he did what was the
usual practice of North Western men and removed the rose
from the vacuum gauge, thus releasing the brakes. Running
without any immediate braking was not as dangerous as it
might sound. Drivers usually had ample warning of when
they had to stop by reason of the distant signal for each
block, and thus was able to slowly 'blow up' the vacuum to
bring the brakes into operation.

It was early evening before we eventually received the
right of way from Northampton and, after crawling through
the middle road of the station, Bill opened her up and we
chuffed our way up the bank towards Roade. The D class of
engine never seemed to make a great deal of fuss, with their
distinctive two sharp beats and two softer ones, and should
one have the misfortune of having a poor steamer, they
would invariably pull a train with only sixty or seventy
pounds of steam showing on the gauge. This engine
appeared to be as the other crew had indicated, but I was
glad I had cleaned the fire as the coal was not good, with the
usual briquettes and slack amongst it. As Bill said, "You can
make a lot of smoke for a few minutes, but a lot of it goes
straight out of the chimney. Good for cleaning the tubes!"

Having topped the bank through Roade Cutting, we
were diverted, almost inevitably, into Hanslope Loop, the
bobby indicating that two trains were in there. Bill had
blown the ejector to restore vacuum as we approached the
loop, and its high-pitched whistle permeated the cab – especially my side as the ejector was situated just in front of my
seat. It was not difficult to understand why men tried to rid
themselves of this intrusive noise. We could see the tail
lamps of the train in front and it slowly dawned on us that he
was moving too, so there would only be that train in front
when we stopped. As we got to the brake van of the train,
Bill gently buffered up, and we went to pay our respects to
the guard – just in case he was someone we knew, and had a
mash of tea on the stove. Neither was the case. However we
learnt that he was a Bletchley man, as were the footplate

crew, and the train was of coal – the 1.30am from Toton to Willesden (I didn't ask which day!). We returned to our engine and began to get some half decent coal forward from the back of the tender.

It didn't seem long before we heard the couplings being tightened of the train in front as it moved off, and we followed, stopping at the signal. Bill went through the brake release procedure again, ready for our next move. When the guard had told us that the crew were all from Bletchley, Bill and I had exchanged knowing glances. We guessed that they would require relieving at their home depot, which might mean there would not be another crew for us, thereby allowing us to sneak through Bletchley to begin a 'nice little earner'! With this in mind, when we stopped at the signal I made my way across the tracks to the box to ask the bobby if he would inform Bletchley that we were 'right away' through that location should there be a road for us.

Whether this ruse worked or not, within half an hour we were given the green signal and, gathering the train together, Bill soon had us trundling at a good pace towards Castlethorpe and the troughs, where I was able to fill the tank. We were now ready for any eventuality. Wolverton signals were green and, as we approached Loughton – wonder of wonders – they had us right away with the distant signal below the home signal off too, which meant we were signalled right through Bletchley. Bill gave her more regulator, and I gave her a firing. She was steaming really well now that she had some fairly decent coal in her belly.

So on we galloped, travelling at about 30mph, the exhaust chopping off nicely at the chimney. The only fly in the ointment was that, not having stopped at Bletchley, we had not been able to mash our can of tea. However, I had the usual square whiskey bottle of Camp coffee on the coffee plate above the firehole door, and Bill was similarly supplied.

In what seemed very quick time we were approaching Linslade Tunnel, and then we were through Leighton Buzzard – greens all the way. Bill by this time was sitting with his back to the side of the cab, facing in to the footplate, perched on the half-moon shaped seat of this type of engine, a seat on which it was really impossible to sit with any degree of comfort. He had utilised his strap, which several drivers carried (formally window straps of carriages which had been replaced), and had secured himself on the seat by hooking the strap on to the now defunct blackout sheet hooks on the cab side. I could see his eyelids drooping and knew he was about to have 'forty winks' before we got to Tring and the down grade towards Watford, which might demand more attention – especially regarding braking.

I fired the engine again and looked ahead. Still greens all the way, both for us on the up slow, and for whoever was signalled on the up fast, the electric distant signals showing quite clearly in the darkness. I took a swig from my bottle of coffee and decided to have a sandwich before the climb through Tring Cutting, where I would need to be firing again. Taking my food tin from the tender locker, I perched

on my seat and automatically leaned out to glance at the signals ahead at Sears Crossing.

For a split second what I saw did not register; the home signal was on and we were signalled into the loop! I jumped up, my tin crashing to the footplate as I yelled to Bill. I pulled the regulator closed and pulled the brake handle over in almost one movement, and began screwing the handbrake on as hard as I could. Bill, who had come to in a flurry of movement, had released himself from the strap, and had wound the reversing wheel into back gear, and was opening and closing the regulator to create added resistance to our forward progress. By this time I was working the sanding handle in an effort to prevent her from picking up her wheels and skidding.

Suddenly we slewed into the loop with a horrid lurch. The brakes were gradually biting but there was not much chance of us being able to stop the train before reaching the end of the loop, which was of only one train length. Bill by now was giving three short blasts on the whistle in the hope that the guard might hear it and be able to give a little help in braking, also, the signalman might become aware of our plight and open the points at the end of the loop to allow us to return to the slow line and stop safely.

All was to no avail. Although the brakes were now biting, and actually working against the wheels, which were spinning in reverse as Bill manipulated the regulator, the weight of the train was too much. I could dimly make out the stop block looming ever nearer as we still moved forward at about five miles an hour. I remember wondering if I should jump, but heard Bill yelling to hang on, then with a sickening crunch we hit the stops. Our momentum seemed to be checked for a brief second, and then pandemonium as engine and tender bucked as we headed downwards for what seemed an age, but in reality was only a few seconds. I was hanging on to the handrail, and I think I again thought of jumping, but it was black unknown out there, but, before my mind could grasp what to do, the tender appeared to fold up towards the cab as the engine levelled out and the tender was still following the downward path the engine had taken.

Suddenly all was relatively silent. We had stopped. The footplate was knee-deep in coal and the air thick with dust, but we were more or less upright. We both began yelling to each other regarding our wellbeing, but found we were relatively unharmed physically, but I guess both badly shaken. I remember we both burst out laughing – a high-pitched nervous cackle. Bill regained his composure first and said, "Bloody hell, I bet the guard's dead", knowing that the cumulative effect of the sudden buffering up of all those loose couplings would create a terrific impact on the brake van.

By this time I was regaining my senses, and anger was replacing my fear of a few minutes earlier. I knew I had to go to the signal box, not only to carry out rule 55, but also to remonstrate with the 'low life' bobby who, having had us signalled through his section, had changed his mind for some reason and diverted us into the loop. First, though, I had to find out if the guard was alright. Bill by this time was attempting to work one of the injectors, but was having little success – the feed pipes from the tender had been damaged, although we didn't know this at the time.

I remember my surprise as I went to step down from the footplate, when instead of finding steps beneath my feet I felt earth! The engine had embedded itself nearly up to the framing in the field in which we had ended our forward momentum. I groped my way back onto railway property and along the train, noting that, in addition to the engine and tender, there were four wagons also either in the field or in the bit of no-man's-land between where the stops had been and the broken fence of the field. As far as I could ascertain in the dim light of the night sky, there appeared to be only two or three other wagons off the rails.

As I got towards the rear of the train, I heard shouting which I guessed was coming from the signal box on the other side of the tracks, but which was obscured by the wagons; then I heard another voice also shouting something to the effect of being alright , but guessing the engine had hit the stops. The first voice shouted something else, but all I managed to hear was, "Too fast". I called out then, saying that we were okay but were in the field. Then I saw the glow of a handlamp between the wagons and croaked, "Are you the guard?", as I scrambled between the wagons to confront the figure holding the lamp. "Of course I am", the figure replied. I suppose I heaved a sigh of relief, and said, "Christ, we thought you'd be dead". "Yes, that was a bloody rough shunt you gave me" he rejoined, "Did I hear you shout you were through the stops?" I explained as calmly as I could that we were not only through the stops, but also through the fence, and had ploughed up half of the farmer's field beyond.

I asked if he had seen the distant signal at green, but he replied that he had been sitting on the right-hand locker and had seen nothing. It seemed amazing to me that he appeared not to be hurt, but he later admitted he had been asleep on the locker and when the impact came he guessed he had merely slid along the locker before being dumped on the floor, wondering where the hell he was, his only injury being a bruised ankle, probably caused by an impact with a wall support or when he hit the floor. His biggest grievance was that his stove had toppled over with the impact and the reason why he had been so long in 'surfacing' was that he had tried to re-assemble it, the van being full of smoke, requiring the doors to be left open, and thus letting in the cold night air!

I told him I was going to the box to 'have a go' at the bobby, and he came with me. After my mouthing a few choice expletives when I got in the box, the signalman defended himself, saying that he had us signalled into the loop all the time in order to let a parcel train overtake us, and he showed us the entry in his log book. There was, of course, no way of knowing when that entry was made. The parcels train had apparently gone past as I was crawling out

of the field. I did not believe all that he said, but, without the backing of the guard, realised that Bill and I had no way of refuting what he alleged. What was asked of him at the subsequent enquiry, and what I had not thought of at the time, was why, after obviously hearing the whistling and the following impact, he had not attempted to stop the parcels train in case our train was fouling the running line. His reply was to the effect that he could see that the up slow line had not been affected.

As I was signing the log book, having placed the link over the loop signal to protect the train, we heard the engine whistle and I realised that Bill must be in some sort of difficulty. I left the box to return to the engine as I heard the guard asking the bobby to boil some water for tea as we were shaken up. He followed me down the steps, saying that he ought to see what had happened to 'his' train. When I got to the engine, it was to find Bill busy throwing out the fire with the clinker shovel. Without the injectors working, the water level in the boiler would soon get dangerously low. Luckily we were on a more or less even keel, plus, being submerged in the field as we were, no air was getting through the dampers, and as the fire appeared to be dying, there appeared to be no cause for immediate panic. However, I took over from Bill, who had, I noted, shovelled quite a lot of the coal from the footplate into the field, thus giving a reasonable space to stand comfortably to work the clinker shovel. He went to report to Control. Having finished baling out the fire, I put the clinker shovel back in its rack and sat on my seat. Suddenly I felt overwhelmingly tired and dejected – what a lousy end to what had been a very pleasant trip.

Eventually Bill returned, saying we were to go to the box and await instructions. He had apparently also blitzed the signalman, but the man had not altered his assertions. Control had, of course, been informed and assistance requested. There was nothing more we could do. We gathered our bags and coats together with Bill's handlamp (remarkably seemingly intact) from the locker, there being no sign of our bottles or my sandwich tin (they were probably under the coal or in the field somewhere) and made our way to the signal-box where the guard had made a can of tea, which, I might add, had never tasted sweeter. The guard imparted the news that an empty wagon train on the down slow would be stopped to give the three of us a lift back to Bletchley.

There being something of an atmosphere in the box, after I had also mashed my can of tea, we adjourned to the brake van – which was by now clear of smoke – and enjoyed the rest of the tea. It was indeed nectar. I had a mouth like the back end of a camel, and the guard had said that when he had seen us in the light of the signal box we looked like a couple of miners, so black were we. So, some twenty minutes later, the three of us scrambled into the brake van of the train which had been slowed for us, made our way to Bletchley, and thence to our respective home depots. Bill and I had to make written reports on our arrival at

Northampton shed, amid some rather ribald comments from colleagues who had heard of our misfortune via the 'grapevine'.

Then it was back to my digs on my bicycle, and some breakfast after I had filled the copper in the kitchen and lit the fire under it. But I had to wait until the children had gone to school, and auntie to her shopping, before I could drag the tin bath in from the yard and give myself a good wash down before falling into bed. I was too weary to trudge to the public baths.

The postscript to the episode is that some three weeks later, Bill and I, together with the guard and the signalman, were summoned to Rugby, where in a small room above the station our statements, together with the log book from Sears Crossing box, were examined. We were questioned in turn by the three men sitting behind a table. Also present, but taking no part, was the NUR representative, all four of us being in that union. After some deliberation, during which we all sat outside in a corridor, it was declared that the cause of the accident had been the lack of observation of the driver, coupled with the rather imprudent speed with which he entered the loop line. I could see the veins in Bill's

neck standing out, but he said nothing. I, too, was criticised for lack of observation and assistance to the driver in not bringing to his attention the speed of the train as we approached the loop. Our assertion that the signals had been altered was not accepted, although I swear to this day that that is what happened.

Bill and I were each to be deducted three days pay, spread over three weeks beginning in two weeks time. Although I considered it to be an unjust decision, it was a less severe way of imposing the sanction. The timing of the final deduction almost coincided with the removal of the engine from its rather undignified position in the field at Sears Crossing, where it had remained until a weekend closure of the slow lines could be arranged to facilitate the use of the Rugby and Willesden breakdown cranes.

I guess the loss of those three days pay hurt me almost as much as the later incident at that location hurt Her Majesty's Post Office. Just think, if the signal box and manually-operated signals had been retained at that location into the mid-sixties, the Great Train Robbery might never have happened!

Sears Crossing box, with the loop line the furthest to be seen (right). I don't think the 'bobby' standing on his verandah was the one I remember, but he looks just as supercilious – 'this domain is mine, I'm in charge' – as his colleague did.
COLLECTION MIKE WILLIAMS

This is Oxford Street. Letts Road was on the right, near where the distant car is seen parked. Rickard Street was the first on the left along Letts Road. The Gees' house was on the corner of Letts Road and Rickard Street.

G. ONLEY

CHAPTER FIFTEEN
SPECIAL LINK STILL

BILL Allen and I, although still rostered together, had weeks at a time when not working together. Bill was a deputy shed foreman and was so employed as and when necessary, which meant that at those times I was detailed to be mate to other drivers. About this time, too, I had left my uncle's house – with three growing children it was a little cramped – and taken lodgings with George Gee, one of the fire droppers at the shed, who lived in a street close to the loco shed, and where I was within easy reach of the 'knocker up'. Living outside the knocking-up area had meant I'd had to rely on my alarm clock to awaken me at some of the unearthly hours we had to book on for duty. Sometimes I had been so tired that I had slept through the sound of the alarm, and missed my duty, either attending the depot when I did eventually wake up, or, what was more usual, taking the day off as being sick. Now, I would have no excuse for not being on time for duty.

George, with his wife and two children, although living in an old house, had the luxury of an inside bathroom and toilet, and I had my own attic room. George, in addition to being employed by the railway, had his own 'business'. He owned a horse and cart with which he did general carting for various people, and he also had a large allotment on Hunsbury Hill. However, he did not grow things as such, but had a small piggery and a chicken run there, plus a motor-driven saw bench with which he cut up disposed-of railway sleepers which he bought cheaply from the CMD and sold them as firewood. It became my lot when off duty to give him assistance in both the sawing and the chopping of the chunks of sawn sleeper into kindling sticks and tying them into bundles to be hawked around the locality of Far Cotton. The best of the sleepers were sawn into planks for fencing, which was also quite lucrative. The horse and cart were also stabled at the allotments after their daily routine, so I sometimes helped with the feeding of the horse, chickens, and the pigs.

One of the perks of living at George's was that he occasionally had one of his pigs butchered, and he always had a side of bacon hanging at the top of the cellar steps, from which I was able to slice a couple of thick rashers, which, together with an egg (or two), made a tasty meal when arriving home from night duty, and before falling into bed. I think Mrs. Gee charged me £3 10s for my lodgings, about half of my weekly pay, which for a single man left me an adequate amount for my needs.

George's chickens were not the only providers of food for our table. When I was detailed to be with a driver on the local trip trains, it was often a case of not having enough room in my sandwich tin or bag in which to store produce I was given. Perhaps I should explain more fully. These 'trippers', usually of not more than half-a-dozen wagons, not only had wagons for, and shunted, the various station yards along whichever route they were operating, but also carried water for the several crossing keepers cottages situated at minor roads and farm tracks, etc. along that section of line. This water was conveyed in milk churns, usually stored on the verandah of the brake van, the train being stopped so the van was adjacent to the cottage, and, should the male occupant of the cottage not be at home (either out 'moonlighting' or poaching) when the train arrived, the fireman and the guard would carry the churn to the house and exchange it for the empty one which would be returned to the van. That done, the occupant of the cottage would invariably request some coal, which entailed reversing the train so the engine was at the cottage, and the fireman heaving a quantity of coal to the ground, usually enough to last until the next visit, but not enough to initiate investigation should it be seen by anyone in authority.

In exchange for this service, the lady of the house would very often provide a hatful of eggs, or perhaps mushrooms, tomatoes, or vegetables grown in their 'garden' scratched out of part of the lineside area. These goodies were shared between the three of us, which usually meant that at the end of the day we took home quite an amount of 'shopping'. I had heard of cases of the crossing keeper's wife or daughter offering other services too, but had no personal experience of such hospitality. Having seen the 'beauty' of some of them, all I can say is that one would need to be a desperate man to indulge!

One such 'crone' resided at a crossing-cum-smallholding not far from Rugby on the line to Coventry, and she was known among the footplate fraternity as 'Black Bess'. Although this crossing was not on a Northampton tripper route, it was well known that if a 'crow' on the whistle was given on the approach to the crossing, Bess would appear from her house, which was set back from the line, holding her skirts above her head, showing the scarcity of underwear in her wardrobe, and the infrequency of the water supply, or application thereof. However, footplate crews invariably lobbed a lump of coal in her direction as they passed, but she was quite spry even with (or because of) her skirts being held aloft, and I don't think she was ever hit!

While still rostered with Bill Allen, I had a month with Joe Placket (Bill Placket's older brother) in No. 6 Link, whose regular fireman was off sick because of a broken ankle sustained when his foot became caught in slipping coals when he was in the tender breaking coal, and he fell, twisting his trapped foot. Joe was a somewhat dour man, very different to his brother, but quite pleasant. He did enjoy his pint of ale, and seemed to have a nose for the nearest pub should we be held at signals anywhere in the vicinity of a village or hamlet with a hostelry not too far from the railway. He would tell me to "Give a crow when the bobby's ready", and off he would potter. I would do as he said, and he would be back on the footplate within five or six minutes, and we were on our way. Should I know that the location of the pub was ahead of us, after giving the crow, I would begin to ease the train towards where I knew

143

Blisworth again, with a train of empties in the down loop being passed by an express. A chalk train can also be seen in the sidings.

W. J. S. MEREDITH

he would appear at the lineside and he would scramble aboard as the train drifted past.

While with him we had several runs to Bescot, a suburb of Birmingham, and also to the Coventry/Nuneaton collieries – empties there and full wagons back – en route for London. This latter venue was also on Joe's rostered route schedule, as was Colwick and Beeston, both suburbs of Nottingham, which were both detailed as double-trip workings. However, the former was the only lodging location to which I went with Joe. Again, the trains consisted mainly of empty wagons with a few mixed freight wagons amongst them. The return trains were again a mixture of coal and general freight. The lodge at Colwick was with a lady who was a railway widow – as at Oxford some years previously – and her name, if I remember it correctly, was Mrs. Louise Black – "Louie to you fellows" she had said. Her home, which was in a terrace not far from the LNER shed, and not dissimilar to the Oxford house, was spotless, and we had our own rooms – luxury. I remember she also had a small dog on which she doted, and which on another occasion, when lodging there with another driver, Don Foster, received an undeserved scolding when Don surreptitiously placed an imitation turd on Mrs Black's freshly Blanco'd hearth in the living room one early morning.

Our engines over the route to Colwick and return were nearly always our old D's, or WD Austerities – 2.8.0 s – which were stabled at the LNE shed. On one of the days of that week we had failed our D engine at Colwick because one of the injectors would not work. On booking on that evening for our return trip, we were allocated an ex WD Austerity. What an old bone-shaker she turned out to be. Notwithstanding that, she was a reasonable steamer, and the footplate was far more comfortable than that of a D. All went well on that return journey. We were reversed into the sidings at Melton Mowbray to await the passenger train to Market Harborough, and as usual Joe disappeared to the 'local', leaving the usual instructions, while I filled the tank. He returned after hearing the 'crow', and we set off for Welham sidings where it was normal to shunt some wagons off, and pick up others. It was at Welham, while I was eating a sandwich, that one of the gauge glasses of the cylinder lubricator located on my side of the footplate suddenly shattered, showering me with hot water and oil. I grabbed my thick jacket hanging nearby and used it to try to block the steam, etc, gushing from the broken glass while I attempted to close the valve to the lubricator. That done, I examined my sore arm where the hot oil had quickly raised a blister. A handkerchief tied around it had to suffice until I reached home, and I had a sore arm and a scar for sometime afterwards. There should have been a wooden holder with spare glasses in one of the tender lockers, but no such luck this time, and we could not isolate the broken part without turning off the whole lubricator. With no cylinder lubrication, we weren't sure how she would behave, but decided to press on to Northampton, but while we filled the tank at 'Harborough Joe poured some thick oil down the blast pipe in the smokebox on the assumption that some would filter

down into the valves and cylinders. It must have worked because she made it to Northampton okay, but was certainly wheezing loudly by the time we got to the Up Sidings there. So, another failure. Two in one trip, not a good record.

It was while with Joe Placket that I learned of the little subterfuge operated by a crossing keeper close to Market Harborough. This crossing was near sidings used to store carriages, and the occupant of the cottage – which was normally lit by oil lamps and/or candles – had 'wired' his home for electricity. He 'acquired' some fittings and bulbs from within various carriages over a period of time, ran a hidden cable from the cottage to the sidings, and plugged into the battery box of any suitable carriage, making sure he disconnected the carriages before they were required for use. His deviousness was only 'officially' discovered some years later when the surveyor's staff called to discuss redecorating the cottage, although suspicion had been aroused when guards examining their train before departure to the station were frequently devoid of lighting because of flat batteries. Ingenious, eh? The railway hierarchy apparently didn't see it that way, and he and his wife lost their home and occupation.

It was towards the end of the 1940s that some excitement was generated among the footplate men when oil tanks were installed at our depot, adjacent to the water softening plant. The rumour that we were to be equipped with oil-burning engines quickly spread around the loco shed, and the thought of just turning a few handles instead of shovelling coal was looked forward to with some anticipation. Hopes were dashed, however, when, before oil was delivered or engines converted, a world shortage of oil frustrated the scheme.

One day I was with Jack Petit (brother of Fred) and we were shunting at the exchange sidings at Blisworth prior to taking a train to Woodford & Hinton on the old GCR via Towcester. We had one of the class 3 0-6-0 Midland-type engines. I liked the class 3s better than the 4s. They invariably steamed more freely, and appeared to be just as powerful. Anyway, Jack was talking with our guard, and I had alighted from the engine to stretch my legs and decided to walk along the shunting neck to where there was a large corrugated-iron structure, painted green, with emblazoned on two sides in large white letters – BBC – which, of course, attracted people's attention. However, the building had no connection with the national broadcasting service, but instead housed the Blisworth Bacon Company. I had often wondered what it was like inside, and this day saw that the door was ajar, so I ventured through the doorway. Inside were three or perhaps four large vat-type containers with mincing machinery going round in them driven by belts running on pulleys in the roof, and obviously worked by a diesel engine in an adjacent shed. There were two men in the building engaged in stirring the glutinous-looking mixture in the vats. I passed the time of day with them, and learned that it was sausage-meat in the vats. As we talked, and while I was looking at the machinery in the roof, I saw a rat running along the girders. As it jumped onto one of the spindles, it lost its footing and plummeted down into one of the vats. I shouted out what had happened, but the men merely laughed, and one said, "That's alright, he'll soon be mixed in". I left the building vowing never to eat sausages again – but of course I did, but not for a long time after that incident.

Bill Allen and I were back together on one occasion and were working a train from our Down Sidings to Bushbury, near Wolverhampton. Ours was a mixed traffic train of some fifty wagons, and as usual we had one of our many Ds, and it was night time. Leaving the yard at sometime after 2am, we knew we were following a train for Bescot headed by a 'Crab', which left the sidings a few minutes before us, so Bill took his time in leaving the sidings and progressing towards No. 5 box. Sure enough we were held at the signals there for some minutes before setting off again. We were also held at the colour light signal on the approach to Althorpe Park. I pushed the plunger on the lineside box to indicate to the bobby that we were at the signal, and settled on my seat, trying to keep warm as the wind whistled across the footplate. Both Bill and I were sitting facing each other – which was the most comfortable position on a D – and just talking and half dozing. We had been there for some twenty minutes, and were wondering what the fellow in front was doing to take so long in clearing the section, when there was a sudden movement on the steps of the engine and a hatless wild-eyed face appeared between the handrails mouthing "I'm in the field".

After helping the man onto the footplate and calming him with a drop of my still-warm tea, we learned that he was the guard of the train in front, which had been having problems in climbing the bank, seemingly with slipping as the guard said there had been a lot of snatching and buffering up as they slowly progressed. Suddenly there had been a vicious snatch, and almost at once he felt his brake van rolling backwards. Before he could apply his hand brake, he had careered through the trap points and plummeted into the nearby field, together with several wagons. The one nearest the brake van was a bogie bolster on which were rails, some of which had gone into the van following the impact in the field.

I got my torch from the locker, and we all went to see the carnage, the trap points being some hundred yards ahead of us. We could make out the wagons in the field by the light of my torch, but could also see that the trap points were fouled by two of the wagons, so there was nowhere for us to go except backwards. It was decided that I would go back to inform our guard, and he would have to walk back to No. 5 box to inform Control, and get assistance. When I got to our brake van, I found the guard asleep on the locker, as had the other guard been, no doubt, otherwise he would have been injured, or worse, by the rails which had impaled his vehicle.

After enlightening our guard of what was up ahead, I decided that I would walk back to No. 5 as I knew the score, and, taking his fog shots, I told him to go to the engine to inform Cock, while I put the shots down at the

appropriate places to protect the train. It was quite a walk, but I made good time as I had my torch. The signalman was not unduly surprised that something was amiss as it had taken so long for the Bescot train to clear the section ahead. Luckily, there was no train behind us at No. 5's signals, so Control quickly organised the Down Side shunt engine to approach our train and pull it back wrong line to the sidings. The wrong line order written by the bobby was handed by me to the driver of the shunt – Ernie Beasley, with whom I travelled to the rear of our train – the detonators echoing as we ran over them.

When we got to the train, the guard was back at his van and, after explaining what was to happen, he coupled the brake to Ernie's engine. Telling them we would give a crow when I got to our engine and acquainted Bill with the news, I made my way forward. On reaching the engine, it was to learn that the fireman of the Bescot train had walked back to find out what had happened, he and his driver suspecting the worst as they suddenly were able to pull their train easily. I was able to enlighten the guard, who was still sitting with Bill, that he was to inform his driver to take what was left of their train forward to Long Buckby where it would be stabled in the siding to await another brake van being provided. With that, we gave the crow, and began to drift back to the Down Sidings.

Once there, we learned that Control had decided that we should take our train to Market Harborough, where, with the assistance of the Banker engine, we would run round the train, the brake van being transferred to the other end, and make our way to Rugby, and onward from there. There was only one thing wrong with this decision as far as we were concerned – the journey from 'Harborough to Rugby would be tender first, and we had no blackout sheet on this occasion. So, Bill telephoned from the sidings box to the shed at 'Harborough requesting that the turntable road be kept clear in order that we could make use of it within the next hour. And that is what we did, also filling the tank while on the shed, before setting off once more in the direction of Rugby. As it happened, we were relieved there, and made our way home on the cushions. All in all quite an interesting night. Having the diversionary routes was so beneficial in those days, as indicated by the fact that we were able to make our way round the obstruction and get to the destination via a different line. As the railways were later fragmented, such escape routes became fewer and fewer.

We learned later that the Northampton breakdown train and crew attended the scene of the derailment, managing to move the wagons obstructing the line, allowing the platelayers to repair the points, etc. Those wagons in the field were left until the next weekend when the Rugby crane cleared the mess.

Bill and I continued to be rostered together through the end of the 40s and early 1950s, although not infrequently separated when Bill was on foreman duty. I suppose he must have been quite well appreciated in that capacity by those in command (meaning Control, etc.) as I remember that on one occasion he was able to convince them that his way of operating was the best. It happened, I think, in early 1950. We were detailed to go engine and brake to Banbury to collect a train comprising the contents of a farm, the farmer moving lock stock and barrel to somewhere in Lincolnshire, or Norfolk, I can't now remember which. We were to take the train as far as Peterborough. Our engine was 44491, and I had acquired one of the ever-diminishing number of blackout sheets, as we would be tender first for some part of the journey, with the inevitable discomfort that would entail on this somewhat cold day. Bill decided we should go tender first to Blisworth, engine first to Banbury, tender first back to Blisworth, and engine first to Northampton and continuing to Peterborough. We could then turn there before travelling back home as light engine.

All went as planned until we got to Banbury. There we discovered that the first vehicle of the train was a composite guards/luggage-van, in which the farmer and family were housed, together with what looked like most of their household furniture, and they wanted heat. The two young boys were happily ensconced on the guard seats on either side of the vehicle, whilst the adults were sitting on what was obviously their sofa. There was no steam heating pipe on the front of the engine, so we had to make use of the turntable, which luckily was still operative, although it was a shoulders-to-the-bar job. After getting water, we backed onto the train and I coupled up, connecting the heater and vacuum pipes, and making sure the vehicle behind the 'family' one was also screw coupled to prevent as much as possible the buffering-up and jolting which occurs on wagon trains.

Looking back along the train, which was in the cattle dock siding, I could see a long flat-bed wagon on which was a tractor, and what I supposed was the family car; also there were several cattle wagons, and sheeted open wagons. The brake van we had brought with us was now surplus to requirements as there was a brake van already attached at the rear of the train. The guard came to the engine to inform us that we had seventeen vehicles, nine of them being screw-coupled, and I helped him tighten these.

While I was so engaged, Bill had disappeared. When he reappeared some minutes later, he had the smirk on his face that I knew so well, and his ruddy cheeks were aglow with self-satisfaction. He explained that he had been phoning Control, because "if we go to Blisworth like this, once there, the farmer's family will be on the wrong end of the train, with no heat once we run round, and we will be tender first all the way to Peterborough. Control have agreed that it'll be better via Verney and Bletchley so we will be engine first all the way".

This news was met by the guard with something akin to dismay as he explained that he didn't know the road to Verney Junction. Bill told him not to worry as we would look after him should the necessity arise, and so we shortly set off on the journey to Peterborough. For my part I was looking forward to travelling on a line over which I had not been previously, but as I exchanged staffs at Cockley Brake Junction,

Bill shouted to the bobby, "How far does this take us?", and I realised he didn't know the road either! The signalman somewhat quizzically shouted after us, "Only as far as Brackley I'm afraid". Bill waved to him with a huge grin on his face, as if he was just pulling the man's leg, and we accelerated round the bend onto this new branch. "How do we know when we're getting towards Brackley", I queried. He replied in his usual pseudo nonchalant manner to the effect we should just look out for signals. At least I thought, we have brakes on the first four of our vehicles, including the coach next to the engine, so should be able to stop reasonably easily.

So in what seemed a very short time we saw signals and buildings in front of us, and Bill closed the regulator, and began braking slightly, although the signals were off. As I made ready to exchange the staff as we drifted through the station, and the bobby came down his steps to cross the line, Bill said, "Just say 'Buckingham next stop, eh', and see what he says?". I did as I was told as the staff was slapped into my hand, but the bobby just grinned and made his way back towards his box. "Ah well", said Bill, "I know Buckingham is on this line, and it's bigger than this place, so it's bound to have a box there". With that, he opened up again, and we trundled onwards. Soon we passed under what was obviously a railway bridge, which Bill guessed was the LNER line. Onwards again until I spotted another station on the horizon. Signals were off, and there appeared to be no passing loop, so we assumed there would be no signal-box. In fact the signals were obviously for the level crossing nearby, with another one not far away. The tiny station was Fulwell & Westbury which we saw on the name boards.

Buckingham was soon reached, a much larger town, and again Bill slowed down in order to get our bearings regarding the position of the signal box. It was similar to Brackley, being on the exit end of the station, and on the other platform. I exchanged staffs, with no comment, and we continued towards what we guessed would be Verney, and on to somewhat more familiar ground. One more little station eventually loomed up, but again we could see no passing loop or signals, so onwards we drifted, and were soon approaching what was obviously Verney Junction. We still had green signals, but Bill slowed down as we rounded the bend on to the Bletchley line, and I dropped off the staff to the bobby as he appeared near his box. Now it would be straightforward, both of us now knowing where we were, and where we were going.

At Bletchley, there was a short wait before we were signalled across to the down slow, and then a clear run to Roade – with a dip of the scoop at Castlethorpe troughs – and another short wait before being signalled to Blisworth, and down the bank to Northampton, and on through to Peterborough East, where a LNER engine was waiting on the old shed road to take the train forward. Another very heavy push round on the turntable, this one requiring inch perfect positioning for a non-heart-bursting exercise, but with the guard's help it was soon completed. Then with him on board we set off for home. Our guard, whom I only knew as Sid, thanked Bill for the trip over the Buckingham route, saying that he would sign for it when he got back to his office, to which Bill replied that he would too. This left Sid open-mouthed for a few seconds, until he realised – as he thought – that Bill was kidding. Bill never let on! I never said a word!

Our engine on that trip – 4491 – had steamed satisfactorily, but with such a light train one would expect it to. However, as we had turned onto the Oxford to Bletchley line at Verney Junction my mind had drifted back some three years or so, when, with the same engine I had experienced an anything but comfortable working day on a troop train from Oxford to Leicester. My driver on this day was 'Bud' Halford, and we had taken our train of ten coaches to Oxford where we were to be loaded with troops due for 'demob'. Even on the journey to Oxford I had been struggling to maintain anything like a full head of steam, so after shunting the train into the station road and going on shed to turn and get water, I had a good go at cleaning the fire and raking the ash pan. I even opened the smokebox door to ascertain if any tubes were blocked with a build-up of ash. All appeared clear in there.

The journey back to Bletchley could be described as traumatic. We stopped three times because of lack of steam, on what was fairly level going, and only limped along when we *were* moving. At Bletchley we were thankfully routed on to the slow line, and stopped in the station on the pretext of requiring water, and I was able to regain some steam with the blower hard on. After handing me the chain of the bag and turning on the water slightly, Bud disappeared somewhere. It was then that I became aware of several items of tablewear on the tender. I collected five metal mugs, and three knives, all obviously hurled at the engine by disgruntled men being delayed from leaving their life in His Majesty's armed forces. Strangely though, none of the men came to the engine while we were in Bletchley station. After I had turned off the water, and deposited the bag into its position by the column, Bud returned with what looked like links of a wagon coupling chain. He proceeded to take the 'wheel spanner' from our tool bucket, and with the appropriate other spanner opened the smokebox door. Having told me to turn off the blower, he placed the spanner across the blast pipe and hung the links on either end of the spanner so that they were hanging on opposite sides of the blast pipe. He tightened the lugs of the smokebox door, and said, "We'll see if that does any good to the cold old bastard".

By now the engine was blowing off steam, so, having still got our signals at green, we set off again. This was my first experience of being on a 'jimmied' engine, and I was not sure what to expect. I soon realised there was a strange roar, with almost a whistle, from the chimney, plus, I soon noted, a difference in the firebox. The fire appeared brighter, with the coals almost dancing as I fired over the half-opened flap door. The old girl's steaming was certainly much improved,

and she almost held her own against the injector as we roared our way along, but I was firing almost continuously to keep the back of the firebox built up. This I did not mind, because it was rewarding in that we now had enough steam to power the train along as was required. I topped the tank up over Castlethorpe troughs, and we had a good run down the bank through Hunsbury Hill tunnel and Northampton, thence onto the 'Harborough branch. We stopped for water at Market Harborough, as for some reason the engine appeared to be using more than one would expect. However, I had had no real problem with steaming since we had left Bletchley, and our journey to Leicester continued in a similar fashion. There, I quickly uncoupled and we went to the shed to turn. While I was operating the turntable Bud busied himself in removing the 'jimmy'. With the aid of the coal pick he deposited the two links by the side of the line, and with the shovel rescued our wheel spanner from where it had fallen in the ashes of the smokebox. It looked somewhat the worse for wear! With the tank filled again, we booked off shed and travelled light engine to Northampton and off duty. That was the only time I knowingly worked a jimmied engine, but had heard of it being a not unusual method of improving the performance of an engine, especially in the days before superheated steam. I can certainly vouch for its effectiveness on that occasion.

Bill and I also not infrequently had other little escapades when rules were slightly bent. One such incident was one night when we happened to be on 'shed turners' duties. These, as I think I have already explained, consisted of marshalling the engines on the shed roads in the order in which they would be required for their next turn of duty after they had been disposed (coaled, watered, fire cleaned, etc.) The final job of the night was to take the engine rostered for the morning train to Stratford-on-Avon, to Blisworth for the crew who were stationed there, and then make our way back to Northampton by the first train. On this particular day, Bill and I were wanting to travel to Walsall, on my motorcycle, to see the 'Cobblers' (Northampton) play in a cup match. We therefore wanted to end our shift as early as possible. Bill found out that the Blisworth driver was to be a man who was known as 'Weary Willie', who lived at the cottage adjacent to Rothersthorpe Crossing. At the appropriate time we booked the engine off shed, informing the bobby at Duston Junction West (via the phone) where we were going and what we intended, and travelled to the crossing. There Bill knocked on Willie's door, made sure he was awake, told him his engine was outside so he had better 'get his skates on', and we then walked back to the loco depot. We booked off some one and a half hours earlier than we would have had we worked 'by the book'. Our trip to Walsall was cold but pleasant – especially so as on the return journey we stopped at an hotel at Solihull kept by Bill's sister, where we enjoyed much appreciated hospitality. The Cobblers? Oh, the usual performance!

CHAPTER SIXTEEN

ANOTHER CHANGE OF DRIVER

Willesden Loco Depot in 1947. No. 3527 is typical of the old Midland class 2 freight engines used for station pilot and for empty stock movements at Euston. They were not infrequently used for banking the train up Camden Bank after having earlier brought the stock into the platform.

H. C. CASSERLEY

DURING the winter of 1950/51 I lost one Bill and re-found another. I left Bill Allen and was posted with Bill Placket again.

It was during this period that the LM(R) were experimenting with the two new diesels – 10000 and 10001 – on various types of trains following their use on the Scottish expresses. One night Bill and I had eventually reached Willesden with a wagon train and had deposited the engine on the shed by about 3am. We were already on overtime, and were told to make our way home by whatever means were available. Together with a set of Bletchley men who were in a similar situation, we made our way to the canteen for a snack, and to await the Old Oak Common to Rugby semi-fast goods which was usually headed by one of our old Ds. It was the normal custom for the driver of this train – which invariably was utilised by homeward-bound crews from Bletchley, Northampton, and Rugby to travel in the brake van – to give a crow on the whistle when he received the green signal from the junction. This gave time for the crews to finish their drinks, amble out to the lineside, and scramble into the van without too much trouble as the train slowly rumbled past. On this particular night we heard a long hoot, not unlike the sound of a class 8 whistle, and thought the driver had forgotten to sound a crow. We left the canteen a little more quickly than normal, realising that an 8 would probably pick up the train more quickly than a D, and so were spaced along the track, giving each man time enough to readily grab a handrail and run before leaping for the running board in the dark, and so not impede the next

man. As we stood there in our positions, we could see the running lights of the train – middle up and down – as it approached in the distance, but could not see any plume of smoke and steam silhouetted in the lights of the yard. It dawned on us then that the engine was a diesel, and my, what a diesel. Instead of the normal eight to ten mph of the steam engine's approach, this train's brake van was travelling at about thirty mph as it passed us – with the guard on his verandah shouting, "I'll have a bit of peace tonight – cheerio fellers". So, it was back to the canteen for a while to await the first electric into Euston, and later, a more comfortable ride home in a passenger train. Another 'little earner'!

I was by this time almost twenty-three, the youngest age one could be a driver, only three places of seniority from being made a 'passed fireman', and was studying reasonably well for this eventuality. However, as we lost more work through the increase in road traffic, and the beginning of line closures, the 'dead man's shoes' syndrome began to take effect. I remained those frustratingly close three places away from being a passed fireman until I left the railway some four years later.

It was during this period of the early 1950s (probably 1952 in my case) that several of the single firemen at Northampton were seconded to Willesden and also Wellingborough for periods of duty. I had two sessions of a month each at Willesden, lodging in the dreaded hostel, which to my pleasant surprise had been improved somewhat since my early experiences of its squalor. However, I did not eat there, as since the end of the war a new canteen had been

May 1945, and the end of the war in Europe, saw many ex-WD 'Austerities' going to the Continent for use on the very depleted system over there, and others returning to Britain for refurbishment and redeployment. Two are shown here in the roundhouse at Willesden, together with a Black Five and a 'Crab'.
H. C. CASSERLEY

A line-up of Midland class 2 engines in the up side carriage sidings at Euston, awaiting their call to collect the stock of trains that had arrived at the terminus in 1946. This was the time when we ate our 'snap' and when the cheeky sparrows would descend on the footplate.
H. C. CASSERLEY

built adjacent to the loco shed, and I had also found a hostelry not far north of the railway where one could partake of very reasonably priced meals. Norman Quennell (who was one of those seconded at the same time as myself) and I used to enjoy a game of dominoes with the locals there during the evenings, if our shifts coincided. It was while at Willesden that I took to wearing a clip-on bow tie (my attempt at being 'jack-the-lad' I suppose), but very soon disposed of this item of apparel because of the ribbing I received from the Londoners. "Oo's the geezer wiv the flutterbye?" would be a common remark, or "Oo's 'e think 'e is, bleedin' Antny Eden?". I would furtively unclip the offending article and stuff it in my pocket after hearing such comments, but I did wear it for quite a time when back at Northampton.

Our duties while at Willesden were mainly on the carriage shunters/bankers at Euston, although I did have a few runs on the North London Line to Devons Road, to where we mainly took wagons of coal, and returned with empties. Again the drivers with whom I was detailed were mainly older men, although a couple of times I had a passed fireman as my driver. I never really grasped where we were in relation to the areas of London, as nearly all of these journeys were in the dark, plus we appeared to go via varying routes on occasions, but I did relate to Hackney when we went through it, as one of the evacuee girls with whom I was friendly during the war came from there. There were also

trips to Broad Street yard, near Liverpool Street station, with cattle trains, the animals in which, I was told, were due for the nearby abattoir, and from there to Smithfield meat market. A mixed bag of engines were employed over these routes from Jinties through Midland class 4s to Ds and Stanier 8s. Other trips were to what I was told were exchange sidings at Acton on the Western Region, and to a similar siding at Sheepcote Junction on the Southern.

The days spent in the bustling activities of the Euston area were quite interesting, and not without amusement. These duties entailed pulling the coaches off recently arrived trains and taking them to the carriage sidings to be serviced, marshalling other trains and taking them into the station at whichever platform they were required. There we had time to leisurely watch the prospective passengers arriving, sometimes with someone to see them off – many an affectionate embrace was witnessed at those times; then, should it be required, banking the train up Camden Bank (one in seventy-seven or so) to Primrose Hill Tunnel, before making the way back towards Euston, either via the shed roads, or via the 'subway' route to the up side carriage shed road. Refreshment time when on these duties was quite amusing as the local sparrows would congregate on the handrails of our engine – usually these would be a Midland type 2 0–6–0, or a 2–6–2 tank – which, with this latter type of engine, surprised me even more at the audacity of these feathered

Euston again, after rebuilding, with one of the more modern tank engines which gradually replaced the old class 2 freight engines, waiting to bank the train out of platform 14. The fireman on these workings had to be very circumspect, in that he had to have enough fire and steam for the job in hand, but not cause either smoke or noise within the station. Not always easily done.

R. J. ESSERY

Unrebuilt 'Baby Scot' No. 5510 on the early evening commuter train to Bletchley, leaving Platform 7 or 8 at Euston in 1959. COLLECTION R. S. CARPENTER

Near the top of Camden bank, with, on the right, the engine line from the shed, then what was sometimes called the carriage roads, to the left of which we see the self-evident electric line into Euston (from which a branch went off left under the bridge at left foreground). The up and down fast and slow lines feature in the top left. I hope my memory serves me something near correctly – apologies if I'm wrong. D. LAWRENCE

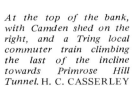

At the top of the bank, with Camden shed on the right, and a Tring local commuter train climbing the last of the incline towards Primrose Hill Tunnel. H. C. CASSERLEY

Saltley in April 1956. H. C. CASSERLEY

Cricklewood on 6th June 1954.
COLLECTION R. J. ESSERY

friends, who would come right inside the footplate of the tank engine, and seemingly be almost ready to perch on the sandwich tin and help themselves if they were not given the requisite amount of crumbs with the required alacrity.

The Wellingborough secondment was entirely different, but was only for three weeks. Being only ten miles from Northampton, I was able to reside at home (my father had cancer and so had to relinquish his pub landlord occupation and my family had returned to Northampton), and travel to Wellingborough for duty. Even if my shifts did not coincide with suitable passenger trains by which I could travel to and fro, I had my motorcycle and often used that for conve-

nience sake. It was while employed on this secondment that I was introduced to firing on Garratts.

These really were 'rock burning monsters' (a name often given by LNW men to the way Midland men thrashed their Jubilees over the hills on the Midland main line). The Garratts had such a deep firebox that one could shovel a couple of tons of coal into it without it showing any signs of getting up to the rim plate! However, the three that I fired during this period were good steamers, and the trips to Kentish Town and return were no great hardship – except when on one occasion the revolving coal bunker (on I think 7994) jammed as I was turning it, and stuck just about half

Berkhamsted in August 1948.
H. C. CASSERLEY

Three of the Garratts on which I worked while seconded to Wellingborough.   H. C. CASSERLEY

way round. It took the driver, Horace Clarke, several minutes to free it again. In the meantime I was restricted to firing by hand with the largest pieces of coal I could pull from within the bunker. Luckily it was on a return trip with a string of empties, so the engine was not working too hard. However, it was somewhat disconcerting, and certainly put me off utilising that mechanism for getting coal forwards in the bunker. The others were (again if my scrawl in my old diaries I have read correctly), 7970 and 7981, all of them Toton (18A) engines.

Another journey was also memorable, although for a different reason. This one was with a class 8 (48191–15A) on a train of iron ore for Clay Cross in the north of Nottinghamshire, and was via the Corby, Melton Mowbray, and Nottingham line. My driver this day was named Arthur Glazebridge, a man in his late thirties who was still a passed fireman. After preparation of the engine and booking off shed, we picked up the train at Finedon Road sidings. From there, with only thirty-eight and a brake, we made good progress through Kettering, and on to the branch line at Glendon Junction. However, when we got to Corby we were stopped by signals at the station, and approached by the station master who informed us that the signalman at Gretton had reported a door of a carriage of a train in front of us being open, and it was feared that someone had fallen from that train in Corby Tunnel. We were to be joined by a couple of men – a porter and a platelayer – and to go slowly to, and through, the tunnel in case there was a body in there. I naively enquired if we should take a stretcher from the station 'first aid' store-box, whereupon the platelayer said, "If someone's fallen out of an express in the tunnel we'd be better taking a couple of buckets or a sack". I kept quiet after that rebuff. However, armed with what appeared to be a car headlamp wired to a car battery, and, I noted, a couple of sacks, the platelayer squatted on the framing of the engine by the side of the smokebox, while the porter rode on the footplate, and off we gently went at no more than walking pace. As we entered the tunnel the 'headlamp' was switched on, and we on the footplate craned our necks to look forward in anticipation of seeing something gruesome. Nothing; not an

arm or leg, or even a pool of blood. As we emerged from the other end of what I guessed was the mile and a half long tunnel, I suppose we all emitted a collective sigh of relief at not having to be involved in the task of retrieving bits of a human body. There was nothing of note along the line from the tunnel to Gretton station.

On arrival at Gretton our findings, or rather lack of them, were relayed to the station staff and thence to the signalman. The porter and the platelayer, together with his artefacts, adjourned to the opposite platform to await transport back to Corby, and we prepared for our journey onwards. This we shortly did, and were soon trundling along Harringworth Viaduct which spans the River Welland valley, but looks far more imposing from the Market Harborough to Peterborough line which passes (I should say 'passed' as this line now does not exist) under a bridge just north of the end of the viaduct. These were another couple of tunnels before reaching Oakham, where we were informed that the express from which it had been feared someone had fallen, had been examined at Melton Mowbray, and the open door had been found to have a defective lock.

After filling the tank, we trundled on – through Melton (under the old GN/LNW line to Nottingham), where we had to back into the sidings to allow a passenger train to overtake us, and on to what I was informed by driver Arthur was West Bridgford, before entering the environs of Nottingham itself. Here we appeared to go round the city on its westerly side, until we reached Radford, where we were unexpectedly relieved by a set of Kirkby-in-Ashfield men.

Having reported to Control, we were told to make our way home 'on the cushions', which, bearing in mind we had nearly eight hours duty done, was not unexpected. An altogether eventful day, and a day on which I had seen a little more of the vast network of railways that existed at that time. I did get to Clay Cross eventually, but it was when I was back at my home depot, and was via the Midland main line, with a train originating, I believe, from the newly re-opened quarries on the Blisworth to Towcester branch.

CHAPTER SEVENTEEN
THE BEGINNING OF THE END

BY the 1950s several branch lines were closing, or losing their passenger services, whilst sometimes retaining a spasmodic freight service. Two such closures that affected train crews at Northampton, and of course the Blisworth men, were those of the Banbury branch, and the Stratford-upon-Avon branch – or more especially our end of it as far as Woodford Halse. Soon to be gone for ever were those pleasant days out along these lines, with a one- or two-coach train, waiting at stations should a regular passenger be a little late, or someone had phoned to say they were bringing a parcel that they wanted to catch that particular train; or shunting off a wagon or two here, picking up others there, and collecting a few eggs or mushrooms, and/or garden produce in exchange for a few knobs of coal. Making friends with the albino blackbird at Byfield, who loved Spam, or watching the kingfishers swooping along the stream at Helmdon was another pleasant diversion, especially during summer days. The workings of those two branches of the 'Dilly Dally', as we used to call them, epitomised what life was like on a country railway, now sadly but a memory for those privileged to have experienced it.

However, there were still plenty of freight workings on the lines around Northampton, and beyond, as shown by the following list of my duties during three months or so of 1951 while in the special link with Bill Placket. (Bill was driver unless otherwise stated.)

Day/Date Hours worked	Engine/Shed	Destination	Train Type	Driver
Mon. 15.1.51	8136 of 18B	Wigston	Mixed Goods	Bill Placket
10.30am to 5.50pm (7.20)	8915 of 1C	Northampton	Light Engine	
Tues. 16.1.51	8365 of 15A	Leicester	Coal Empties	
9.40am to 5.55pm (8.15)				
Wed. 17.1.51	8614 of 16A	Leicester	Coal Empties	
6.40am to 4.25pm (9.45)				
Thurs. 18.1.51	5371 of 12A	Rugby	Fitted Goods	
2.30pm to 9.30pm (9.00)	5025 of 1A	Northampton	Empty Stock	
Fri. 19.1.51	8534 of 4B	Up Side	Shunting	
12.15pm to 8.05pm (7.50)				
Sat. 20.1.51	8194 of 18A	Leicester	Coal empties	
9.10am to 8.50pm (11.40)				
Mon. 22.1.51	8927 of 2B	Bletchley	Coal	
6.35am to 4.25pm (9.50)	8915 of 1C	Northampton	Mixed Goods	
Wed. 24.1.51	8658 of 1A	Leicester	Coal Empties	
2.45am to 2.05pm (11.20)				
Thurs. 25.1.51	9126 of 8A	Rugby	Mixed Goods	
2.15am to 10.40am (8.25)				
Fri. 26.1.51	90323 of 38A	Bletchley	Coal	
12.55am to 12.50pm (11.55)				
Sat. 27.1.51	8176 of 18A	Bletchley	Coal	
1.00am to 7.00am (6.00)	8141 of 15B	Northampton	Iron Ore Empties	
Sun. 28.1.51	7299 of 4B	Bridge Street	Shunting	
1.40am to 8.35am (6.55)				
Mon. 29.1.51	5004 of 2A	Rugby	Mixed Goods	
1.30am to 12.50pm (11.20)				
Tues. 30.1.51	8493 of 18D	Rugby	Mixed Goods	
1.00am to 8.45am (7.45)				
Wed. 31.1.51	8674 of 3A	Bletchley	Mixed Goods	
4.00am to 1.40pm (9.40)				
Thurs. 1.2.51	2931 of 1A	Leicester	Mixed Goods	
7.50am to 4.25pm (8.35)				
Fri. 2.2.51	8634 of 1A	Leicester	Coal Empties	
4.55am to 2.35pm (9.40)				
Sat. 3.2.51	8324 of 18A	Leicester	Coal Empties	
6.40am to 6.15pm (11.35)				
Mon. 5.2.51	3453 of 18A	Leicester	Coal Empties	
7.50am to 5.00pm (9.10)	8493 of 18D	Northampton	Coal	
Tues. 6.2.51	2747 of 1A	Wigston	Mixed Goods	
7.50am to 7.40pm (11.50)	9145 of 1C	Northampton	Coal	
Wed. 7.2.51	2812 of 1A	Leicester	Mixed Goods	Cliff Breakspear
7.50am to 6.55pm (11.05)	9448 of 4A	Northampton	Coal	
Fri. 9.2.51	3795 of 18A	Leicester	Coal Empties	Bill Placket
7.50am to 4.25pm (8.35)				
Sat. 10.2.51	8656 of 1A	Kilsby Bridge	Coal Empties	
7.50am to 3.45pm (7.55)	9432 of 2B	Northampton	Coal	
Sun. 11.2.51	9270 of 4B	Rugby Branch	Local Ballast	Sid Clarke

Date	Hours	Engine	Destination	Work	Driver
Mon. 12.2.51	7.45am to 3.45pm (8.00)	3821 of 18A	Leicester	Coal	Bill Placket
Tues. 13.2.51	12.40pm to 10.55pm (10.15)	3820 of 18A	Leicester	Coal Empties	
Wed. 14.2.51	12.40pm to 3.40am (15.00)	9287 of 4A	Bletchley	Coal	
Thurs. 15.2.51	3.50pm to 1.55am (10.05)	9323 of 1C	Northampton	Mixed Goods	
	2.05pm to 9.55pm (7.50)	8426 of 4B	Northampton	Breakdown Train	
Fri. 16.2.51		8638 of 18A	Leicester	Coal Empties	
Sat. 17.2.51	12.40pm to 10.45pm (10.05)	90672 of 38A	Bletchley	Coal	
Mon. 19.2.51	3.30pm to 1.35am (10.05)	8325 of 1A	Market Harboro.	Coal Empties	
Tues 20.2.51	7.28am to 4.35pm (9.07)	4287 of 15C	Market Harboro.	Coal Empties	
	10.10am to 6.10pm (8.00)	90122 of 38A	Northampton	Coal	
Wed. 21.2.51		8081 of 16C	Leicester	Coal Empties	
Thurs. 22.2.51	12noon to 10.45pm (10.45)	531 of 9D	Bletchley	Parcel train	
Fri. 23.2.51	11.55am to 7.00pm (7.05)	8362 of 18A	Bletchley	Coal	
	9.00am to 5.15pm (8.15)	9323 of 1C	Northampton	Mixed Goods	
Mon. 26.2.51		8476 of 1A	Rugby	Coal Empties	
	10.30am to 5.35pm (7.05)	8195 of 18A	Northampton	Coal	
Tues. 27.2.51		8625 of 15A	Irthlingborough	Iron Ore Empties	
	9.40am to 5.25pm (7.45)	8151 of 15A	Bletchley	Iron Ore	
Wed.28.2.51		8387 of 18A	Leicester	Coal Empties	
	6.40am to 4.25pm (9.45)	4713 of 2A	Northampton	Fitted Freight	
Thurs. 1.3.51		8304 of 18A	Leicester	Coal Empties	
Fri. 2.3.51	2.30pm to 10.45pm (8.45)	9271 of 4B	Up Side	Shunting	
Sat. 3.3.51	12.35pm to 8.05pm (7.30)	8200 of 18A	Leicester	Coal Empties	
Mon. 5.3.51	9.10am to 8.40pm (11.30)	3804 of 18A	Blisworth	Light Engine	Bud Halford
	2.30am to 11.50am (9.20)		Irthlingborough	Iron Ore Empties	
Wed. 7.3.51		8658 of 1A	Leicester	Coal Empties	Bill Placket
Thurs. 8.3.51	2.45am to 12.10pm (9.25)	9433 of 2A	Bletchley	Mixed Goods	
Fri. 9.3.51	12.55am to 11.00am (10.05)	90369 of 38A	Bletchley	Coal	
Sat. 10.3.51	12.55am to 1.40pm (12.45)	90122 of 38A	Bletchley	Coal	
Mon. 12.3.51	1.50am to 12.25pm (10.30)	8445 of 4B	Blisworth	Light Engine	
	1.30am to 9.25am (7.55)		Irthlingborough	Iron Ore Empties	
Tues. 13.3.51		8445 of 4B	Rugby	Mixed Goods	
	12.30am to 8.15am (7.45)	5017 of 8A	Northampton	Mixed Goods	
Wed. 14.3.51		8657 of 1A	Bletchley	Coal	
Thurs. 15.3.51	4.00am to 1.55pm (9.55)	8626 of 1A	Wigston	Coal Empties	
	7.50am to 4.45pm (8.55)	8602 of 1A	Northampton	Coal	
Fri. 16.3.51		4287 of 15C	Wigston	Coal Empties	
	4.55am to 2.10pm (9.15)	8610 of 1A	Northampton	Coal	
Sat. 17.3.51		8196 of 18A	Leicester	Coal Empties	
Mon. 19.3.51	6.40am to 4.20pm (9.40)	8433 of 1A	Leicester	Coal Empties	
Tues. 20.3.51	7.50am to 5.45pm (9.55)	5495 of 8B	Rugby	Mixed Goods	
Wed.21.3.51	7.50am to 3.35pm (7.45)	8628 of 1A	Leicester	Coal Empties	
Sat 24.3.51	7.50am to 4.35pm (8.45)	8518 of 1A	Market Harboro	Coal Empties	
	7.50am to 6.00pm (10.10)	8642 of 19A	Northampton	Coal	
Tues. 27.3.51		8709 of 15C	Leicester	Coal Empties	
Wed.28.3.51	12.40pm to 9.30pm (8.50)	8102 of 16A	Market Harboro.	Coal Empties	
	12.40pm to 9.35pm (8.55)	9126 of 1C	Northampton	Coal	
Thurs. 29.3.51		8325 of 1A	Leicester	Coal Empties	
Fri. 30.3.51	1.25pm to 2.00am (12.35)	9385 of 2B	Wellingboro.	Local Tripper	
Sat. 31.3.51	2.10pm to 9.55pm (7.45)	90491 of 38D	Willesden	Coal	
	3.30pm to 9.20am (17.50)				

The work had become mundane on most of the duty shifts – a far cry from those days when I first began firing, when each day was looked upon as something of an adventure. The shifts that footplate men were called upon to work were, I would hazard a guess, some of the worst of any industry in the world, and for a young man were very detrimental to any sort of social life he might wish to follow. However, because of the amount of overtime accrued, wages were relatively good, and mine averaged between £7 and £9 per week during the final few years of my railway service – certainly much more than I received when I joined the police force in 1956.

One of the regular night time workings was the 'ghost train', called as such because it always ran at night, and rarely brought attention to itself because it flitted along at a fairly fast speed for a wagon train. This, as far as I can recall, was the precursor of the fully vacuum-brake-fitted wagon trains, and consisted of about 16 forty-ton hopper wagons loaded with crushed coal, which ran from Toton to Stonebridge Park railway power station, which mainly provided electricity for the LMS/BR(M) electric line from Euston to Watford.

This was a double-trip lodging job for Toton men, but on the odd occasion when some hold-up occurred, creating exceptional delays, the men were relieved en route, usually at Northampton. Then, depending on the dictum from Control, they either had to continue forward on the cushions for lodging and their return working (the usual option), or return home on the cushions if they were very much on overtime. Whichever way Control decided did not please them as it curtailed both their overtime aspirations and also their mileage money. However, one morning I was with Arthur Cherry and we relieved the Toton men at No. 3 Box at about 7am, they already being on overtime. Apparently they had been delayed several hours by a derailment at Wigston, near Leicester. Our engine was a class 8, and, after

The engine board now appears to be on the canal side wall of the shed. In my time at the loco it was on the wall to the right (off picture) at right-angles to the present position, and between the booking-on lobby and the door to the office and Gaffer's office. The structure on the right of the picture is unknown to me.
G. ONLEY

filling the tank, we were soon away and up the bank to Roade. It was often usual for this train to be routed via the main line once that location was reached, but as it was now 'commuter time' of the day, and also the time when the over-night sleepers were approaching London from the north, we were kept to the slow line. Notwithstanding this fact, we made very good time as far as Tring, and had been galloping along at between what I estimated as 40 to 50mph. The engine was steaming well, and the ride really comfortable. A well-kept Toton engine – 8201 I believe.

From Tring we were obviously on the block behind a local passenger train, and Arthur reduced our speed in order to tally with it as near as possible. In spite of us being slightly delayed because of this, we arrived in the sidings at Stonebridge Park before 10am, but even so the delayed arrival of the coal had been noticed, and we were quickly uncoupled, whereupon one of the shunting diesels was soon on scene and busy with the unloading procedure.

Having taken the engine on Willesden shed, and snacked in the canteen, we were detailed to relieve a train of empty wagons from Devons Road bound for Toton which was coming from the North London Line. In less than an hour of arriving at Willesden we were on our way home – but this time with one of their old Ds – 9122. Our run home was uneventful, but as we descended the bank from Roade, Arthur chuckled to himself and commented that should it be

Midland men who relieved us it would no doubt be amusing to see their long faces when they saw the class of engine they had. As it happened, it was a set of our own men who took over from us at Northampton, and we made our way back to the loco shed and off duty.

One of the most fascinating engines that used to ply to and from Euston was 6202 – the 'turbomotive' as it was called. Should you be trundling along the slow line during the night and about to be overtaken by a train headed by this engine, even though it could not be seen, you should always know it was that particular engine because of the unique sound it made – a sort of fluttering air vibration. Unfortunately, it was frequently out of service because of malfunctions, and was finally converted to a normal type of engine, but its new life was short-lived as it was one of the engines involved in the crash at Harrow in 1952 and was cut up.

That incident caused havoc on the lines to and from London. I happened to be with Bill Gadsden on that foggy night, and we were working a wagon train to Willesden, but were stuck at Tring for hours before finally being relieved by Bletchley men who had been sent to us by bus. We too had to utilise that form of transport to make our way back to Bletchley, and thence home via the brake van of a train from Oxford. Another eighteen-hour day, but thankful we had not been trundling through Harrow & Wealdstone at the moment of that horrific accident.

CHAPTER EIGHTEEN

THE FREIGHT LINKS

IN April 1951 I was posted with George Iliffe in No. 7 link, the first of the 'goods links'. The work was very similar to that of No. 8 link – the Special Link, although there were some slightly more diverse routes over which we operated on occasions, and we would be on the same working all of the week – most weeks. George was a man in his fifties, with a very sardonic sense of humour, and was frequently attempting to 'wind people up'. Although I did not get many driving 'turns', we got on really well and I enjoyed my time with him. In May, George went on holiday, and for the first week I had Jack Pettit as my driver. On the 17th while shunting at Banbury with engine 4491, we knocked over the shunter and it was feared he had suffered internal injuries. He was taken to hospital by ambulance, and of course more writing ensued. Next day, to everyone's relief, we learned that his injuries were not too serious, and in fact he was back on duty in less than two weeks. Apparently the accident occurred when, after shunting off one wagon into a siding, he had operated the points for us to back into another siding, and was crossing over the line behind the engine as we set slowly back. His shunting pole hook became caught under the rail somehow and stopped his forward motion. Before he could extricate the pole – or more sensibly drop the pole – he was hit by the buffer, luckily knocking him out of the path of the engine. Neither Jack, nor myself had seen the incident, and only became aware something was amiss when we heard his shout.

The second week of George's holiday I had Stan Richards as driver. Luckily nothing untoward happened that week. The following week, however, when George had returned, we were on the Rugby local tripper. On the Thursday, while shunting the sidings at Long Buckby with engine 9030, we were directed into a siding which had more wagons in than we thought, the consequence being that the stops were pushed back about a yard beyond their original position. Apart from there being a rather heavy buffering up, we knew nothing about it until the guard came to the engine with the information. More writing!

Another incident occurred in early June. That week's working was on mixed freight trains, firstly from Northampton to Wellingborough, and a return working with a similar train through to Rugby. On the Tuesday we had engine 8638 of 18A to Wellingborough, and returned with 5316 of 4A. All went well until we arrived at Northampton, where, as we negotiated the points near No. 2 box, she became derailed and we came to a sudden stop. Fortunately, we were travelling slowly and only the bogie wheels had come off the road. The local breakdown train, with Archie Harris and the gang, were not long in arriving on scene, having travelled wrong road from No. 1 box via the middle road. With astute use of wooden packing by the gang, and equally astute use of the regulator, George was able to reverse our engine and relatively light train and so regain the rails. Examination of the points revealed that a sheared bolt had somehow fouled the trailing points, causing our bogie wheels to jump the track. The fitters gave the okay as far as our bogie alignment was concerned, and we eventually continued our journey to Rugby. Once there and on the shed, George reported the incident in order that the bogie truck could be properly tested before the engine might be utilised on a fast train. That was the only day of that week that we made any overtime!

Again, although rostered with a regular driver, it was not unusual to have several different drivers during a month's workings. During the time I had George Iliffe for my mate, on occasions I had other drivers for the odd day, or perhaps longer – George did like his days off for attending race meetings! Some of these men were Jack Pettit, Stan Richards, Ken Allan, Fred Elliott, Pete Craddock, Bill Constable, Trevor Jarrett, and Harry Mann.

My time with George did not last long, and in July I was back with Bill Placket in No. 8 link – with our workings mainly as listed previously. We continued together until the latter part of the year with nothing of note occurring during that time, except that my father died during the autumn. In the spring of 1952 I began my secondment to Willesden and later to Wellingborough, about which I have already written.

In January 1953 I was posted with George Carter, back in No. 7 link, and so resumed more or less regular weeks workings, although during this month I had Punch Pointer as my driver while George was learning the road to, I think, Stratford. In February while on a mixed freight from Willesden to Beeston with 4480 of 16A, we failed at Wigston with a hot crank pin in the driver's side crosshead. She was making a terrible noise as we descended the bank from Kibworth. With the train stabled in the loop, we took her on the shed and prepared another engine, 4034 of 15C, and worked our train forward to Leicester, where we were relieved and sent home on the cushions.

It was during this early part of the year, while we were working an empty wagon train to Toton and were 'on the block' after we had passed Kegworth and approaching Trent Junction, that water was flooding over the railway, and was nearly up to rail height. As we stood at the signal, we could see eels swimming along the 'six-foot'. George was all for taking the shovel and bucket and trying to catch one or two, but when he tested the depth of the water with his boot, he realised he would soon have wet feet, so abandoned his thoughts of an eel pie for supper.

March 1st saw me on a Sunday excursion to Leeds with Frank Paling, for an advertised visit to the Variety Palace. This was a usual 'short rest' double-trip working. The engine was 5091 – one of our own – but she was in poor order, so what should have been a pleasant day turned out not to be so. She was a very rough rider, and not a brilliant steamer either. Even Frank said that she was a 'green bastard', after trying his hand on the shovel.

The rest of the week with George we were on the Bescot run, changing trains with Bescot men at Coventry and working back to Northampton. Engines were: Monday 8713 (3A) & 5394 (2A); Tuesday 8679 (3A) & 4862 (2A); Wednesday 8766 (3A) & 4713 (2A); Thursday 8705 (3A) & 8441 (2E); but on Friday we had 5738 *Samson* (3B), obviously being worked towards her home shed, and we returned with 2787 (1A).

On Saturday we had 8716 (2B) on a Stetchford train. I was under the weather and felt as if I had the flu. In fact George did nearly all the work. Thankfully we came home on the cushions, and the 'flu' turned out to be something the medical profession called 'erythema nodosum', an illness initially associated with rheumatic fever, and I had five weeks off work before joining George again.

On my return to work on the 13th of April, I was surprisingly still rostered with George Carter, but was posted on late turn (2–10pm) disposing until I was seen by the railway doctor on Friday at Euston (Drummond Street). I was passed fit by the doctor, and back with George the following week on the Peterborough tripper with engines 4242, 4391, 64288, 64397 (both ex LNER) and 8422.

At the end of April I was again rostered with George Iliffe, still in 7 Link, but George was off duty, so I was on shed duties for one of the days. On the following day, the 28th, I was with Stan Watts on double-trip Manchester with engine 4867 (2A) there and 2925 (1A) back that night. A very pleasant trip, although the lodge seemed to have deteriorated somewhat since my last visit. I was still awoken by the sea lions! The rest of the week George and I were on Willesden coal trains with engines 8679, 8205 (both 1A), and 8361 (18A). And so we continued, working through the link's twelve weeks duties – runs to Willesden (maybe cut short at Bletchley), Birmingham (various locations), and Nottingham (Toton or Beeston, with the possibility of only getting as far as Leicester).

During this time I was not always with George. Other drivers with whom I worked included Les Agutter, Edgar Williamson, Wilf Saunders, George Quartermain and Joe Briddon. It was while with Edgar on the 27th August with our Black Five 5401 on an excursion to a Wembley Ice Hockey evening that our engine failed at Bletchley on the return run with a broken valve! She had been making very strange-sounding beats from the chimney, plus other somewhat disturbing noises, shortly after passing Tring. Luckily there was a spare engine on shed at Bletchley, 5089 (1A), so we were not delayed too long.

At the end of September I was back in No. 8 link with Cock Allen, working the usual relief of men on overtime etc., but of course he was otherwise engaged at times, and I had such men as Fred Pettit, Joe Hasdell, Walter Gardner, Ted Fell, Bill Tarry, Norman Jackson, Frank Dring, George Hibbert, Bill Gadsden, Les Oldham, Tommy Moore, Sandy Webster, George Williams (of Blisworth), Bill Middleton, and Chris Whittaker, etc.

On the 25th of October Bill Allen and I were again on an excursion to Blackpool (for the lights). Our engine was one of our Black Fives, 5331, and another super trip ensued. This time the night was beautifully clear, so no problem with seeing the signals at Preston, or anywhere else for that matter. Again we were somewhat inundated with bottles of beer and even a couple of bottles from Yates Wine Bar!

The only other thing of note that I remember of the latter part of that year, was when on the Irthlingborough iron ore empties with engine 8364 (15A), we 'parked' the brake van on the top of the stops at Wellingborough London Road when reversing into the sidings. Unfortunately, we were unable to rectify the situation as the buffers of the van had become 'hooked' over the cross beam (made of pieces of defunct rail) of the stop block. We reported it to the signalman, just in case he hadn't heard the noise, and beat a retreat after putting the excess wagons in another siding, leaving the damage in the capable hands of the local breakdown gang.

So life continued interestingly. Although still rostered with Cock Allen, there were many times when we were not together for a week at a time, he being on his foreman's duties, or our rest days not coinciding. When we were together it was the usual laugh a minute; Cock was always 'winding' someone up!

On a Sunday at the end of July I was detailed with Jockey Smith on a short rest double-trip to Llandudno. Our engine was 5547 (10B Preston, I think), a Baby Scot, my favourite class of engine, although unfortunately not a 'namer'! A pleasant trip, although the tender was loaded with poor coal, so she wasn't steaming too well towards the end of the run into North Wales. However, we thoroughly cleaned the fire and ashpan on Llandudno shed before eating our meal, and attempting to find a 'club' where we could purchase a pint or two of beer, Wales being more or less 'dry' on Sundays at that time. Our run home was much better as I had found a wagon of decent-looking coal at the shed, and had heaved a few hundredweight onto our tender before we returned to the station to hook on to our train of twelve carriages for the journey home. All in all a nice little earner – 7.30am to 1.45am (18hrs 15mins), which with mileage accrued something over 30 hours pay!

After my holidays in August, when Norman Quennell and I toured Devon and Cornwall in his new car (the first of us four 'railway friends' to move on to four wheels) my less than good luck returned. Firstly, I fell while climbing from a tender onto the footplate, and again hurt my ribs, this time on the hand brake mounting. After a week in pain, I reported the accident, and went for an X-ray. Just one cracked rib, but it certainly made shovelling painful. Even laughing was to be avoided! Then I had a 'dear John' letter from my girl friend, a nurse in London. Several weeks later I had a spill from my motorcycle and damaged my wrists. Another visit to the hospital and an X-ray – impacted bones was the diagnosis. 'Keep them strapped up', was the advice given. Another painful two or three weeks.

CHAPTER NINETEEN
TOWARDS THE END

IT must have been much less than a year after that trauma that I found myself posted with a driver named Bill Cornelius, a somewhat laconic man with a wry sense of humour. Notwithstanding that, we got on quite well with each other, and he was a very good engineman. He told me a somewhat amusing story, which I now relate just to show that it was not only Bill Allen and I that got into scrapes culminating in a visit to the red carpet room at Rugby.

The incident occurred on the 'Harborough branch at a time when everything was 'on the block'. Bill Cornelius and his fireman, whom I think he said was Doug Phipps, were on a train of mixed goods headed by an old D and on their way to Welham sidings. Having finally arrived at Brixworth after darkness had fallen, they were informed by the bobby that they were required to draw forward and back into the sidings there, 'out of the way', while up and down passenger trains were given clear lines. Bill dutifully drew forward and was stopped by the red hand lamp signal given by the guard, who, when the points were set, called them backwards with his white hand lamp signal. So they backed slowly into the station yard, Dougie (because the guard was on his side of the train) relaying instructions to Bill. Eventually they were given a green signal by the guard, which of course meant 'slow down even more'. Bill did so, but then the guard's signal disappeared so Bill fully applied the brakes, but as he did so there was a thump as the wagons buffered up sharply. As the train stopped, Dougie went to see what, if anything, had happened. When he got to the rear of the train, it was to find the brake van and a wagon inside the goods shed, with the smashed shed doors and part of the wall to which they had been affixed adorning the sides of the vehicles. The guard was apparently bewailing the fact that his lamp had gone out as he tried to change the signal from green to red.

The tale ended with the three of them appearing at Rugby, where they in turn relayed their story of the incident to the investigating officers. When it was the turn of the guard (whose name I can only remember as Ronnie) to give his version, he was asked what he did when his lamp was extinguished. He said, "I struck a match and waved it violently", which apparently caused one of the panel to suffer a slight coughing attack. No disciplinary sanctions were imposed, although it transpired that they should not have been backing into the goods shed road, but the one next to it. Bill said of the actual incident, that when he drew the train forward a little way, the brake van emerged from the debris little the worse for wear, and they eventually resumed their journey to Welham.

My time with Bill Cornelius was quite prolonged as there was little movement regarding promotion – it had almost become the state of waiting for 'dead men's shoes'. I too was becoming somewhat restless, perhaps more so by frequently being told by personnel at the shed that a man of my height would find better employment in the police force. In fact

two of our firemen, Glynn Hughes and Ginger Chapman, had already made that move, Glynn joining the Metropolitan Police, and Ginger the local force. Although I was somewhat tempted by the idea, the thought of joining the local force did not appeal – I knew too many fellows, who, although not what one would class as criminally inclined, were not averse to a little 'borrowing' of commodities which were not really theirs. The idea of policing in areas where one might meet them, or even apprehend them, could perhaps prove somewhat embarrassing. Joining the London force was more attractive, but home circumstances had changed. My family had returned from Leamington Spa, and father had died of cancer, leaving mother with two children younger than I, my brother being only twelve years old. I had therefore returned to live in the family home, and agreed that I would make no 'career move' until he had left school and gained employment. With this decision made, I knuckled down to doing the job in hand.

Of course, although being rostered with Bill Cornelius, again it did not mean I was with him every shift; in fact it was often the case that we were with other colleagues for perhaps a week at a time. I spent a few days with Steve Powell, who it transpired was a distant relative of my mother. One of our trips was to Bescot with one of their old Ds, 9077, on a train of mixed goods, most of which consisted of empty coal wagons. We soon discovered that when hard at work, she was such a rough rider that the fireman's side injector steam valve – which seemed not to pull out fully – kept closing, which was somewhat disconcerting when I was otherwise engaged in firing or coal cracking, etc. The injector on the driver's side would not work at all, merely blowing steam, the water feed appearing to be blocked. The non-discovery of that fault before we left the shed was my error, but one rarely tried both injectors, especially when the boiler was nearly always full to the whistle when on shed. However, Steve was not over critical, saying that we could fail her at Rugby if things got worse, but that he would rather 'dump' her back at her home shed for them to sort out. As it happened, I was able to overcome the difficulty of the closing steam valve with a length of string (always carried in my bag, my Boy Scout training I suppose) which I was able to secure to the steam valve handle and with a loop at the other end which I could secure to a 'blackout sheet' hook on the back of the cab roof.

In such state we clanged and wheezed our way to Bescot, and finally deposited her on the shed there. Steve filled in the appropriate 'failure' form, and after a mash and a sandwich, we collected another of that depot's Ds for the return journey. This one was 9308, and you can be sure that everything was fully checked before we took to the road. The train this time was for Willesden and, although classed as mixed goods, mainly consisted of coal. This engine,

The shed from the 'Blisworth line', showing the coaling and ash plants that became operative in about late 1955. Note the dilapidated fence along the loco yard. COLLECTION R. J. ESSERY

Another view of the shed from the canal towpath. The new water tank can be seen above the shed roof. G. ONLEY

A picture obviously taken from the coaling plant, showing the new ash plant. The old coaling stage had been situated somewhere in the foreground with the water tank above it. The wagons were on a slight hump to assist the coalers in shovelling coal onto tenders.   G. ONLEY

A ground level view of the ash plant, with dear old 1219 on No. 10 road, and a two-coach diesel unit on the down running line. A strange view to my eyes.   G. ONLEY

'Crab' No. 2710 in the shed. Note the electricity switch on the post — such luxury!

G. ONLEY

A view looking out of the shed — no sign of a 'D' anywhere!   G. ONLEY

A scene reminiscent of my 'fitting' days, with water cascading from the engine during a boiler washout.   G. ONLEY

An engine on the ash pit, obviously during disposal. Note the ash bucket, either going up for emptying or coming back down into the pit.

G. ONLEY

The coaling plant, with a wagon on the 'tipper'
mechanism.   R. J. ESSERY

Another view of the coaling plant, with an engine near the 'tipper', perhaps positioning a wagon there. Note the capstan — not known in my day.
G. ONLEY

A Class 8 on the turntable, with what appears to be the now redundant steam crane on the left.
G. ONLEY

A Compound and other engines apparently stored on the turntable road in October 1954. As mentioned in the text, a turntable was not a necessity at Northampton shed because it was situated within a triangle of lines. Note the cabin on the right, which was that used by the female labourers during the war as their rest room.
H. C. CASSERLEY

A view of the shed — in wintertime? Plenty of coal present and seemingly plenty of motive power, but again not a 'D' in sight.   G. ONLEY

A more or less overhead view of the turntable.   G. ONLEY

Bridge Street Junction signal box, with 2160 about to book on shed, the bobby beginning to open his window to give the crew the 'time on'.

R. J. ESSERY and R. GAMMAGE

Another view of the 'new' layout at the loco, showing the coaling plant and the new water tank, plus the water softening plant (not new, of course). The redundant oil storage tanks that were positioned somewhere near where the water tank is now shown had been removed. Note that the breakdown train was apparently coming on or going off the shed, attached to a double-cabbed 'D'.
R. K. BLENCOWE

A 'Jinty', 'dobbin' or 'humpy', whatever you wish to call them, on a trip from the up sidings to Far Cotton yard, approaching Bridge Street Junction pulling its load over the 1 in 35 crest of the canal bridge. The brake van had just cleared Duston North Junction (the box and gantry can be seen far right).
R. GAMMAGE

A Standard 2—10—0 on an iron ore train ex-Irthlingborough pits, approaching Bridge Street Junction box on its way to Oxford and Ebbw Vale steelworks. In my day, these trains were worked by Midland 'Long Toms' 0—8—0s, with Wellingborough men on double trip to Oxford, perhaps lodging where Bosco and I did!

R. GAMMAGE

although not in the best of condition, rode quite well, and it was something of a pleasure to be able to squat on the seat without being bumped off it with every turn of the big end. Back at Northampton, we were relieved by Bletchley men at No. 3 box and made our way on the mile and a half walk to the loco shed and off duty, having done just over nine hours that day.

The majority of work, as in the Special Link, was of a mundane nature, mostly on wagon trains heading to or from Willesden, Birmingham, or Nottingham, with perhaps slightly added interest being provided by being switched via a diversionary route to or from the latter location. On occasions when something was amiss on the Midland main line, trains for Toton were diverted at Market Harborough onto the LNW/GN line to Colwick or Beeston. This usually was met with approval by Northampton men as it meant they would not be relieved at Leicester, thus ensuring them of at least a little overtime money in the pay tin – which seemed to be the ultimate goal of all of us.

Similarly when working back from Leicester, should anything be wrong on the line to Market Harborough, or the branch to Northampton from there, an alternative route was to be switched at Wigston onto the branch to Rugby, and thence to Northampton from there. The 'diversionary' routes around the Birmingham area were quite numerous, but several of the Northampton men were conversant with them, and some interesting trips were to be had around not only Bescot, but also Stetchford, Aston, etc.

So life continued in its somewhat mundane fashion into 1955, when my occasional periods of bad luck continued to catch up with me. While with George Carter one night in the new year, I had my second injury of note on the footplate. We were on the tender of a D getting coal forward

while awaiting the start of a journey from the Up Sidings loop. I was shovelling coal from the back and middle part of the tender, and George was cracking it up with the coal pick, when a flake of coal hit my right eye causing me not a little discomfort. It put an end to our endeavours, but we carried on to finish our run to Bletchley. This was one occasion when I was very glad to be relieved there. On return to our shed, we reported the incident and, because the eye was so red and inflamed, I was told to attend the hospital. This I did, but as it was the middle of the night, little was done except for drops put in the eye, and a pad and bandage put on it. Next day I re-attended the hospital as instructed, when the eye was properly examined. It was then found that the cornea had been cut, and several minute pieces of coal were embedded in it. Some of those fragments are still in the eye, but have caused no undue concern, although the sight in that eye has deteriorated more than my left eye over the years. The outcome of this little episode was that after a week off duty, I was taken off main-line footplate duties for over two weeks until the eye had healed, and I had attended Euston for an eyesight test. So, back on shed work was my lot for that time, mainly assisting the shed turner or labouring, but at least on day shifts, which was good for my social life!

1955 was really the 'final straw' as far as my 'railway career' was concerned. This was the year when the ASLEF Union took their members on strike over a pay dispute. This lasted for two weeks, and the outcome was that drivers were awarded, I think, two shillings and sixpence rise (enough for a packet of cigarettes). The firemen got nothing.

However, I and about 90 other men, from a total of 300 or more at our depot, belonged to the NUR (I having joined that union while with the fitting staff and had not

A 'picket line' during the 1955 ASLEF strike, seemingly positioned somewhere in Main Road near the shed approach path, but perhaps on the opposite side of the road, near the school entrance, by reason of the background view. From left to right: Driver Jockerill (for whom I fired on several occasions), Frank Jones, D. Jones, J. McCulloch and Sid Hall (who was a cleaner and fireman like me). His father (Henry) was also a driver. CTY. CYRIL GREEN

considered it worthwhile to change when I moved over to the 'footplate side') who were not on strike, although several men did 'come out in sympathy', as it was termed. I was not one of them, and neither was Cock Allen, and we teamed up again for the two weeks, having what I can only call an adventurous time. We perhaps would be running commuter trains to Euston in the mornings, and then returning with empty wagon trains from Willesden, probably running without brakes on an old D at about 40mph, knowing we had a clear road. Having been relieved (or exchanged trains) at Northampton, we would then take a coal train to Willesden, before returning with a commuter train in the evening – all within ten or eleven hours duty. Trains to other destinations in differing directions were organised similarly. I thought it great fun, with invariably the word 'Scab' chalked by someone on the cab side.

The only drawback was when going through the pickets at either Castle Station, or outside the loco depot, where feelings were sometimes quite high, and one or two punches thrown. I hadn't realised just how much bad feeling had been roused until the strike ended, and my mate, Bill Cornelius, who was an ASLEF man, and had been on strike, resumed work. He showed great animosity towards me and did not speak to me for more than two months. It was, to say the least, most uncomfortable and frustrating; two men working in close proximity to each other, each relying on the other for proper working of the engine, and yet to be incommunicado. He gave no help with tank filling, fire cleaning, or getting coal forward, which did not worry me unduly. I continued to speak to him as normally as was possible, and to inform him of signal positions when he could not see them from his side of the engine, but would receive only a grunt as acknowledgement.

It was about this time that I had another prang on my motorbike and hurt my wrists. Again I eventually attended hospital, and an X-ray showed I had impacted some of the bones in my wrist. However, instructions were given to strap both of them and carry on, as no actual bones were broken. So, another few weeks of painful firing. Having prior to this become really disillusioned with railway employment, I had made tentative enquiries about joining the police force. Two other firemen, as I have mentioned above, had already done so – Glynn Hughes had joined the London force, and Ginger Chapman the local borough force. Having chatted to Ginger in a pub where we happened to meet one evening, and received favourable accounts of his new life, I had sent for enrolment forms from the Metropolitan Police, not wanting to join the local force, as already explained. It was not so bad for Ginger as he had spent a relatively short time on the railway before changing his occupation, thus probably not knowing some of the activities of certain of his former colleagues. However, having sent off the forms and received an invitation to attend for an interview, the damage to my wrists delayed my acceptance of the invitation until the new year (1956).

Me at the age of 26 or so, shortly before leaving the railway to join the police.

During the early part of 1956, Bill appeared to have regained much of his old cheerfulness and laconic sense of humour. In fact I think he was somewhat disappointed that I was considering leaving the railway, and began to query whether it was because of his attitude following the strike that had 'pushed' me to the decision. I tried to convince him that he was not the cause, merely that our work was decreasing, and promotion was stagnant, and if I didn't leave home now, I probably never would. My young brother had now left school, and I had assisted in his getting work at an advertising firm who specialised in shoe advertisements, which entailed technical drawing, an art in which my brother excelled.

So it was that in early April I attended London for an interview/examination at a building in Beak Street off Regent Street, and eventually received acceptance to join the Metropolitan Police – which I did on May 6th. So, my thirteen-plus years of railway service ended, with me still a fireman. I have obviously looked back with nostalgia over the years, but in reality, once I got onto the promotion ladder in the police force, I wished I had left the railway when I was younger. However, hindsight is wonderful, and in truth I did enjoy most of my days on the railway, and I certainly came to know some real characters amongst my workmates.

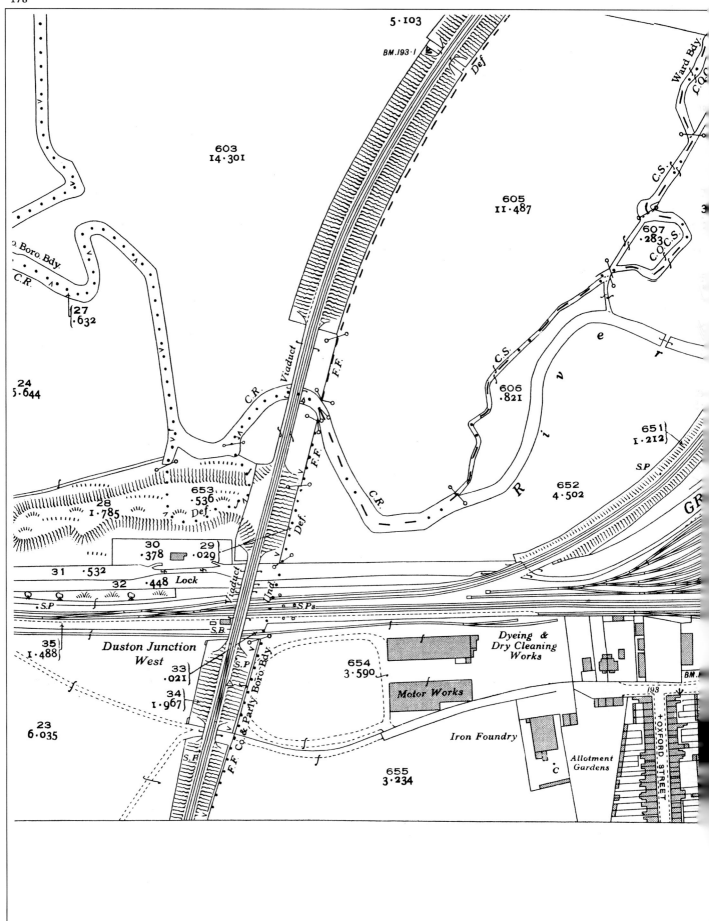

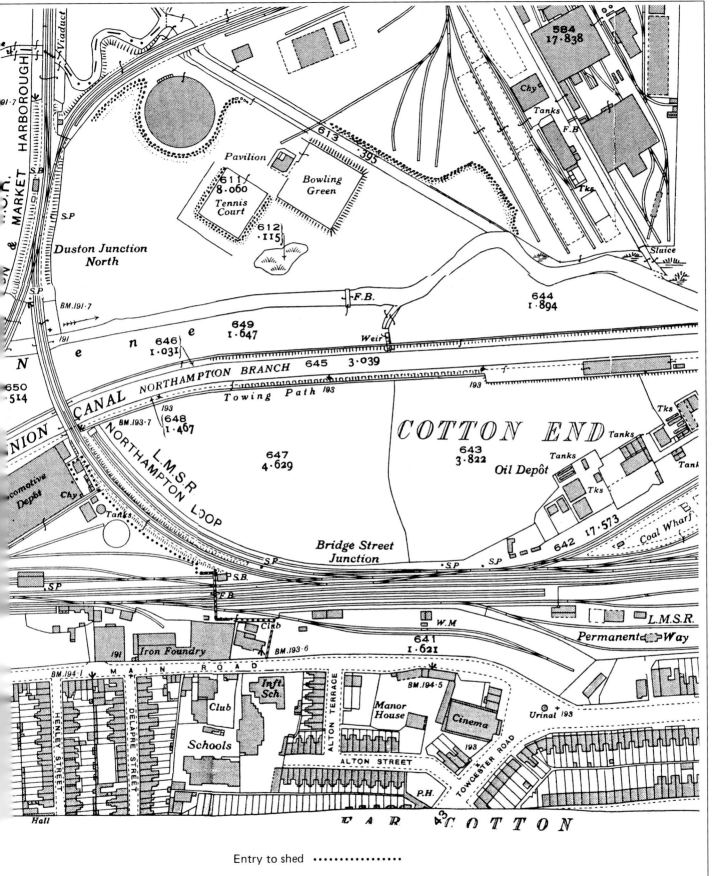

Entry to shed ················

The maps on the following pages are taken from 25-inch Ordnance Survey maps for 1938.

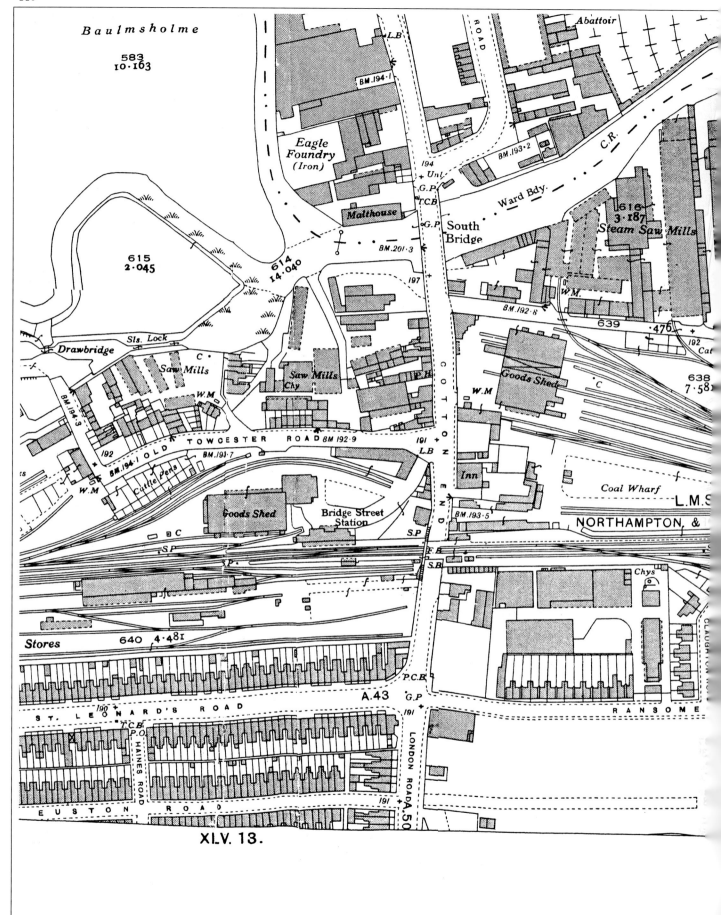

Baulmsholme

583
10·163

Eagle
Foundry
(Iron)

BM.194·1

LB

ROAD

Abattoir

C.R.

BM.193·2

194
+ Unl
G.P
TCB

Ward Bdy.

616
3·187

Steam Saw Mills

Malthouse

G.P

*South
Bridge*

BM.201·3

W.M.

639   ·476

192
Cat

615
2·045

614
14·040

197

BM.192·8

Sls. Lock

Drawbridge

C

Saw Mills

W.M.

BM.194·3

Goods Shed

C

638
7·58

*Saw Mills
Chy*

P.H.

W.M.

192

Cattle Pens

BM.194·

OLD   TOWCESTER   ROAD

BM.193·7

BM.192·9

191
LB

COTTON   END

Inn

Coal Wharf

L.M.S

W.M.

B C

Goods Shed

*Bridge Street
Station*

S.P

BM.193·5

NORTHAMPTON, &

SP

P.

f

f

f

S.P
F.B.
S.B.

Chys

Stores

640   4·481

CLAUGHTON

P.C.B

A.43

G.P

RANSOME

ST.   LEONARD'S   ROAD

190

191 +

LONDON ROAD A.50

TCB
P.O

HAINES   ROAD

EUSTON   ROAD

191

XLV. 13.

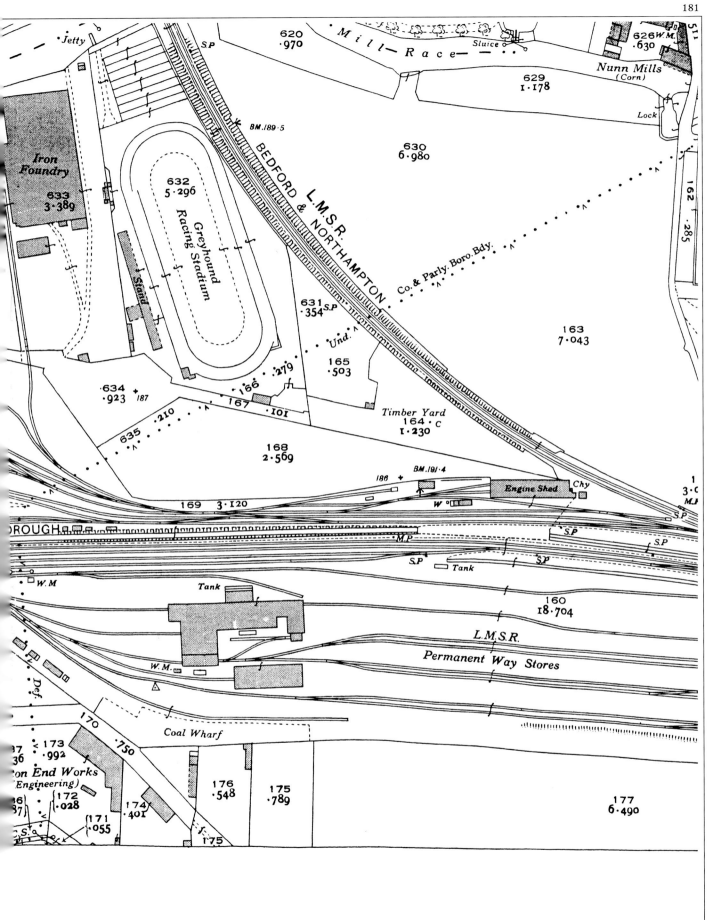

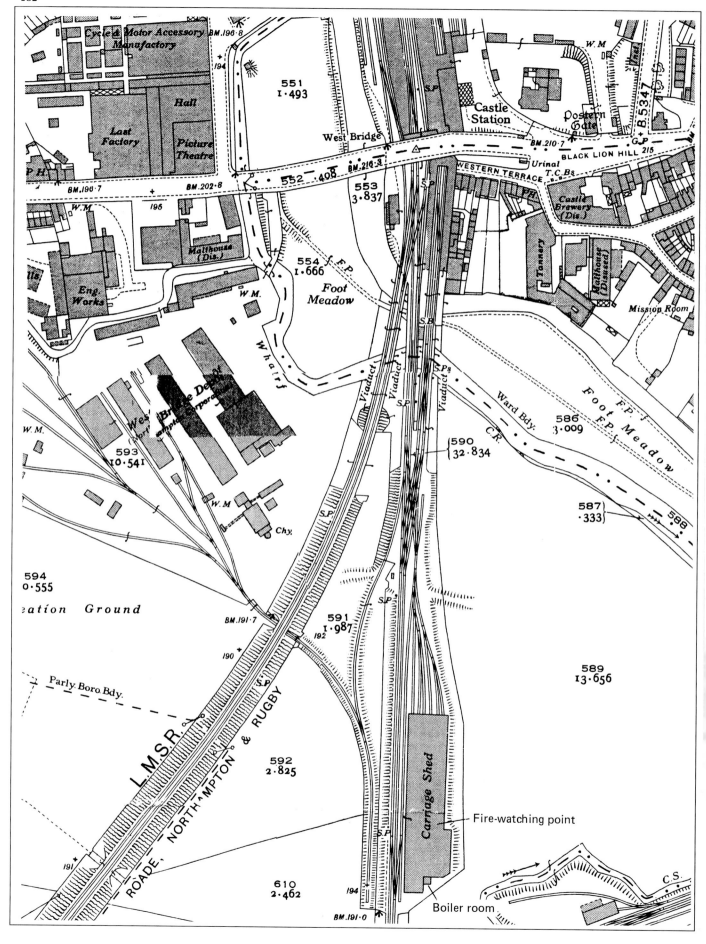

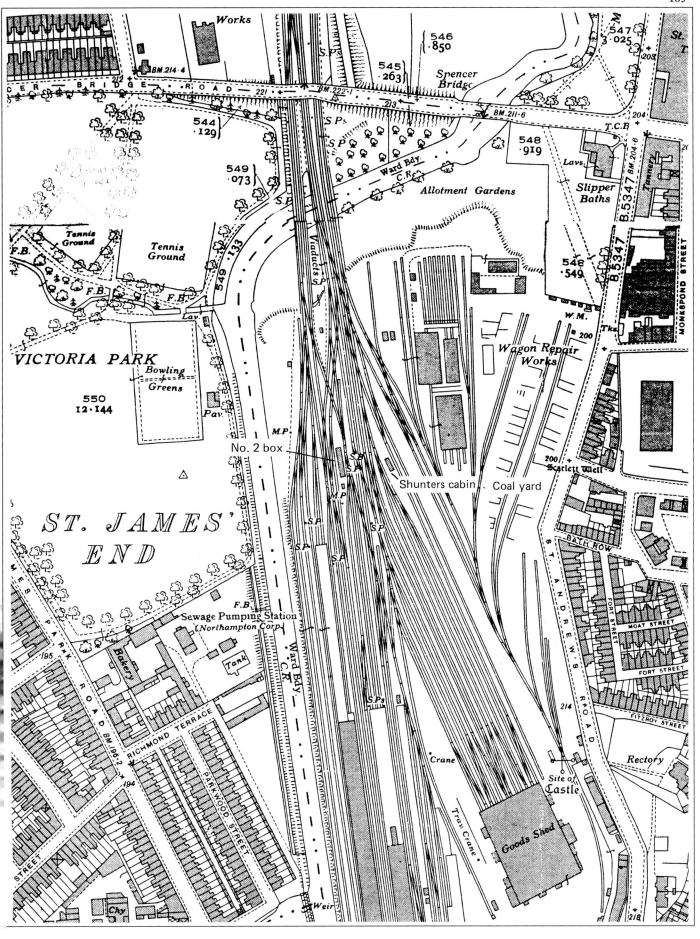

Works

546
·850

545
·263

Spencer
Bridge

BM.214·4

CER BRIDGE ROAD 221 BM.222·1 213 BM.211·6 M 547 3·025 St. T.

T.C.B. 204

544
·129

SPs

SP

SPs

SP

548
·919

Lavs.

T.C.B.

Slipper
Baths

Tanner

B.5347 BM.204·6

549
·073

SP

Ward Bdy.

C.R.

Allotment Gardens

Viaducts SP

W.M.

548
·549

B.5347

Tennis
Ground

Tennis
Ground

549·133

F.B.

F.B.

F.B.

Lav.

Wagon Repair
Works

200

VICTORIA PARK

Bowling
Greens

Pav.

200

Scarlett Well

Tks.

MONKSPOND STREET

550
12·144

M.P.

No. 2 box

SP
SP

Shunters cabin   Coal yard

BATH ROW

MP

SP

SP

ST. JAMES'
END

SP

SP

ST ANDREW'S ROAD

FORT STREET

MOAT STREET

FORT STREET

F.B.

PARK ROAD BM.196·2

Sewage Pumping Station
(Northampton Corp)

Baker's

Tank

Ward Bdy.
C.R.

FITZROY STREET

195

RICHMOND TERRACE

PARKWOOD STREET

214

Rectory

194

Crane

Site of
Castle

MES PARK ROAD

SPs

Trav. Crane

Goods Shed

STREET

Chy.

Weir

218

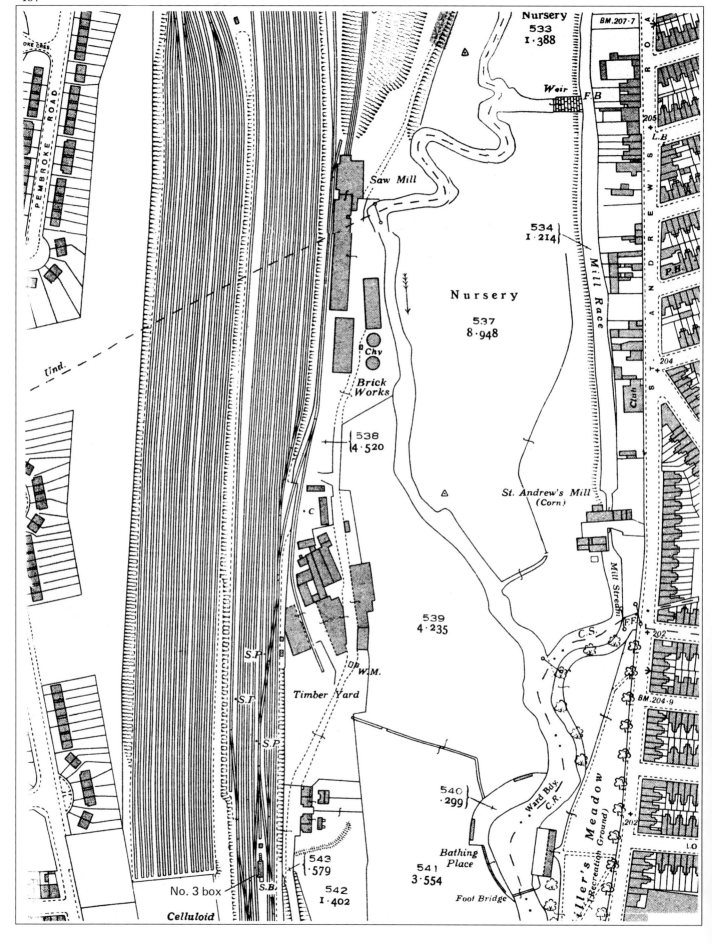

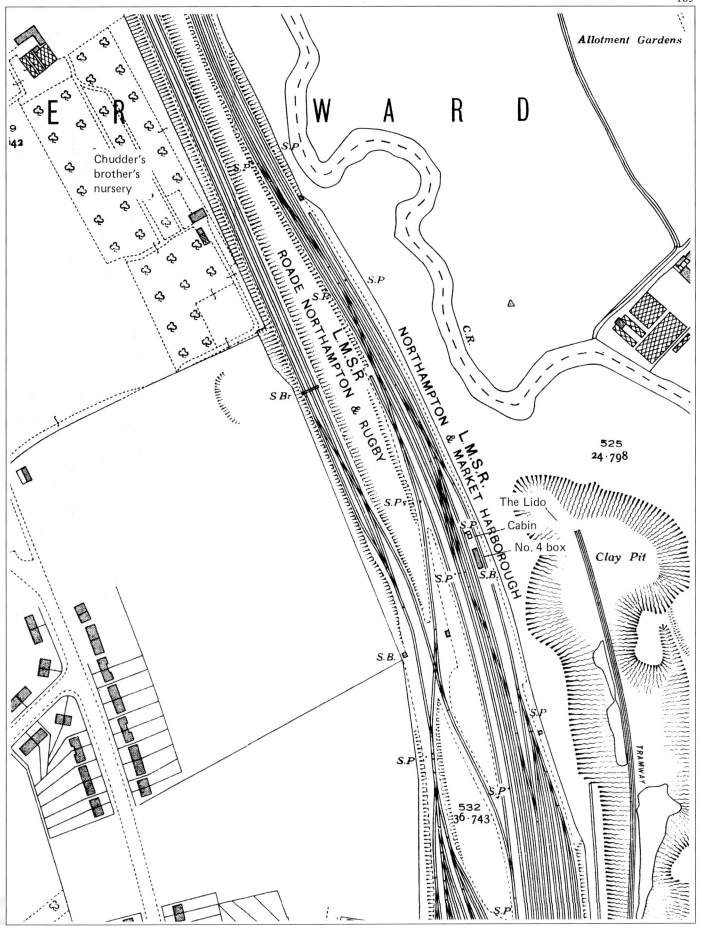

Allotment Gardens

W A R D

E R

Chudder's
brother's
nursery

ROADE NORTHAMPTON

L.M.S.R.

NORTHAMPTON & RUGBY

NORTHAMPTON & MARKET HARBOROUGH

L.M.S.R.

S.P

S.P

S.P

S.P

C.R.

S Br

S.Ps

S.P

S.B.

S.P

S.P

S.B.

The Lido
Cabin
No. 4 box

525
24·798

Clay Pit

TRAMWAY

S.P

S.P

S.P

532
36·743

S.P

A fine shot of the inside of the cab of a 'D' with the driver perched on his 'half-moon' seat holding the partly open regulator. There was also another 'arm' of the regulator handle at right-angles to that being held by the driver, and this can be seen protruding upwards towards the cab roof. The vacuum brake handle above the driver's hand incorporated the ejector valve. The position of the handle is shown in the ejector working position. To operate the brakes, it would be pushed towards the fireman's side. Note the corresponding handle on the fireman's side, joined by a metal bar. The two injector steam valves above this bar were opened by pulling them towards the tender. The water valves were on the tender. The driver's tea can was hanging on the boiler gauge glass shut-off valve — a similar valve was on the other gauge glass and the check valves can be seen below the glasses. The vacuum gauge was in the corner above the driver's hat, and the reversing gear in front of his left side. Below the steam gauge on the fireman's side, the ejector mechanism is just apparent with its bell-like housing, from where the intrusive whining whistle emanated. Just in front of that can be seen the blower handle, the position of which indicates that the blower was on. The 'fizzle' pipe and valve can be seen and to the right of that the 'pull/push' sanding lever. Note that the train was on a single line, hence the 'staff' lodged on top of the sander lever. The half-moon seat is easily seen, but someone had repositioned the fitting so that it was further from the cab side, thus giving more posterior room! The lever below the fizzle pipe valve, to the right of the injector pipe, was the water inlet adjuster valve — not often required to be moved — with below that, protruding upwards, the back damper lever. The front damper lever and that of the cylinder water cocks were below and in front of the fireman's seat, and often awkward to operate without use of one's foot. A 'buffer' lamp can be seen at that location. The bracket attached to the cab side above the 'bell' of the ejector, was for holding the metal container of the warning flags and detonators, but, as appears on this occasion, it was normally kept in the tool bucket in the tender oil locker. On the tender on the driver's side is what looks like a brake stick — used for pegging down wagon brakes — so perhaps there were gradients on this line which necessitated such action to assist with the engine braking.

J. M. BENTLEY

ACKNOWLEDGEMENTS

The publishers would like to record their sincerest thanks to Richard Coleman, Patrick Rawlinson and Graham Onley for so generously allowing access to their photographic collections, which have proved invaluable in illustrating this volume. David Hanson, John Meredith and Richard Casserley were kind enough to allow reproduction of their fathers' photos whilst R. J. Essery, Roger Carpenter, Rod Blencowe and Mike Williams managed to plug some frustrating gaps. Thanks are also due to Brian Bibb, Jacquie Pryce of the *Northampton Chronicle and Echo*, Terry Bracher of Northampton Library, and Chris Turner who co-ordinated much of the picture research with his usual dedication.